The Resurrection of Christ

AN ESSAY IN BIBLICAL THEOLOGY

The

RESURRECTION OF CHRIST.

A. MICHAEL RAMSEY

Van Mildert Professor of Divinity in the University
of Durham and Canon of Durham Cathedral

PHILADELPHIA: The Westminster Press

Copyright, MCMXLVI, by
The Westminster Press

Preface

IT IS the purpose of this book to examine the place of the Resurrection in the Gospel preached by the Apostles and in the theology that created the New Testament, and to discuss the historical character of the event from which both the Gospel and the theology sprang. In recent years there has been no lack of treatment of the historical problems of the narratives of the Resurrection; but these problems have too often been discussed in separation from the Gospel with which the history is bound up and from the theology which made the story of Easter worth the telling.

The Resurrection of Christ is the point where the paths of history and theology meet in a way that is crucial for the understanding of both; and the handling of this stupendous theme in a book is fraught with special dangers. I shall not be surprised if I am told that my treatment of the history is vitiated by presuppositions or that my exposition of the doctrine is cramped by the use of historical criticism. But it is hardly possible that both charges can be true. As to presuppositions, it is impossible to write history without them; and those who have disclaimed presuppositions in writing about Jesus of Nazareth have always used them. In this book I have striven to combine the use of critical methods with but one modest presupposition, namely, that the historical event was such as to account for the theology of Resurrection which runs through the New Testament. For a Christian the words " theology " and " Resurrection " are uniquely linked, since his God is the living God of the Bible who raised Jesus Christ from the dead, and hath raised us together with Him.

I hope that my references to other books and writers give some indication of my awareness of my debt to them. I would also thank a former teacher, Canon Balmforth, and a former pupil, the Rev. C. F. Evans, for their criticism and counsel.

A. M. RAMSEY

October 1944

Contents

		Page
I.	THE RESURRECTION AND THE NEW TESTAMENT	9
II.	ACCORDING TO THE SCRIPTURES	21
III.	HISTORY AND BELIEF	35
IV.	HISTORY AND CRITICISM	47
V.	THE EVIDENCE OF THE GOSPELS	59
VI.	THE THEOLOGY OF THE GOSPEL NARRATIVES	75
VII.	THE RESURRECTION AND THE CHURCH	91
VIII.	THE RESURRECTION OF THE DEAD	103
IX.	CONCLUSION	117
	NOTE (A) — THE ASCENSION	122
	NOTE (B) — APPEARANCE AND VISION	124
	INDEX OF NAMES	125
	INDEX OF SUBJECTS	126

Chapter One

THE RESURRECTION AND THE NEW TESTAMENT

I

THE writer of this book remembers receiving something of a shock when it was first his privilege to attend the lectures of the late Sir Edwyn Hoskyns. The lecturer began with the declaration that as our subject was the Theology and Ethics of the New Testament we must begin with the passages about the Resurrection. It seemed to contradict all the obvious preconceptions. Was it not right to trace first the beginnings of the ministry of Jesus, the events of His life and the words of His teaching? Here, surely, the essence of the Gospel might be found, and as a finale the Resurrection comes so as to seal and confirm the message. No. The Resurrection is a true starting-place for the study of the making and the meaning of the New Testament.

We are tempted to believe that, although the Resurrection may be the climax of the Gospel, there is yet a Gospel that stands upon its own feet and may be understood and appreciated before we pass on to the Resurrection. The first disciples did not find it so. For them the Gospel without the Resurrection was not merely a Gospel without its final chapter: it was not a Gospel at all. Jesus Christ had, it is true, taught and done great things: but He did not allow the disciples to rest in these things. He led them on to paradox, perplexity and darkness; and there He left them. There too they would have remained, had He not been raised from death. But His Resurrection threw its own light backwards upon the death and the ministry that went before; it illuminated the paradoxes and disclosed the unity of His words and deeds. As Scott Holland said: " In the Resurrection it was not only the Lord who was raised from the dead. His life on earth rose with Him; it was lifted up into its real light." [1]

[1] *On Behalf of Belief*, p. 12.

It is a desperate procedure to try to build a Christian Gospel upon the words of Jesus in Galilee apart from the climax of Calvary, Easter and Pentecost. If we do so, we are professing to know Jesus better than the first disciples knew Him; and the Marcan record shews us how complete was their perplexity before the Resurrection gave them the key. Every oral tradition about Jesus was handed down, every written record of Him was made only by those who already acknowledged Him as Lord, risen from the dead.

It is therefore both historically and theologically necessary to " begin with the Resurrection." For from it, in direct order of historical fact, there came Christian preaching, Christian worship, Christian belief. Of the preaching much will be said in the pages that follow. As to the worship, the most stupendous change followed the Resurrection: Hebrew monotheists, without forsaking their monotheism, worshipped Jesus as Lord. As to the belief, there meets us throughout the Apostolic writings a close connection between the Resurrection and the Christian belief in God. The God of the Christians is essentially the God who raised Jesus Christ from the dead. In Paul's words they " believe on him that raised Jesus our Lord from the dead " (Rom. iv. 24). In Peter's words they are " believers in God, which raised him from the dead and gave him glory; so that your faith and hope might be in God " (1 Peter i. 21). Christian theism is Resurrection-theism. Similarly Christian ethics are Resurrection ethics, defined and made possible by men being " raised together with Christ " (Col. iii. 1). What is perhaps the earliest known Christian hymn contains the words,

" Awake, thou that sleepest, and arise from the dead, and Christ shall shine upon thee." (Eph. v. 14.)

2

The Gospel of God appears in Galilee: but in the end it is clear that Calvary and the Resurrection are its centre. For Jesus Christ came not only to preach a Gospel but to *be* a Gospel, and He is the Gospel of God in all that He did for the deliverance of mankind.

The Greek word " *evangelion,*" that lies behind the word " gospel " in our English versions, is very rare; and its meaning in the

New Testament is apparent only when we turn to the Old Testament, where the corresponding verb is specially used for God's coming intervention to deliver His people. The word tells of the good news that God is come, bringing (to use the Biblical words) salvation, righteousness, remission of sins, peace, mercy. " O thou that tellest good tidings to Zion, get thee up into the high mountain; O thou that tellest good tidings to Jerusalem, lift up thy voice with strength; lift it up, be not afraid; say unto the cities of Judah, Behold your God! Behold, the Lord GOD will come as a mighty one, and his arm shall rule for him: behold his reward is with him, and his recompense before him " (Isa. xl. 9–10; cf. lii. 7; lxi. 1). It is passages such as this that provide the background for the understanding of the words of the preaching of Jesus in Galilee: " The time is fulfilled and the Kingdom of God is at hand; repent ye, and believe in the Gospel " (Mark i. 14).

Thus the good news that Jesus proclaimed was the coming of the Reign of God. The Reign had come. Both the teaching and the mighty works of the Messiah bore witness to it. The teaching unfolded the righteousness of the Kingdom, and summoned men and women to receive it. The mighty works asserted the claims of the Kingdom over the whole range of human life. The healing of the sick; the exorcism of devils; the restoration of the maimed, the deaf, the dumb, and the blind; the feeding of the hungry; the forgiveness of sinners; all these had their place among the works of the Kingdom. But though the Kingdom was indeed here in the midst of men, neither the teaching nor the mighty works could enable its coming in all its fulness. For the classic enemies — sin and death — could be dealt with only by a mightier blow, a blow which the death of the Messiah Himself alone could strike. And the righteousness of the Kingdom could not be perfected by a teaching and an example for men to follow; it involved a personal union of men with Christ Himself, a sharing in His own death and risen life. Thus He had a baptism to be baptized with, and He was straitened until it was accomplished. But when it was accomplished there was not only a Gospel in words preached by Jesus but a Gospel in deeds embodied in Jesus Himself, living, dying, conquering death. There is a hint at the identity between the Gospel of Jesus and the person of Jesus in the arresting words " for my sake and the gospel's " (Mark viii. 35; x. 29).

Thus it was that the Gospel preached by Jesus became merged into the Gospel that *is* Jesus. This is the Gospel which the Apostles preach. It is still the Gospel of God (Rom. i. 1; 2 Cor. iv. 4). It is still the Gospel of the Kingdom (Acts, *passim*). But its content is Jesus. The striking phrase "to gospel Jesus" appears (Acts v. 42; viii. 35; xi. 20). They preach His life, death, Resurrection and gift of the Spirit; for all this constitutes the drama of the mighty acts of God who came to deliver and to reign.

We are able to form some picture of the preaching of the Apostles from the speeches recorded in the Acts and from the brief summaries of the basic Christian facts which we find in the Epistles. The speeches of Peter in Jerusalem (Acts ii. 14–36; iii. 12–26; iv. 8–12) and in Caesarea (Acts x. 34–43) and of Paul at Antioch in Pisidia (Acts xiii. 16–41) disclose the common themes of the preaching. The same themes recur; and the evidence of the Epistles confirms the presence of these themes in the earliest teaching of the Church. (*a*) The messianic age is come: " The things which God foreshadowed by the mouth of all the prophets, He thus fulfilled." (*b*) This has happened through the ministry, death, and Resurrection of the Messiah. He came as David's heir. His death was not a mere tragic defeat; it was a part of God's agelong purpose for the deliverance of mankind. It was foretold in the Scriptures. By the Resurrection God vindicated the Christ. (*c*) Jesus, exalted at God's right hand, is Lord. He shares in the sovereignty of God. (*d*) His sovereignty is attested by the outpouring of Holy Spirit upon the disciples. The gift comes from the exalted Jesus Himself. (*e*) The end is at hand, and Jesus will return as judge of the living and the dead. This is the drama wrought by God in the events in Jerusalem whereof the Apostles are witnesses. It implies the coming of the new age, the breaking into history of the powers of the world to come. It impels the Apostles to summon men to repent and to be baptized into the name of Jesus.

Such was the Gospel. With the accounts of the preaching in Acts we can compare the tradition which Paul says that he had received (presumably from Christians in Jerusalem):

" How that Christ died for our sins according to the scriptures; and that he was buried, and that he hath been raised on the third day according to the scriptures: and that he appeared to Cephas, then to the twelve." (1 Cor. xv. 3–5.)

We can compare also the allusions to the content of the Gospel in a number of passages in the Epistles (Gal. iii. 1; 1 Cor. i. 23; Rom. viii. 31–34). The Gospel was one. The same framework of events underlies the primitive preaching in Jerusalem, the preaching of Paul, the final presentation of the Gospel in the four written Gospels. There were of course differences of emphasis. Peter links the offer of forgiveness with " the name of Jesus Christ," that is, with His mission and person in general; Paul links it specially with the Cross. Peter is not recorded as mentioning the burial; Paul includes it in his summary of the tradition he had received. The earliest speeches dwell upon the death and the Resurrection and say nothing of the preceding life and ministry; Peter at Caesarea includes an account of how Jesus was anointed with the Holy Spirit and went about doing good and healing all that were oppressed of the devil (Acts x. 38). But there was one Gospel. In it, amid whatever varieties, the Passion and the Resurrection had the pre-eminent place. And the whole story — ministry, Passion, Resurrection — was told not as a piece of biography but as the drama of God's mighty act as deliverer. It was not that the biographical interest in the Man Jesus came first, and a divine Gospel was subsequently deduced from it. It was that the events were from the first handed down as a divine Gospel, and only within the context of that Gospel did the biographical and human interest in Jesus survive and grow.

3

In the midst, however, of the Apostles' preoccupation with the Word of the Cross and with the glory of the Resurrection they did not lose sight of the earthly ministry of Jesus. Indeed their refusal to lose sight of it is impressive and significant. They knew Christ " no longer after the flesh " (cf. 2 Cor. v. 16); their immediate concern was with the contemporary Christ whom they worshipped; their message dwelt upon the absorbing and heart-rending episodes of a Crucified Messiah and a victory over death. But the words and deeds of the days of His flesh were not forgotten.

The Apostolic writers often give glimpses of the earthly ministry of Jesus. If Paul is concerned with the contemporary Christ, he recalls sayings of Jesus that have been handed down (1 Cor. vii. 10; ix. 14), and he mentions His characteristics that have been remembered — His gentleness, His forbearance, His humility and His refusal to please Himself (2 Cor. x. 1; Phil. ii. 7; Rom. xv. 2–3; cf. 1 Cor. xi. 1). If the writer of Hebrews takes for his theme the heavenly priesthood of Christ, he bids his readers contemplate the Man Jesus in His temptation, His prayers, His strong crying and tears, His godly fear, His endurance and faith. If John dwells upon the eternal Sonship, he insists also that Jesus sat by a well and was weary. The impress of the human life of Jesus rested upon the teaching of the Christians. They handed down His words and deeds, first in oral tradition and finally in written books.

But the earthly ministry was remembered, handed down and taught *never* as a self-contained biography, *always* as a part of the Gospel of God whose climax is the Passion and the Resurrection. The words and deeds of Jesus were narrated with the light of the Resurrection upon them. For the first Christians lived in a double perspective: the risen Jesus at the right hand of God and the Jesus of Galilee and Jerusalem. It is from this double perspective that all the Apostolic literature was written.

There was first the stage of *oral teaching* about Jesus. This stage has been brought into valuable prominence by the modern method of study known as Form-Criticism. The Form-critics attempt to discover, behind the Gospels, the various types of story-telling used in the early communities. Though some of their conclusions have been arbitrary and unjustifiable, they have enabled us to detect certain genuine story-forms. There was the story told for the sake of a saying of Jesus which formed its climax; there was the story told for the sake of a mighty work of Jesus which illustrated some theme of the Gospel; there was the story told in order to meet some problem or difficulty within the early Church. Thus we may picture the telling of the stories about Jesus by the preachers, teachers and catechists in the early communities. But these same communities

worshipped Jesus risen from the dead. While they heard of how
He healed and forgave in Galilee, they knew Him as one who
healed and forgave there in their own midst. They learnt the
stories not as the biographical records of a dead hero, but as illustrations of a Gospel of God, living and active and sharper than any
two-edged sword, and piercing even to the dividing of soul and
spirit.

After some decades there came the *Synoptic Gospels*. In them we
can detect the same double perspective, the perspective of the original events that are recorded and the perspective of the worshipping
Church. Do we find that the later perspective is read back into the
story, and that the narratives are tinged with the devotion to the
risen Jesus and with the " developed " doctrine of the Church? To
some extent we find this; for while the evangelists tell of the
" Rabbi " whom the disciples so addressed in Galilee they are conscious of the " Lord " of Christian doctrine and devotion after the
Resurrection. Yet the impressive fact is that, taking the material in
the Gospels as a whole, the " reading-back " seems so restricted and
the material is often markedly " raw ": it takes us behind the Resurrection and the worshipping Church, and it shews the original awe
and bewilderment and failure of the disciples. But this material,
reflecting as it does the raw reminiscence of the primitive perspective, gets its coherence and its meaning only within the Gospel of
God who raised Jesus from the dead.

Thus the Gospels are works of an entirely novel and unique literary character. They are not biographies, for they pay little attention to the psychology of a hero and to many of those aspects of a
life which are dear to a biographer. They are *Gospels*. They are
written to tell of the events whereby the Reign of God came. The
human story is told, as alone it survived to be told, in the frame of
the Gospel of God. The Gospels reproduce the pattern of the
preaching of the Apostles from the earliest days.

Finally there comes the *Fourth Gospel* bearing the name of John.
Here the double perspective, that has been apparent at every stage
of the Apostolic writings, is seen with a special and deliberate
vividness.

For in this baffling and glorious book we find a blending of an emphasis upon the importance of historical fact with an emphasis upon those aspects of the truth in Jesus Christ that lie beyond the historical events. This blending of two strains puzzles the reader, and has caused the book to be regarded as a kind of problem-piece among the writings about Jesus Christ. Is the author, we ask, giving us good history, supplementing and correcting the history provided by the earlier Gospels? or is he deserting history and leading us into the realms of mystical interpretation? The problem has been baffling, for neither of these alternatives seem wholly to correspond with the author's purpose or wholly to explain all the characteristics of the book.

But when once we have perceived that the double perspective exists in all the Apostolic writings and in all the Apostolic teaching from the earliest days, then the Fourth Gospel appears in a less problematic light. For while it does indeed contain its own problems, its main problem is not a new one. It sums up the inevitable tension in Apostolic Christianity, and enables a truer understanding of that tension. John writes in order that his readers may believe that Jesus is the Christ the Son of God and believing may have life in His name. With this end in view he will not allow his readers to ignore either of the two aspects of Christianity. (*a*) On the one hand he makes it clear that men in every age may be in touch with Jesus Christ, risen and glorified, and may by believing on Him and feeding on Him possess eternal life. " He, the Paraclete, shall glorify me, for He shall take of mine and shall declare it unto you." " Blessed are they that have not seen and yet have believed." The Incarnation was the prelude to the greater works that the disciples would do when Jesus had gone to the Father, and to the closer union between the disciples and Jesus made possible by His departure. Here and now men may dwell in Him, and He in them. (*b*) But at the same time John is at pains to shew that the contemporary Christ is known aright and that union with Him is possible, only if the Christians are in a constant relationship with the historical events of the Word-made-flesh. It is vital that the events really happened, events that men saw and heard and their hands handled. " Back to history " is an avowed motive both in the Gospel and in the First Epistle of John.

These two factors are essential to John's message. If at times he points his readers beyond history to the eternal significance of Jesus, he as often brings them to earth again with his sudden reminders of stark historical fact. But he will not let them rest in history; for the history cannot reveal God or be understood unless it points men beyond itself. Nor will he let them rest in an unhistorical mysticism, for the risen Christ, interpreted by the Paraclete, is known only by those who will believe and treasure the historical events in the flesh.

Thus John draws together the two facts which belong to Christianity from the beginning, the Jesus who lived and died in the flesh and the Jesus who is living, contemporary and life-giving. If he puzzles us by the tension between them, neither the puzzle nor the tension are of his own making. The Fourth Gospel is what it is, not only because of the special tendencies and insights of the writer, but because of the nature of Christianity. From the tension between history and that which is beyond history the Christian never escapes, and within that tension the strength of Christianity lies.

The ministry, the Passion, the Resurrection, the mission of the Paraclete — John presents these in a true unity. He does so by means of the theme of *Life* which runs through his Gospel. The teaching and the works of Jesus, meeting as they do a vast variety of human needs, are united by the single purpose of bringing the gift of Life in answer to the fact of death, both the death of the body and the death of sin. Life and light are the divine answer to death and darkness. The Messiah comes that men may have life, and have it abundantly. His life-giving mission has its climax in His own death and Resurrection which enable the fullest release of life, through the Paraclete, for the disciples and for mankind. Thus John shews the unity of the mission of Christ by expounding it with the glory of the Resurrection upon it. The themes of the ministry in John are really the same in essence as those recorded in the Synoptists; but in John the light of Easter is allowed to shine backwards upon these themes, and the reader feels that this light is never absent from the story.

4

There is yet another tension within the thought of the Apostolic Church; and this is the tension that is created by the contrast between the Crucifixion and the Resurrection. The preachers of the Gospel told their hearers of the humiliation of Jesus done to death between two criminals, and of the "exceeding greatness" of the power of God when "according to the working of the strength of his might" (Eph. i. 19) He raised Jesus from the dead. "He was crucified through weakness, yet he liveth through the power of God" (2 Cor. xiii. 4). We discover as we read the New Testament that the two events, seen first as opposites, are found increasingly to be like the two sides of a single coin. Here again it is John who finally shews us the perfect unity.

To the disciples the contrast between the Reign of God proclaimed by Jesus and the shameful death of the Messiah presented at first an unbearable paradox. But the Resurrection shewed them that the Passion was a part of the divine counsel and a prelude to glory, both for their Master and for themselves. Finally, they came to see that the Passion was not only a necessary prelude, but itself a part of the glory. This truth peeps out at many points in the Apostolic writings, until it blazes into light in the Fourth Gospel.

In the primitive preaching of the Apostles there is only a linking of the death and the exaltation as two stages in the divine drama. Both had their place. Jesus is both Servant and Lord. The same linking appears in Peter's First Epistle; he who once had stumbled at the Messiah's choice of the Cross is now "a witness of the sufferings of Christ who am also a partaker of the glory that shall be revealed" (1 Peter v. 1). Paul, however, sees more than a linking of the two events; they are for him blended together. The risen Christ is for ever "the Christ who has been sacrificed." His theme is "Christ Jesus that died, yea rather that was raised from the dead" (Rom. viii. 34). Christ crucified is "the power of God and the wisdom of God" (1 Cor. i. 24). To worship the risen Jesus is to accept the Cross in virtue of which He triumphed: to believe in the Crucified is to adhere to one who conquers and reigns. Similarly the writer of Hebrews bids his readers to "behold Jesus because of the suffering of death crowned with glory and honour, that by the grace of God he should taste death for every man " (Heb. ii. 9). The exact exegesis of this verse is difficult: we cannot be quite sure whether it speaks of Jesus as crowned with glory after His victory or as going to His death as one who is crowned with glory already. If Pilate's words, " Behold the man," are the " Ecce Homo " of the world which sees only the bruised figure with a crown of thorns, these words in Hebrews are the " Ecce Homo " of the Christian who knows where the glory really is.

This blending of Passion and Resurrection was not a piece of picturesque dramatizing by the early Christians. It corresponded to their own discovery that to share in the sufferings of Christ was to know His triumph. They were " always bearing about in the body the dying of Jesus that the life also of Jesus may be manifested in our body " (2 Cor. iv. 10).

It is, however, in the narratives of the Passion in the Gospels that the drawing together of the two events is most significantly to be seen. In *Mark* the Passion is depicted as an austere and lonely scene: the Messiah dies in utter isolation, and the only word from the Cross is the cry, " My God, my God, why hast thou forsaken me? " Yet the scene is not one of pathos, or tragedy or defeat. The many references to the fulfilment of prophecy declare that here is no haphazard disaster, but a divine act of redemption. Its power shatters the barrier between Jew and Gentile, as is symbolized by the confession of the Roman centurion, " Truly this was the Son of God." Only the Resurrection could have so turned the darkness of Calvary into a light for the Gentiles. *Luke* goes further in drawing Cross and Resurrection together. He shews in the Passion the serenity and the mastery of love whereby the Son of Man reaches out in sympathy and tenderness to those around Him. It is they and not He whose need and plight are pitiable. The gloom of the scene as Mark depicted it is, in Luke, lightened by the love which is already conquering. More still, Luke hints at the connection between the Cross and the glory. It is he who in the story of the Transfiguration links that scene with the Passion by telling how Moses and Elijah appeared in glory and spake of the exodus that Jesus was to fulfil in Jerusalem (Luke ix. 31). It is he who records the words spoken on the way to Emmaus: " Behoved it not the Christ to suffer these things and to enter into his glory? " (Luke xxiv. 26).

It is left to *John* to depict the unity in full measure, and to make the explicit equation of Crucifixion and glory. He uses the word " glory " not a few times in direct reference to the Passion; and his narrative of the Passion reflects this. In the garden the soldiers fall back, awe-struck at the Majesty of Jesus. At the trial Pilate seeks to judge Jesus, but it is Jesus who is his judge. Master of the events, Jesus carries His own Cross to Calvary, freely lays down His own life, and cries, " It is finished," for the victory is His. On the Cross Jesus is King. The Crucifixion is not a defeat needing the Resurrection to reverse it, but a victory which the Resurrection quickly follows and seals. The " glory " seen in the Cross is the eternal glory of the Father and the Son; for that eternal glory is the glory of self-giving love, and Calvary is its supreme revelation.

So it is that the centre of Apostolic Christianity is *Crucifixion-Resurrection;* not Crucifixion alone nor Resurrection alone, nor even Crucifixion as the prelude and Resurrection as the finale, but the blending of the two in a way that is as real to the Gospel as it is defiant to the world. The theme is implicit in the mission of Jesus as the Servant of the LORD, and it becomes increasingly explicit until John says the final word. To say that this theme is the centre of the Gospel is not to belittle the life and words of Jesus that precede it nor the work of the Paraclete that followed it. For Life-through-death is the principle of Jesus' whole life; it is the inward essence of the life of the Christians; and it is the unveiling of the glory of the eternal God. So utterly new and foreign to the expectations of men was this doctrine, that it seems hard to doubt that only historical events could have created it.

Chapter Two

ACCORDING TO THE SCRIPTURES

THE message of the Resurrection was the newest thing in history. Yet those who first believed it attached the utmost importance to its connection with one of the oldest things that they knew, the Scriptures of the Old Testament. This connection is still affirmed when Christians sing in the Eucharistic Creed, " On the third day He rose again according to the Scriptures." Is this affirmation a tiresome survival of the Jewish atmosphere of primitive Christianity, or has it a vital place in the Gospel of the Resurrection?

Paul wrote to the Christians of Corinth to remind them of what he had originally taught them, and he hastened to say that his teaching did not originate with himself: he had " received " the form of it, handed down from an earlier tradition:

" How that Christ died for our sins according to the scriptures; and that he was buried, and that he hath been raised on the third day according to the scriptures: and that he appeared to Cephas, then to the twelve." (I Cor. xv. 3–5.)

According to the Scriptures! The events of the Gospel were to be grasped as the fulfilment of the ancient Scriptures of the Jews. Only thus would they be truly understood. This was indeed a difficult doctrine for the people of a cosmopolitan Greek city like Corinth to swallow. They were to look to Jewry for the understanding of the things of their salvation! Yet, far and wide, converts to Christianity came so to do, for the Gospel was bound up with facts and conceptions that had their roots in the Bible of the Jews. When in the end the Graeco-Roman world was won to Christianity it seemed like the fulfilment of an old prediction that " ten men shall take hold, out of all the languages of the nations, shall even take hold of the skirt of him that is a Jew, saying, We will go with you, for we have heard that God is with you " (Zech. viii. 23).

For the message, " Now hath Christ been raised from the dead," demands that he who would understand it must think *Biblically* about Christ and about death and about Resurrection. The word *Christ* was more than a surname: it meant the anointed Messiah of God, and its background was the view of history which runs through the Bible. God chose Israel to be, in a unique way, His people: He set her free: He revealed Himself to her by His own mighty acts, of which the climax was the coming of the Messiah to vindicate His Kingdom and to draw mankind within its embrace. The word " *death* " meant in the Bible a destiny that was specially connected with sin and with separation from God. And the word " *Resurrection* " when applied to the Messiah meant inevitably an act of divine victory over both death and sin as the means of the coming of the Reign of God. Thus the Resurrection of Christ was no isolated wonder. It was inseparable from the messianic deliverance of mankind into the Kingdom of God.

I

The connection between sin and death in the Old Testament is not confined to a theory about the fall of a historical Adam. It lies deep and widespread in the Biblical attitude to man. For if man is created in the image of God, in order that he may reflect God's own attributes and live in unbroken fellowship with God, then the true and perfect relation of God and man will have no place for death. This is not to say that man was once immortal, nor is it to deny that death is natural and inevitable to man as we know him. But it is to affirm that in the true and perfect manhood death has no place. In Jesus Christ alone both spirit and body were the perfect instrument of the Spirit of God; and some have supposed that Jesus Christ in His perfect manhood was able to pass to a heavenly glory without death, and have thought that the story of the Transfiguration suggests this. But He died because He made Himself utterly one with us and trod the road which our own maimed and mortal manhood has to tread.

Death and sin are thus linked in Biblical thought. Frequently in the Bible two aspects of death are woven together. For the word is used of the cessation of a man's existence upon earth; and it is used also of the separation from God which is, to him that believes in God, the bitterest part (cf. Psa. lxxxviii. 3–5; Isa. xxxvii. 10–18).

As with death, so with life. Life means to exist upon earth as a man; and it also means to be with God (Deut. viii. 3; Isa. xxxviii. 16); for life apart from God barely deserves the name of life at all. This interweaving of the religious and the physical aspects of death and life is one of the distinctive glories of the Biblical view of man. It provides the background for a corresponding belief about the redemption wrought by Jesus Christ; for in this redemption the conquest of death is linked with the conquest of sin, and the bestowal of everlasting life is linked with the bestowal of fellowship with God. In the Reign of God there will be no more death, only because the spirits and bodies of men shall be freed from sin and made alive unto God.

It was in these terms that the Gospel concerning Jesus Christ was proclaimed and understood. The death of Christ was seen in relation to the Biblical meaning of death. It was the deepest point of His loving identification of Himself with mankind. He put Himself beside them, He went the whole way with them, He shared in the darkness of their self-sought separation from God. He plunged beneath the waters of their calamity. But He was raised from death so as to bring to the Father a life that is for ever alive unto God: " the life that he liveth, he liveth unto God." The self-centredness of human life and death finds its answer in Jesus Christ who lives because, and only because, He lives unto God. The victory over death is inseparable from the victory over sin; and the risen Christ is a revelation of manhood finding its perfect end in the life unto God, with spirit and body glorified in perfect obedience to the Spirit of God.

This victory was won in order that the human race might share in it. " Likewise reckon ye yourselves to be dead indeed unto sin but alive unto God through Jesus Christ our Lord." It was not that Christ's Resurrection exemplified an immortality that belongs to all men as they are. It was that He enabled men to be released from sin and death through union with Him, and to become sharers in *His* Resurrection. Their entry into His Resurrection is both here and hereafter. The first Christians knew that they had already become " raised together with Christ " (Col. iii. 1). But they believed also that a fuller entry awaited them after their death, for there would be a final resurrection unto their final destiny. They still must die, for death remains as long as the world shall last. But it remains only as an enemy defeated and spoiled of his power. It is no longer the last word. It has become a road along which those who are Christ's may pass to a fuller sharing in His life.

Thus the Resurrection of Christ meant far more than the addition of a new doctrine concerning the future state to the doctrines which had been held before. It concerned the whole relation of mankind to God and of God to mankind. It was an act that summed up God's purpose in history, conquered sin and death, wrought a new principle of life for this world no less than for the next, and vindicated the righteousness of the God of the Bible. Thus when many of the people of Corinth came to believe in the Resurrection of Christ, they were embracing not just a new idea about immortality but a belief in the God of Israel and the salvation which He had wrought. His Resurrection is the means of mankind's release from *its own* sin and death into *His own* life-unto-God both in this age and in the age to come.

2

The words "according to the Scriptures" had these big implications. But, immediately, they meant the fulfilment of certain passages in the Old Testament. The Resurrection sent the Apostles back to their Bible. There they could see the meaning of the new and marvellous happening. There they could find its relation to the agelong purposes of God.

The Jews had never expected that the Messiah would suffer and die, and thus they had never expected that He would rise again. They never included within their messianic expectations the description of the sufferings of the Servant of the LORD in Isa. liii. To them, there were no Scriptures that foretold either the Messiah's death or the Messiah's Resurrection. Nor had the idea of His Resurrection entered seriously into the expectation of the disciples of Jesus (cf. Mark ix. 10). It seems that the predictions of Jesus gave them no clear conviction, and right up to Easter morning they did not think that the Scriptures in any way foretold the Resurrection. Yet, when once the event had happened, they leaped to the belief

that in the raising of Jesus from death the Scriptures had been fulfilled, and they proclaimed the belief to their fellow-Jews.

Of what Scriptures were the Apostles thinking? They had in
mind proof-texts which they discovered, some of which may seem
to us to be used in ways remote from their original meaning. But
that was not all. Beneath the use of proof-texts was the conviction
that the whole story of God's words and actions in Israel had found
its climax and its key in the death and Resurrection of Christ. In
Scott Holland's words, "The entire body of ancient Scripture
opened its heart to the astonished and rejoicing Apostles." [1]

(*a*) The proof-texts appear often in the preaching of the Apostles.
For the death of Christ, the fifty-third chapter of Isaiah, with its description of the Servant of the LORD who suffered and bare the sin
of many, came quickly into use. For the Resurrection, a variety of
passages were used. There was a passage from the sixteenth Psalm,
quoted by Peter at Pentecost and by Paul in Antioch in Pisidia
(Acts ii. 25–28; xiii. 35):

> " I beheld the LORD always before my face;
>   For he is on my right hand, that I should not be moved;
>   Therefore my heart was glad, and my tongue rejoiced:
>   Moreover my flesh also shall rejoice in hope;
>   Because thou wilt not leave my soul in Hades,
>   Neither wilt thou give thy Holy One to see corruption:
>   Thou madest known unto me the ways of life:
>   Thou shalt make me full of gladness with thy countenance."
>   (Psa. xvi. 8–11.)

There was also a passage from the one hundred and eighteenth
Psalm:

> " The stone which the builders rejected
>   is become the head of the corner.
>   This is the LORD's doing:
>   it is marvellous in our eyes.
>   This is the day which the LORD hath made:
>   we will rejoice and be glad in it."
>   (Psa. cxviii 22–24 quoted Acts iv. 11; 1 Peter ii. 7.)

Yet another Psalm was quoted in reference to the vindication of
Jesus by the Resurrection as Son of God:

[1] *Op. cit.,* p. 28.

" Thou art my Son: this day have I begotten thee." (Psa. ii. 7.)

As to the exaltation of Jesus to heaven, which followed the Resurrection and is sometimes hardly separated from it in thought, the Apostolic writers make frequent use of Psalm cx:

> " The Lord said unto my Lord,
>> Sit thou on my right hand,
>> until I make thine enemies thy footstool." (Psa. cx. 1.)

This Psalm was quoted by Jesus (Mark xii. 36). It was used by Peter (Acts ii. 34); and the imagery of " the right hand of God " recurs again and again in the Apostolic writings. In all these ways the Scriptures, in the belief of the Apostles, " testified beforehand the sufferings of Christ, and the glories that should follow them " (1 Peter i. 11).

Did the Apostles also use proof-texts for the occurrence of the Resurrection *on the third day*? Here the evidence available is very slight. The New Testament contains no actual citation of any proof-text upon this point. The possible references in the Old Testament to a Resurrection on the third day are few and elusive (cf. Jonah i. 17; Hosea vi. 2; 2 Kings xx. 5); and it is therefore unlikely that the Old Testament passages can have created the belief that the Resurrection occurred on the third day. It is far more probable that the event, attested by good evidence, created any use of proof-texts that was made. As to such use of texts, it is possible — some would say it is probable — that the Apostles made use of Hosea's words:

> " Come, and let us return unto the Lord;
>> For he hath torn, and he will heal us:
>> He hath smitten, and he will bind us up.
>> After two days will he revive us;
>> On the third day he will raise us up,
>> And we shall live before him." (Hosea vi. 1–2.)

There is also recorded in Matthew a saying of Jesus:

" As Jonah was three days and three nights in the belly of the whale: so shall the Son of man be three days and three nights in the heart of the earth." (Matt. xii. 40.)

These words may be an elaboration of a simpler saying about the sign of Jonah that occurs in the primitive source (cf. Luke xi. 29–

32). They suggest in God's deliverance of Jonah from his plight a comparison with God's raising of Christ from death. There is no decisive reason why Jesus should not have spoken them.

(*b*) It was, however, not only in terms of proof-texts that the Apostles were thinking. There was a larger fact that lay beneath the use of these texts. The particular passages had their significance because the Scriptures *as a whole* had found fulfilment. What God did of old time, in the call and redemption of Israel, in the catastrophes and deliverances of her history, has now found its climax in the deliverance of Christ from death.

Throughout the Old Testament there had been the strain of a tension which, it seemed, could never be resolved. On the one hand there was the faith of Israel in God's sovereignty and righteousness and faithfulness to His people. On the other hand there were the sufferings of the righteous and the cries of the afflicted. The tension ran through the history of Israel, and it sometimes strained the faith of Israel nearly to the point of breaking. But, now that the Christ has Himself suffered and been raised from death, the tension within the Scriptures is resolved and the unity of the Scriptures has been disclosed. For it is perceived that the sufferings of the Servant of the Lord do not contradict the sovereign power of God; rather are those sufferings the means whereby God has wrought mightily in His purpose to deliver mankind.

Thus the Scriptures, being vindicated by Jesus Christ, seem in divers ways to speak about Him. Passages about the sufferings of the righteous seem to describe His Passion (cf. Psa. xxii). Passages about God's mighty deliverances seem to bear witness to His Resurrection. The Old Testament is found both to foretell Christ and to preach Him.

If the reader will turn to the speech of St. Paul at Antioch in Pisidia (Acts xiii. 16–41), he will see a clear illustration of the two aspects of fulfilment. There is in this speech the characteristic use of proof-texts. St. Paul cites Psa. ii, Psa. xvi, Isa. lv. 3 and Hab. i. 5 in his preaching of the Resurrection. But there is also in this speech that which underlies the use of proof-texts, namely, the conviction of the unity of God's acts in Israel and His acts in Christ.

" Men of Israel, and ye that fear God, hearken. The God of this people Israel *chose* our fathers, and *exalted* the people when they sojourned in the land of Egypt, and with a high arm he *led them forth* out of it. . . . He *gave* them their land . . . he *gave* them judges . . . he *gave* unto them Saul the Son of Kish . . . he *raised up* David to be their king . . . he *brought* unto Israel a Saviour Jesus . . . God *raised him from the dead*. . . . And we bring unto you good tidings of the promise made unto the fathers, how that God hath fulfilled the same unto our children, in that he raised up Jesus. . . . Beware therefore, lest that come upon you, which is spoken in the prophets:

> Behold, ye despisers, and wonder and perish:
> For I work a work in your days,
> A work which we shall in no wise believe, if one
>   declare it unto you."

For the God of Israel is a God who " raises up." In divers ways the word " raise up " is used of His acts in the Old Testament. He raised up prophets, judges, the poor, the nation, the fallen tabernacle of David (Amos ix. 11), a righteous branch (Jer. xxiii. 5), a shepherd in the land (Zech. xi. 16). Israel's history is misunderstood if it is treated primarily as a story of human genius gradually advancing in its ideas about God. It is God who acts, speaking, calling, delivering. The history of Israel is a series of crises wherein in hours of catastrophe God stretches out His arm in judgment and mercy. Finally a day comes when Jesus Christ, identifying Himself with Israel, bears the destiny of Israel with Him to the Cross and the grave; and God raises Him, and with Him Israel, from out of death.

The central theme of the Apostles was not belief in the Resurrection, so much as belief in the God who raised up Jesus. As we have seen, to be a Christian was " to believe on him who raised up Jesus our Lord from the dead " (Rom. iv. 24; cf. 1 Peter i. 21) and New Testament theism is essentially Resurrection-theism. It is sometimes said that the one really important fact is that the life of Jesus continues, and therefore the act whereby this was effected cannot greatly matter. It is indeed impossible to exaggerate the importance of the fact that the life of Jesus continues, and the Apostles dwelt upon this fact constantly. But it was not all that mattered. God had raised Him up, and the Apostles dwelt upon this act of raising; ὁ Θεὸς ἤγειρεν, Χριστὸς ἠγέρθη, those are the characteristic words used.[1] For the act of raising reveals the God of Israel, the God who raises from death, the living God as yet unknown to Athens and Corinth. The Christians came to know

" the exceeding greatness of his power to usward who believe, according to that working of the strength of his might which he wrought in Christ, when he raised him from the dead." (Eph. i. 19–20.)

3

It is not therefore surprising that the Apostles described the Resurrection by likening it to two of the greatest acts of the power of God of which they could read in the Old Testament. God created the world: God led Israel out of Egypt in the Exodus. The Apostles believed that they were witnesses of a new Exodus of Israel, and a new act of creation as momentous as when God said, " Let there be light: and there was light."

THE NEW EXODUS

In Luke's account of the Transfiguration we read that " there talked with him two men which were Moses and Elijah; who appeared in glory and *spake about his exodus* which he was about to fulfil in Jerusalem " (ix. 30–31). The Greek word used is "exodus." The word can mean a man's departure in death, and in the Authorized Version and Revised Version it is here translated " decease." But its normal meaning is simply " going-forth," or " exodus," and such may be the suggestion here. It was of an Exodus of Israel that Moses and Elijah spoke. The Passion, foretold by Jesus six days before, would be the prelude to a new Exodus of the people of God from bondage to freedom.

Such was the belief of the Apostles. Israel in rejecting the Messiah brought doom upon herself. But the Messiah was raised from death to be the head of a new Israel, a spiritual race and nation. As the old Israel looked back to the Exodus from Egypt and kept the Passover to commemorate God's deliverance, so the new Israel looks back to the Exodus from sin and death in the Passion and

[1] Throughout the New Testament the Resurrection is most often described not as Jesus raising Himself but as Jesus being raised or as God raising Him. A notable exception is John x. 17, " I lay down my life that I may take it again."

Resurrection and commemorates God's deliverance in the sacrament of the Body and Blood of Christ.

Thus Peter in his First Epistle reminds his readers that they are participants in a new Exodus. He begins with an outburst of praise for the Resurrection, whereby the Christians were begotten again unto a living hope unto an inheritance in heaven. They have been set free by the blood of Christ, as their fathers believed themselves to have been set free by the lamb of the Passover (i. 18–19). They are, like Israel of old, " an elect race, a royal priesthood, a holy nation, a people for God's own possession " (ii. 9). Paul gives essentially the same picture. The passing through the sea, the eating of the manna from heaven, the drinking of the water from the rock, all have their greater counterpart in the new Exodus of the Christians (cf. 1 Cor. x. 1–4). It is the same God who has wrought deliverance; and from Apostolic times the Church of Christ has found in the Psalms about the Exodus a fitting language for the praises of the God of Israel who is still their God and has led them forth by Jesus Christ, the shepherd raised from death (cf. Heb. xiii. 20).

> " Thy way was in the sea,
> And thy paths in the great waters
> And thy footsteps were not known,
> Thou leadest thy people like a flock
> By the hand of Moses and Aaron." (Psa. lxxvii. 19–20.)

THE NEW CREATION

It was more than a new Exodus which the Apostles found in the Resurrection. It was the begetting of a new race, and the creation of a new world. These things were wrought by the Holy Spirit bestowed by the risen Jesus: they were the immediate impact of the Resurrection.

Here again the Epistle of Peter tells of the new belief. The Resurrection was the source of a new-begetting.

" Blessed be the God and Father of our Lord Jesus Christ who according to his great mercy begat us again unto a living hope by the resurrection of Jesus Christ from the dead." (1 Peter i. 3.)

"S. Peter's language," wrote Dr. Hort in his commentary, " includes the conception of entrance into a new order of existence but combines with it that of a divine parentage: men enter the new life as children of its author." " The hope is living," writes Fr. Thornton, " because it springs up in the new life to which we have been begotten again; and this took place through the resurrection. Our Lord's resurrection is doubtless ' instrumental in our rebirth, because it guarantees both his Messiahship and our immortality.' But this is not simply a forceful way of saying that ' hope was reborn in us.' For the resurrection of Christ was something more than a guarantee of Christian truths. The resurrection was the historical channel through which God acted when he begat us again." [1]

The new birth or begetting is realised in the rite of Christian baptism. It is wrought by the Holy Spirit; it is received by the repentance and faith of the convert: but the impact of the Resurrection alone makes it possible. For the Resurrection both asserts the lordship of Jesus beneath which the convert passes into his new life; and it enables the convert to share in the risen life of Jesus. This relation includes the gift of sonship, for it is the emphatic teaching of the New Testament that men *become* sons of God through the action of the Holy Spirit who reproduces Christ's sonship in them (Rom. viii. 14–15; John i. 12). Christ is thus " the firstborn among many brethren " (Rom. viii. 29); but He is so only because He is " the firstborn from the dead" (Col. i. 18). The great doctrine that Christ is the Second Adam, the author of a new humanity that is being moulded into His own true image, has its basis in the Resurrection. " The first man Adam became a living soul. The last Adam became a life-giving spirit " (1 Cor. xv. 45). The original man possessed the life that God gave to him, but the New Man Christ bestows life upon mankind. A new birth, a new sonship, a new race have their origin in the Resurrection of Christ.

This tremendous language, used by the Apostolic writers, shews that they believe the Resurrection to be not merely a great event upon the plane of history, but an act that breaks into history with the powers of another world. It is akin to the creation in the beginning; and the Gospel is the good news that God is creating a new world.

" For we preach not ourselves, but Christ Jesus as Lord and ourselves as your servants for Jesus' sake. Seeing it is God, that said, Light shall

[1] *The Common Life in the Body of Christ*, p. 197.

shine out of darkness, who shined in our hearts, to give the light of the knowledge of the glory of God in the face of Jesus Christ." (2 Cor. iv. 5–6.)

These words recall the dazzling light that confronted Paul at his conversion. He comes to know that this light betokens a new creation. God spake, and it was done. He spake in the mission, death and Resurrection of Jesus.

"Wherefore if any man is in Christ there is a new creation; the old things are passed away, behold they are become new." (2 Cor. v. 17.)

A new world has dawned, and the Christians belong to it already.
It is not only the spiritual aspect of man that is affected by the Resurrection. In face of the contemporary Hellenistic teaching that the body is irrelevant and is to be left behind in the interests of a purely spiritual salvation, the first Christians insisted that the body, created by God, is also redeemed by God. The body is for the Lord.

"If the Spirit of him that raised up Jesus from the dead dwelleth in you, he that raised up Christ Jesus from the dead shall quicken also your mortal bodies through his Spirit that dwelleth in you." (Rom. viii. 11.)

Both here and hereafter the bodies of the Christians share in the effects of Christ's victory over death.[1] Nor is it man alone that is embraced by the Resurrection; for the deliverance of mankind will be the prelude to the freeing of nature from its present frustration, and

"the creation itself also shall be delivered from the bondage of corruption into the liberty of the glory of the children of God." (Rom. viii. 21.)

The liturgies of Eastern Christendom have echoed the Apostolic belief that all the world is destined to share in the new creation wrought by the Resurrection.

"For meet it is that the heavens should rejoice: and that the earth should be glad, and that the whole world, both visible and invisible, should keep the Feast. For Christ is risen, the everlasting joy.

[1] The implications of the " bodily resurrection " of the Christians are discussed in Chapter Eight of this book.

" Now all things are filled with light, heaven and earth and all the places under the earth. All creation doth celebrate the Resurrection of Christ.

" Rejoice, O creation and bloom like a lily! For Christ as God has risen from the dead! O death, where is thy sting? O grave, where is thy victory?

" As God thou didst arise from the grave in glory, and with thee didst raise the world."

It was in no spirit of dream or of phantasy that the Apostles dared to say that a new creation was being wrought. They were not weaving an academic doctrine or spinning an apocalyptic theory. They were missionaries, immersed in the practical tasks of their calling and grimly realistic about the state of the hostile world. But they knew that in the Resurrection of Christ another world had come, and that they were already its citizens; and they summoned men to enter it with them and to claim it as their own. The old world continued with its contradictions and its sufferings, but by the Cross and the Resurrection these very contradictions and sufferings could be transformed into things fruitful and creative wherein, by faith in the Crucified, the power of God might be found. There was no escaping from the facts of this world. Rather did their membership within the world-to-come enable them to see the facts of this world with the light of the Cross and the Resurrection upon them, and to know that their own tasks were but the working out of a victory that Christ had already won.

All this had been wrought by the God of their fathers and their Scriptures. It was the Lord's doing, and it was marvellous in their eyes.

Chapter Three

HISTORY AND BELIEF

I

THE theology of the Apostles sprang, as we have seen, not from their own theorizing, but from certain historical events which led them to beliefs far removed from their own preconceived notions. The most significant of the events was the Resurrection. What sort of event was this? What in fact happened? Before we turn, as turn we must, to the direct historical evidence, we may ask: What sort of event is postulated by the message which we have seen to pervade the teaching and writing of the Apostles?

Clearly the Apostles' message rested upon an event of *Resurrection* as distinct from an event of *survival*. The distinction is big and important, between a Resurrection and the survival of an immortal soul. In the Platonist doctrine of immortality the body dies, but the soul continues its life. Thus, really and essentially, there is no death for that aspect of man that is deemed to be of eternal importance; the truth is that " in the sight of the unwise they *seem* to have died." Very different is a belief that the continuing life of the soul by itself is a maimed and incomplete life, that death is real with no semblance attaching to it, that Resurrection is the raising from out of death of a life that will be as rich and richer in the unity of soul and body than the life that existed previous to death.

Now the central theme of the Apostolic teaching is bound up with the belief not that Jesus spiritually survived, but that Jesus was raised. (*a*) He truly died. He underwent, so both the Gospels and the Epistles tell us, the whole fact of death in all its bitterness. His soul was exceeding sorrowful even unto death. He tasted of death for sinners, making Himself one with them. He took upon Himself the reality of death in its connection with sin. The death was real and complete. If it could be said of Jesus that " in the sight of the unwise He seemed to have died " and that His essential and complete life survived from the hour of the Crucifixion, then the central theme of the Apostolic Gospel would be rendered void and false. (*b*) Further, it is not only the continuing life of the risen Jesus that matters supremely in New Testament Christianity. For besides the emphasis upon " Jesus Christ the same, yesterday, to-day, and for ever " there is in the Apostolic teaching an equal emphasis upon the *act* of God in raising Him. It is the *act* that reveals the power of the living God; and the Christian life is lived in relation to this initial *act* no less than in relation to the contemporary presence of Jesus. (*c*) Further, the event upon which the Gospel rests is unique, redemptive, creative. It is not that Jesus Christ by surviving death demonstrates that all good men survive it too. The Resurrection is far more than an illustration or an example of human immortality. It is a victory uniquely won, and won in order that mankind may be enabled to share in *Christ's* Resurrection. It does for us what we cannot do for ourselves.

The Gospel therefore postulates as its basis not an illustration of survival but a miracle of Resurrection. Its character as a miracle does not depend upon any portentous happenings that may have accompanied it nor upon its being a "bodily" as distinct from a "spiritual" act. The Resurrection is a miracle because it is a unique redemptive and creative intervention of God; it interrupts the hitherto normal workings of historical cause and effect and the hitherto normal workings of the order of human sinfulness, and ushers in a new stage in the cosmic process. "It is evident," wrote Westcott, "that if the claim to be a miraculous religion is essentially incredible, Apostolic Christianity is simply false."

A miracle may be called an event wrought by God which does not fit into the hitherto observable laws of nature. It resembles in one way the actions of the free wills of men which disturb the dispositions of nature; and it resembles in another way the operations of the grace of God in human lives. It is credible to those who, recognizing the potentialities of free will in man to distort the divine design, do not deny to the living God His own freedom in His work as redeemer. If the Resurrection breaks what appears to be law, it does so in order to vindicate another and a higher aspect of law. As a miracle, it is the disclosure of an order of being new, unknown, transcendental. It is, in the literal sense of the word, a "revelation": it unveils a new level of glorified human life.

Yet though it is a miracle in relation to the observable laws of the world that we know, the Resurrection is, in relation to the new order that it discloses, natural, inevitable, lawful. It shews us perfect human nature glorified through a perfect response to the Spirit of God. It shews us the goal for which human nature was created, and to which it will be raised when the law of the Spirit of life in Christ Jesus sets men free from the law of sin and death (cf. Rom. viii. 2). It shews us both the crown of the purpose of God in the Scriptures, and the crown of His purpose in the created world, wherein new levels of life succeed to old levels and the series of successions arouses what Butler called " the implicit hope of something further."

The miracle of the Resurrection could thus be made known only to those who responded to the new level of spiritual existence which it disclosed. It was not a portent which could be shewn to all and sundry to scare them into belief. Westcott's classic words are worth quoting:

" If then the life of the risen Lord had been simply a renovation or a continuance of the former life, subject to the same conditions and neces-sarily destined to the same inevitable close, then the experience of un-believers would have been sufficient to test, the witness of unbelievers would have been adequate to establish the reality of the Resurrection. But if it was a foreshadowing of new powers of human action, of a new mode of human being, then without a corresponding power of spiritual discernment there could be no testimony to its truth. The world could not see Christ, and Christ could not — there is a divine impossibility — shew Himself to the world. To have proved by incontestable evidence that Christ rose again as Lazarus rose again would have been not to con-firm our faith, but to destroy it irretrievably." [1]

There was in the Resurrection a gentleness and a restraint akin to that which was seen in the ministry and in the Passion.

This is not to say that the appeal to historical evidence is unim-portant. On the contrary, the evidence is of great importance. It may be shewn that certain historical facts are unaccountable apart from the Resurrection, and that different lines of historical testi-mony so converge as to point to the Resurrection with overwhelm-ing probability. But decisive proof can never be provided. Belief in

[1] *The Revelation of the Risen Lord*, pp. 11–12.

the Resurrection, involving as it does the most strict historical considerations, involves also belief in Jesus Christ.

The narratives in the Gospels suggest that a number of factors played their part in leading the Apostles to their belief. It was not the news of the empty tomb alone that convinced them: of itself this news seemed to them to be idle talk. There was need besides the empty tomb for the appearances of Jesus; and here far more was involved than proof by means of visible phenomena. There was the gradual impact of the risen Jesus upon their minds and consciences; and there was the unfolding of the Scriptures so that what they heard and saw became integrated with their faith in God and His righteous purpose for mankind. The tomb, the appearances, the converse of Jesus, the Scriptures — all these had their place in leading the Apostles through fear to wonder, through wonder to faith, and through faith to worship. For their belief included not only a conviction that a certain event had happened, but faith in the God who wrought it and in the Crucified Jesus whom it vindicated.

2

The historical evidence now demands examination. If apologists have sometimes made the mistake of seeking to " prove " the Resurrection, and if historical critics have sometimes made the mistake of investigating the history without due appreciation of the theology with which it was linked from the very first, it would be a no less grievous mistake to rest in theological affirmations and to belittle the scope of scientific historical inquiry. It is by their readiness to welcome such inquiry and to participate in it that the teachers of Christianity make good their claim that the Gospel rests upon fact.

In this chapter therefore the main elements in the historical evidence for the Resurrection will be described: and in the chapters that follow there will be some account of the trend of modern investigation and some fresh examination of the chief problems presented by the narratives in the Gospels.

What is the evidence? It might be claimed that the Apostolic Gospel, which we have already been studying in this book, is in itself evidence, for it bears no marks of having originated in theory or speculation and it bears many marks of having originated in events that created it and gave it its distinctive character. What, however, is the more direct evidence which the historian must investigate?

(*a*) It is important, first, to notice that the Resurrection was not expected. The available evidence suggests that neither the Scriptures nor the words of Jesus had led the disciples to a conviction that He would rise again. If the predictions by Jesus of His Passion went home to the disciples, the predictions of the Resurrection (if indeed He made such predictions explicitly) caused no clear expectation.

There are first the three "formal" predictions of the Resurrection recorded by Mark. Thrice, after foretelling the Passion, Jesus is said to have added the words "and after three days rise again" (Mark viii. 31; ix. 31; x. 34). Matthew and Luke, in editing the passages, alter the words "after three days" to "on the third day." [1] The predictions are full of detail, mentioning the delivery of Jesus by the Jews to the Gentiles, the mocking, the scourging, the Crucifixion, the Resurrection. It is possible, as many scholars are inclined to think, that the words have been elaborated and formalized in the light of knowledge after the event.

Yet it is likely that predictions of a rising again were made by Jesus. Mark ix. 10 depicts the disciples "questioning among themselves what the rising again from the dead should mean"; and besides the three "formal" predictions there are other more allusive ones. (1) There is the injunction not to make known the Transfiguration "save when the Son of Man should have risen again from the dead" (Mark ix. 9). (2) There is the saying on the night before the Passion, "Howbeit, after I am raised up, I will go before you into Galilee" (Mark xiv. 28). (3) There is a puzzling saying, in answer to a warning that Herod seeks to kill Him, "Behold, I cast out devils and perform cures today and tomorrow, and the

[1] There is evidence that the phrase "the third day" sometimes bore the meaning of "a very short time," i.e., before a visitor had become a resident or before a dead body had begun to suffer decay. Thus it is possible that Jesus so used the phrase as to convey to the disciples that death and defeat would after a very short space be followed by victory. Cf. John xvi. 17, "a little while, and ye shall see me."

third day I am perfected " (Luke xiii. 32), a saying which may originally have had no reference to the rising again on the third day.
(4) There is the saying, peculiar to Matthew, where the coming
burial of Jesus in the earth is likened to the sojourn of Jonah for
three days and nights in the belly of a whale (Matt. xii. 40; contrast Luke xi. 29–30). If genuine, this saying might have conveyed
to the disciples no more than that there would be for Jesus a humiliation and a deliverance akin to that of Jonah of old. (5) There was
also the saying recorded in the Fourth Gospel, " Destroy this temple, and in three days I will raise it up " (John ii. 18–19), a saying
that has a counterpart in the Synoptists who record that Jesus at
His trial was accused of threatening to destroy the temple and to
build another in three days (Mark xiv. 58). As we shall see, the
saying anticipates the destruction of the old order symbolized by
the temple and its replacement by the risen Christ with His Body
and Temple, the new Israel. Such are the predictions which the
Gospels record.

The predictions are mysterious, elusive: the more so because Jesus
made predictions in other kinds of imagery too. He spoke of the
coming of the Son of Man in glory (Mark xiv. 62), of the coming
of the Kingdom of God in power (Mark ix. 1), of the banquet in
the Kingdom of God with the disciples (Mark xiv. 25), of " that
day" (Luke x. 12), of the " day of the Son of Man " (Matt. xxiv.
27–39; Luke xvii. 26–27), as well as of a rising " on the third day."
Perhaps the varied imagery depicted one and the same event, a
coming of the Reign of God into history in a manner that defied
exact description. A divine victory was coming, beyond the Passion.
But meanwhile the disciples were, it seems, left bewildered as to
what to expect. The predictions of the Passion filled their minds
with dark forebodings; and beyond this point their minds could
hardly move.

The disciples were not anticipating the Resurrection. It is possible to dismiss at the outset any view that their belief in it sprang
from a projection of their own expectations.

(b) Next, there is the evidence provided by the existence of the
Church in spite of the catastrophe of Good Friday. What happened,
so as to change the disciples from survivors of a cause that was
broken and crushed into men who could bid the nation to repent

and be baptized into the name of Christ, and could proclaim even the Crucifixion itself to be a Gospel?

This is a question that the historian cannot avoid. If he advances the hypothesis that the disciples were led to imagine a great event by the projection of their own hopes and preconceptions, he will be met by the evidence that the belief in the Resurrection stretched the disciples far beyond their own presuppositions and turned these presuppositions upside down. If he advances the hypothesis that the personality of Jesus had so gripped them and His teaching had so influenced them that they were unable to think of Him as dead and gone and were convinced that He lived on, he will be met by the evidence that the centre of their preaching was not the personality and teaching of Jesus but the Cross and the Resurrection. It must not be forgotten that the teaching and ministry of Jesus did not provide the disciples with a Gospel, and led them from puzzle to paradox until the Resurrection gave them a key. The whole claim of Jesus to proclaim and to embody the Reign of God breaks down in deceit or in failure if Calvary is the end. Without the Resurrection the historian has the problem of Jesus, no less than the problem of the Church, to explain.

(c) There is the evidence that the disciples became subject to the impact of Jesus Christ moulding their minds and hearts. This is evidence from religious experience, and it is beset by the difficulties and limitations which belong to such evidence. But evidence it is. In the case of Saul of Tarsus the impact began while he was persecuting the disciples of the Crucified Jesus. He records the reversal that he underwent: the revolution of his entire relation to God, to Christ, to the world, and to himself. He exemplified this revolution in every part of a life of action, thought and suffering; and he ascribed it to an unwanted and unexpected act of Christ. "For neither did I receive it from man, neither was I taught it, but it came to me through revelation of Jesus Christ" (Gal. i. 12); "I was apprehended by Christ Jesus" (Phil. iii. 12). The testimony cannot easily be dismissed, for it is corroborated by the testimony of other Apostles, and it is related not to a narrow field of religion or emotion but to the whole of a life wherein thinking, feeling and action were made creative under the new and unexpected impulse.

(d) There is the evidence that Jesus appeared to the disciples.

We find this evidence in Paul's statements about himself, in the tradition that Paul received concerning other Apostles, and in the narratives in the Gospels.

Paul distinguishes the appearances of the risen Jesus to him from visions of a mystical sort which he had at other times. He sometimes experienced " visions and revelations of the Lord " and in one of these he was caught up into the third heaven (2 Cor. xii. 2). He was careful to attach small importance to these experiences and to be reticent about them. But he speaks in a totally different manner about the claim that, at the beginning of his discipleship, he saw Jesus. It was an appearance of Jesus akin to the appearances to the other Apostles (1 Cor. xv. 8). " Am I not an apostle? Have I not seen Jesus Christ? " (1 Cor. ix. 1). He could not be reticent about that appearance of Jesus which was the basis of his mission and his authority.

The accounts of Paul's conversion in the Acts (chs. ix; xxii; xxvi) differ from one another in some details, but they are congruous with Paul's own evidence in his Epistles and they " really present a perfectly harmonious picture, that Saul beheld an external vision of Christ in His risen glory; that it came to him suddenly and without; that it was so far from his thoughts and anticipations that he utterly failed to recognize who it was that appeared before him; that it was only in answer to his bewildered exclamation ' who art thou, Lord? ' that he was told ' I am Jesus of Nazareth whom thou persecutest '; that he trembled and was astonished, and in utter helplessness appealed for further knowledge, ' Lord, what wilt thou have me to do? ' " [1]

But it is not only to the appearance of Jesus to himself that Paul refers. He records, and amplifies, the primitive tradition of the appearances to the eleven and to others. He gives the " list " in 1 Cor. xv.

" He appeared to Cephas: then to the twelve: then he appeared unto five hundred brethren at once, of whom the greater part remain until now, but some are fallen asleep: then he appeared to James: then to all the apostles: and last of all, as unto one born out of due time, he appeared to me also." (1 Cor. xv. 5–8.)

[1] Sparrow-Simpson, *Our Lord's Resurrection*, pp. 117–118.

It is not clear at what point in this list Paul is passing from the primitive tradition to supplementary information of his own. But plainly the appearances to Cephas and to the twelve belong to the primitive tradition. Paul would have learnt this tradition when he made his first visit to Jerusalem after his conversion and saw Peter, possibly not more than nine years after the Crucifixion. Here indeed is early evidence. It is not surprising that the tradition, in the brief form here used, makes no mention of the appearances to the women, for it was the testimony of the Apostles that would be held to have a special authority. To the Corinthians, mention of the evidence of women quite unknown to them would carry little weight.

The evidence here cited by Paul appears some decades later in ampler form in the narratives in the Gospels. The appearance to Cephas is alluded to in Luke; the appearance to the Apostles is described by Luke and John; an appearance to a larger number of disciples in Galilee is described by Matthew; there is no mention of an appearance to James.

(e) There is, lastly, the evidence that the women found the tomb empty upon the third day after the Crucifixion and reported the news to the Apostles. This evidence is set forth in the Gospels. Mark describes the visit of the women; John follows a separate tradition of a visit by Mary Magdalene alone. According to John — and some MSS. of Luke — Apostles came to the tomb to verify the news for themselves.

There is no reference to this evidence in documents earlier than the Gospels; and the question arises, Did the empty tomb have a place in the primitive tradition? It seems that although the primitive tradition as we know it does not mention the *evidence* about the empty tomb, it none the less implied the belief in it. The words of the tradition, as Paul reproduces it, seem incomprehensible unless they mean that the body of Jesus was raised up.

"How that Christ died . . . and that he was buried . . . and that he hath been raised again on the third day."

Died — buried — raised: the words are used very strangely unless they mean that what was buried was raised up. What otherwise is the point of the reference to the burial? In default of the very strongest evidence that Paul meant something different and was using words in a most unnatural way, the sentence must refer to a raising up of the body. The most radical of critics, Schmiedel, and the most scientific of critics, Lake, agreed that the *belief* in the empty tomb is implied in these words.

It is, however, sometimes said that Paul cannot have known of the evidence about the discovery of the empty tomb, or else he would have alluded to this evidence in 1 Cor. xv. This suggestion was long ago answered by Lake: " Was there any reason why St. Paul should have supplied these details had he known them? Surely not. He was not trying to convince the Corinthians that the Lord was risen: he was reminding them that he had already convinced them." [1] It is therefore impossible to draw any conclusion that Paul must or must not have known about the women's story. What is clear is that the tradition as he received it meant the death and the burial and the raising up of Jesus from the tomb. But the evidence for the empty tomb is not here cited; and it is only in the Gospels that we find it set forth.

Such are the main factors in the evidence for the Resurrection. The event itself no man saw, and no evangelist has dared to describe, though the writer of the Apocryphal " Gospel of Peter " so dared. But the evidence that points to the event is the existence of the Church, the experience of the earliest Christians, the records of the appearances of Jesus, and the records of the empty tomb. Though the evidence about the empty tomb is not cited in the earlier documents, the belief that the Resurrection was *on the third day* has a place in the earliest known tradition (1 Cor. xv. 4). It is unlikely [2] that Old Testament passages created this belief. It is far more likely that an event itself created it. For there is the early evidence also that the first day of the week replaced the seventh day because it was the day upon which the Lord rose again (1 Cor. xvi. 2; Acts xx. 7).

---

[1] *The Historical Evidence for the Resurrection of Jesus Christ,* p. 194.
[2] And Kirsopp Lake agreed, *op. cit.,* p. 112.

3

Of the evidence that has been described different factors have had their special importance for different occasions and needs. To the Apostles themselves it was perhaps the appearances that mattered most. To them the most thrilling fact was that Jesus had shewn Himself to them alive and had spoken with them. This evidence was overwhelming and compelling; and it was more than evidence: it was the risen Jesus Himself. But for subsequent believers the story of the empty tomb would have an increased significance; for it was not enough to rely upon the testimony of the religious experiences of particular men, and the story of the empty tomb was the clearest witness to the Act which preceded any and and all experiences of the risen Jesus, to the ἠγέρθη, " He was raised," which preceded the ὤφθη, " He was seen."

For centuries the empty tomb became the great evidential symbol that far more had happened than either the survival of the soul of Jesus or certain religious experiences of the Apostles: sin and death had been conquered by the Resurrection of Jesus from out of death. But in modern times the historical criticism of the Gospels has given rise to the question, Was the belief in the empty tomb a false inference and an unwarranted addition to a primitive Gospel in which originally it had no place?

Chapter Four

HISTORY AND CRITICISM

I

FOR many centuries there was little tendency within the Christian Church to doubt any part of the body of evidence for the Resurrection which the New Testament contains. The empty tomb and the appearances both had their place in the defence and in the interpretation of Christian belief. The belief was that the body of Jesus was raised from the tomb, not so as to return to the former mode of life but so as to be "glorified." It was no longer subject to the laws of its former existence; it became the perfect instrument of the spirit. It was — to borrow the phrase by which Paul described the risen body of the Christians — "raised a spiritual body."

This belief was congruous both with the empty tomb and with Paul's doctrine of the spiritual body. It was also congruous with two seemingly contrary features in the narratives of the appearances. On the one hand the narratives describe Jesus as acting in a manner reminiscent of the conditions of His life during His earthly ministry. He invites the disciples to touch Him: He breaks bread and eats with them: He walks with them. He assures them in all these ways that He is the same Jesus whom they have known before. On the other hand there are features of the narratives which suggest a mode of life new and utterly unlike the former mode. He is seen only by disciples; He is recognized by them gradually; He appears suddenly and as suddenly disappears. These aspects of the story suggest that, if the risen life is indeed bodily, it is bodily with a difference.

Now this twofold aspect of the narratives was taken by orthodox teachers to be evidence of a twofold truth. First, the risen Jesus is the same Jesus, and He enabled the disciples, by the only means that can be imagined, to know that He was the same Jesus whose victory over death had been complete. Yet, though He was the same, He had entered a new mode of being. Into this new mode of being all that had belonged to Him before is taken up and transformed. What previously had been marvellous was now normal, what previously had been normal was now marvellous.

If some theologians, both in the ancient Church and subsequently, took the appearances as manifestations of the risen Body in its essential state, there was another tradition which insisted that the visibility and tangibility by which He made Himself known to the disciples were evidential accommodations made for the disciples' sake. This tradition had celebrated exponents in the ancient Church, notably John Chrysostom in his commentaries. It was upheld by Bishop Westcott: " A little reflection will show that the special outward forms in which the Lord was pleased to make Himself known were no more necessarily connected with His glorified person than the robes which he wore." [1] Yet Westcott was equally firm in his belief that the glorified body was the body that had been raised from the tomb, for " it is not that Christ's soul lives on divested of the essence as of the accidents of the earthly garments in which it was for a time arrayed. It is not that His body, torn and mutilated, is restored such as it was to its former vigour and beauty. But in Him soul and body in the union of a perfect manhood are seen triumphant over the last penalty of sin." [2]

Westcott's teaching represents the historic faith of the Church as presented in a spirit of scholarly orthodoxy in the latter decades of the last century. His teaching is of abiding importance. It is in keeping both with the Gospels and with St. Paul. It is, like the work of his master Origen, both profoundly orthodox and strangely modern. It holds to the New Testament belief that the spiritual and the material are not at permanent variance; both are created by God who wills that both shall be redeemed and exalted. It is congruous also with those factors in modern science and philosophy which suggest that the continuity of a body lies not in the identity of the particles which compose it but in the identity of its organization or " form " in relation to the person whose it is. Westcott's teaching may yet be found to outlive the theories which the succeeding half-century has produced.

---

[1] *The Gospel of the Resurrection*, p. 112.
[2] *The Revelation of the Risen Lord*, p. 10.

2

In the past hundred years the evidence for the Resurrection, like every part of the records concerning the origins of Christianity, has been subjected to the methods of historical criticism and research. It had been usual to accept the Gospels as inspired documents of uniform value and authority for the events which they describe; and the task of the historian would be almost limited to attempts to harmonize and to interpret what was recorded. But the application of a rigorous historical science to the Gospels involved the method of treating them "like other books." Their literary sources were unravelled; the tendencies of the different writers or editors were detected; and a frank examination was made of the possibility that the historical material may have been embroidered by legendary elements or by theological motives. In particular the question had to be faced: how far did the early Christians read back developments of doctrine and devotion into their records of the events?

In the case of the Resurrection the scope for such investigations is obviously great. The accounts of the appearances of Jesus are difficult to harmonize into a coherent story. The events of the first Easter morning are difficult to form into a consecutive plan. Above all, is it possible that the Apostles' belief that the *body* of Jesus had been raised from the tomb was a false inference derived from Jewish presuppositions as to what a Resurrection meant, whereas in fact the Resurrection was a survival of the spirit of Jesus? It is around this question that historical research has specially moved.

The attempts of scholars throughout more than a century to discover the real events of Easter have gone hand in hand with the attempts to discover the real Jesus of history behind the figure described in the New Testament and worshipped by the primitive Church. It is a story full of scholarly achievement, of devotion to Jesus, of zeal for truth. But it is also a story full of the blinding effects of the presuppositions sometimes held by historians who are convinced that they are working without any presuppositions at all. Here it is possible only to record some of the types of conclusions reached by those who have applied the methods of critical science to the narratives of the Resurrection.

(*a*) First of all there comes into view the line of writers, from Strauss onwards, who have concluded that the appearances of Jesus recorded in the Gospels were simply visions generated by the imaginations of the disciples out of an intense state of emotion or expectancy. In a state of fervent devotion they imagined that they saw Jesus. " *Ce qui a ressuscité Jésus, c'est l'amour,*" wrote Renan in describing how the over-wrought feelings of Mary Magdalene led her to think that she saw her Master. *Strauss* and *Renan* were among the nineteenth-century biographers of Jesus who upheld this " subjective-vision " theory, as it is sometimes called. Among later critical writers who reached this conclusion were *Schmiedel*, whose article on " Resurrection and Ascension narratives " in the *Encyclopedia Biblica* is perhaps the most radical treatment of the problem that has been published, and *Montefiore*, the devout and learned liberal Jew, in his commentary upon the Synoptic Gospels.

It has not been difficult to point out the weaknesses that are involved in this theory. It contradicts some very marked features of the narratives — the slowness of the disciples to grasp that Jesus was alive and to recognize Him, the way in which the appearance so far from reflecting the disciples' own spiritual ideas led them beyond themselves into utterly new and unexpected apprehensions of truth. The theory of course dispenses with the idea of *Resurrection* altogether. Some of those who have held it have combined it with a belief in the immortality of the soul or spirit of Jesus, urging that the disciples should have inferred from the character of their Lord that His life would inevitably continue after death. Their hallucinations thus might serve both to aid and to express their faith in His survival.

(*b*) There has, however, been another vision-theory less remote from the main stream of Christian belief. This is the theory of writers who have believed that the residuum of fact behind the narratives consists not in visions generated by the disciples but in visions imparted by God Himself, so as to assure the disciples that Jesus was alive and that His gracious activity was with them in a new and enhanced manner.

This view will long be associated with the name of *Theodor Keim.* In his vast *History of Jesus of Nazara* (1867–1872), the most

attractive of the great "liberal" lives of Jesus, Keim criticized the
theory of subjective-visions and set forth his belief that God-given
visions were granted to the disciples. "We find ourselves in the
midst of impossibilities when we make the ordained of God to
end, or when we leave the matter to the chance-play of visions,
that he is awaked from the dead for the dead. The evidence that
Jesus was alive, the *telegram from heaven,* was necessary after an
earthly downfall which was unexampled and, in the childhood of
the human race, would be convincing. The evidence that he was
alive was therefore given by his own impulsion and by the will of
God. The Christianity of today owes to this evidence, first its Lord
and then its own existence: the latter, because it rejoices in him,
and because it sees its own future. . . . Thus, though much has
fallen away, the faith-fortress of the resurrection of Jesus remains." [1]

The phrase "telegram from heaven" became well-known as a
description of this line of interpretation. Amongst English scholars
who have expounded it, a special prominence belongs to Dr.
Streeter, in his essay in the volume entitled *Foundations* (1910).
Streeter believed that the Resurrection of the body of Jesus from
the tomb involved intolerable difficulties concerning the nature of
the future life, and he interpreted the Resurrection to mean that
the spirit of Jesus survived and was able to convey to the disciples
the certainty of His presence with them, "possibly showing Himself to them in some form such as might be covered by St. Paul's
phrase a 'spiritual body'; possibly through some psychological
channel similar to that which explains the mysterious means of
communication between persons commonly known as telepathy;
or possibly in some way of which we have at present no conception. On such a view the appearances to the disciples can only be
called visions, if by visions we mean something directly caused by
the Lord Himself, veritably alive and personally in communion
with them." Streeter claimed that the Resurrection, thus interpreted, was unique and miraculous and implied an intervention
of the power of God altogether beyond our experience. "It is the
Lord's doing, and it is marvellous in our eyes." But he believed that
the event thus interpreted was nearer to our experience and there-

[1] English trans., vol. vi, pp. 364–365.

fore more credible than the traditional belief that the body was raised and glorified.

But though Streeter, like other exponents of this interpretation, rejected the belief that the body was raised, yet, unlike them, he held that the evidence for the empty tomb was historically convincing. The tomb, he believed, was found empty by the women, not because the body had been raised, but because it had been mysteriously removed by human hands. None the less " the discovery of the empty tomb was to some extent a factor in confirming the Apostles in their belief in the Resurrection " (p. 135). It is here that the most difficult feature of Streeter's theory appears. A mistaken inference on the part of the disciples, who ascribed to the power of God what was really an act of unknown human interference with the tomb, was partly the cause of their belief! Here indeed is something hard to believe: that a kind of " providential falsehood " had a place in the revelation of the Resurrection to the disciples and in the historical basis of the Christian faith.

(c) But the interpretation of the Resurrection on these lines as a purely " spiritual " happening has generally been linked with the rejection of the evidence that the body was raised from the tomb. And here is the crucial point. Many scholars, observing signs of development within the tradition, have maintained that the story of the discovery of the empty grave by the women may be a distorted and fanciful version of what really happened on Easter morning.

Foremost among scholars who reached this conclusion was Dr. Kirsopp Lake. His book, *The Historical Evidence for the Resurrection of Jesus Christ* (1907), is the most thorough of all attempts to trace the growth of the primitive traditions. If it provides the historical student with the most valuable setting out of the main problems, it also throws the most valuable light upon the question of the relation between historical study and doctrinal presuppositions.

Lake's preliminary contention was that the appearances of Jesus were in Galilee and not in Jerusalem. The disciples had fled to Galilee after the Crucifixion. There Jesus appeared to them. On returning to Jerusalem they found that the women were telling a story of how they had visited the tomb of Jesus and found it to be empty. The women's story strengthened the disciples in their belief that

Jesus lived, and led them to be sure that there had been a Resurrection of His body. The disciples' story in turn encouraged the women in their belief that they had seen the tomb of Jesus empty. But was the story told by the women (cf. Mark xvi. 1–8) a true interpretation of what they saw? We cannot be quite certain. It is possible, Lake contends, that the women visited the wrong grave, and that a young man directed them to the right one: " He is not here: behold the place where they laid him " (the words " he is risen " being an addition to the story). It is possible, Lake goes on, that the women's report was mingled with misunderstanding; and that it all went back to a visit to the wrong grave and an encounter with a stranger which caused them to run away in terror.

Lake therefore would reject the historicity of the empty tomb. But towards the close of his discussion he makes a very important observation:

" The historical evidence is such that it can be fairly interpreted consistently with either of the two doctrinal positions . . . but it does not support either. The story of the empty tomb must be fought out on doctrinal, not on historical or critical grounds." [1]

The evidence, Lake tells us, is inconclusive: our decision will rest upon our doctrinal prejudice. It depends upon whether our view of the future life is " the resurrection of a material body " or " the unbroken survival of personal life." Upon this our interpretation of the historical question will rest. Lake himself believes in " the unbroken survival of personal life," and his decision about the Resurrection of Christ accords with his presupposition.

These words of Lake are of the utmost significance. The author of the most scientific treatment of the historical problem that has been written, in this and perhaps in any language, admits in the end that a decision cannot be made without recourse to religious presupposition.

3

From this sketch of some of the chief theories which have arisen in the historical study of the evidence for the Resurrection one certainty at least emerges: the investigation of the historical problem

[1] P. 253.

has again and again been interwoven with doctrinal and philosophical considerations. Sometimes the presence of presuppositions,
whether traditional or modern, is acknowledged, as Kirsopp Lake
has shewn us. But often writers about Jesus Christ have claimed
to be conducting a purely historical investigation in strict impar-
tiality; and yet decisive, though unconscious, presuppositions have
been present. Too often writers of the school which has been most
certain of its freedom from presuppositions have been slow to examine and to criticize the presuppositions which they have employed.

For the whole question of presuppositions is an exceedingly difficult one. It would seem to be the greatest gain when historians can
eschew the presuppositions derived from ancient orthodoxy and
can investigate the origins of Christianity in a spirit of detached
and impartial inquiry. Yet the avowal of a historian that he is
working without presuppositions has so often, in the field of New
Testament study, opened the way to the dominance of new presuppositions. Indeed history without presuppositions is impossible:
a historian must needs bring to his task a certain view of the world
and a certain mental furniture of his own. The historian of Jesus
Christ, confronted with unique occurrences in the documents, may
explain them in the light of presuppositions derived from a belief
in the uniqueness of Jesus Christ in relation to a redemption — and
perhaps a supernatural and cosmic redemption — wrought through
Him by God. Or he may explain them away in the light of presuppositions which demand that Jesus Christ be fitted into certain natu-
ralistic beliefs about the world, man and religion. Or he may em-
ploy a variety of other presuppositions. But what does not exist is a
historical procedure wherein presuppositions have no place at all.

Now in the study of the Resurrection certain presuppositions
have occurred again and again. If by some they are held unconsciously, they are described plainly by the commentator upon St.
Luke in the new edition of the *Cambridge Bible for Schools and
Colleges*. He includes in his discussion of the historical problem
these words:

" The modern mind cannot accept the idea of a bodily resurrection
for humanity. The future life is viewed as a spiritual, not as a physical

existence; in which personality, not the physical organism survives. Apart therefore from the question of the miraculous, the story of the empty tomb seems unnecessary, inconsequent, even crude; in Lake's words 'an improper inference from the fact of the Resurrection.'" [1]

Here indeed are some highly questionable propositions. It is not clear that the "modern mind," as exemplified in science and philosophy, is in sympathy with the sharp antithesis between "personality" and "physical organism." Nor is it clear that what happens for "mankind" in general must determine what should fittingly happen for Jesus Christ, for may not the Resurrection have been not a typical survival to illustrate the fact that all good men survive but a unique redemptive act whereby death was conquered for our sake?

It seems that three presuppositions are here apparent, and they have indeed often been adopted. (a) The one notion is that the body has no place in man's future life. Into this notion the interpretation of our Lord's Resurrection must be fitted. (b) The second notion is that the human race is destined for a spiritual immortality through the survival of the soul after death. Into this notion Jesus Christ as a member of the human race must be fitted. Neither of these notions is peculiarly modern, and it needs demonstration that the most modern science or philosophy tends to support them. These two notions are used in conjunction with a third. (c) This is the notion that the Resurrection of Jesus is not, as the Apostles taught, the unique spring and source of our resurrection but rather an exemplary edifying symbol of our survival after death. What is normal for righteous men is thus the norm of the Resurrection of Jesus.

It is here that the real distinction lies. The real issue is not between a "bodily" and a "spiritual" event: for the orthodox may err in clinging to the inadequate word "bodily" as greatly as the modernist may err in clinging to the inadequate word "spiritual." The issue is rather between two different beliefs about the Gospel. According to the one belief Jesus Christ is interpreted within the series of evolution and history in such a way that the transcendental and redemptive aspects of the Gospel receive less than their proper

[1] H. K. Luce, S. Luke, p. 366.

place: the Resurrection is an example to us that if we are good we may, like Jesus, survive death. According to the other belief the Resurrection is a divine intervention, transcendent and creative, whereby a new creation is inaugurated in the life of mankind and the world. For such a Gospel the story of the empty tomb can never be " unnecessary, inconsequent, even crude."

Now it would be unfair to say that the interpretation of the Resurrection, along the lines of Keim or Streeter, as an exaltation of the spirit of Jesus, necessarily misses the transcendental and redemptive meaning of the Gospel. Such an interpretation *may* conserve the uniqueness of the event as more than a survival. As its most recent exponent has urged: " It is sometimes said that mere visions of Jesus, even if objective, might establish the fact that he had survived death, but not that he had conquered it. But if Jesus survived death in such a sort as to be able to energize and inspire his disciples, he *had* conquered it; nor would the resuscitation of his material body make the conquest more real or glorious." [1] True, to think thus of the Resurrection does not inevitably imply a departure from a belief in its uniqueness and its redemptive character. None the less two things can be said. (*a*) It is hard to see how the Apostles or their converts could have been convinced of a redemptive victory over death by Jesus had they believed that His body was corrupted in the grave. (*b*) The view of a spiritual survival of Jesus held by a long line of scholars has been frankly linked with the presuppositions that we have described. These presuppositions have often been decisive in the handling of the evidence about the tomb. The criticism which rejects the empty tomb as *a priori* incredible or inconsequent or crude has its roots in a philosophy which is far removed from the New Testament. For the Gospel in the New Testament involves the freedom of the living God and an act of new creation which includes the bodily no less than the spiritual life of man.

4

It is with history that we are concerned. What happened? That is what Christians desire to know. In seeking the answer there is

[1] C. J. Cadoux, *The Historic Mission of Jesus*, 1941, p. 282.

need for the most scientific approach to historical truth that is possible.

But the era of historical criticism has disclosed faults of method which it is now possible to detect. It was a great gain when liberal theology linked the belief in Creation to the facts of the evolution of nature and man, and so enabled us to study afresh the divine action in the processes of nature and in the gradual movement of history. But it was the fault of liberal theology sometimes to go far towards eliminating the other aspect of the divine action, namely, the unique and transcendental work of God whose redemption is a breaking into history from above. This fault in theological thinking begat presuppositions fatal to the handling of the history of Jesus.

Now it would be none the less fatal for us to go behind the methods of historical criticism and to rest in doctrinal affirmations. *Non tali auxilio.* In connection with the Resurrection narratives no difficulty must be ignored; and the possibility must be faced that, here as elsewhere, unreliable and legendary elements may have found their way into the traditions and the documents. The technique of literary and historical criticism, the analysis of sources and of the work of editors, must be employed to the full.

But to discard presuppositions altogether would be an impossible adventure; and rather than claim to discard presuppositions the present writer would ask sympathy for two very modest presuppositions. The one is that the Biblical belief in the living God, creator, redeemer, transcendent, is true. The other is that the events must be such as account for the Gospel which the Apostles preached and by which the first Christians lived. We would not use these presuppositions for the pressing of historical conclusions; but we would so bear them in mind as to avoid a sort of inhibition if the converging lines of evidence seem to point to a supernatural event at the climax of the story of Christ. Thus if the evidence is pointing us towards a Resurrection of an utterly unique sort we will not be incredulous, for the Christ is Himself a unique and transcendent fact in history. If the evidence is pointing us towards a miracle we will not be troubled, for the miracle will mean not only a breach of the laws that have been perceived in this world but a manifestation of the purpose of the creator of a new world and the redeemer

of our own. And if the evidence is pointing us towards an act
wherein spirit and body are strangely blended and exalted, our
minds will have no terrors: for the message of the New Testament
is pervaded through and through by the belief that the spiritual and
the material are interwoven in the purpose of the Word-made-flesh.
Why is it judged incredible with you, if God should raise the dead?

Chapter Five

THE EVIDENCE OF THE GOSPELS

THE NATURE OF THE PROBLEM

THE narratives of the Resurrection present a number of difficult questions, and it is important that in studying them we should see where the problem really lies. The scholars of an older generation were concerned to construct, if possible, a harmony of the events recorded by the four evangelists; and the credibility of the records has often been thought to depend upon the possibility of such a harmony being made. Today, new knowledge of the character and composition of the Gospels seems to shew that such a harmony is not to be expected, and that the absence of it need not impugn the historical worth of the traditions which the Gospels contain. The task is rather to discover the primitive traditions that lie behind the narratives, to detect the ways in which these traditions may have been developed or corrupted, and to trace the methods and motives with which the evangelists have woven the traditions into frameworks of their own.

The process behind the making of the Gospels falls into several stages. (*a*) There was first the oral tradition of the deeds and words of Jesus, handed down by Christian teachers through several decades. Stories would be told in the Christian communities of the things which Jesus had taught and done. Inevitably the stories would be strung together, not necessarily in chronological or biographical order, but in shapes or plans suitable for the purposes of teaching about the various themes of the Gospel. Inevitably also there would be embellishments made in the stories during this process of oral tradition. (*b*) There was finally the work of the evangelists who took the traditions that had come down to them, now partly in written sources as well as in oral form, and moulded these traditions into continuous narratives of the events of the Gospel. Here too we can detect embellishments made by different evangelists as editors, and we can trace the special tendencies of each evangelist as he edits the traditions into his own framework. As often as not the framework may be arbitrary, and we cannot harmonize the frameworks of the evangelists one with another. Yet all these facts do not lead us to doubt that the Gospels preserve for us true accounts of the deeds and sayings of Jesus. For we can sometimes see in the material a primitive perspective that takes us behind the developments in the theology of the Apostolic age. We can trace the primitive themes of the words and deeds of Jesus as recorded in several distinct "blocks" of tradition. And we can compare these results with our other evidence concerning the Gospel which the Apostles preached in the earliest days.

Now the Resurrection narratives seem to have been built up in much the same way as the other narratives in the Gospels; and the problems are not dissimilar. We can detect some of the early stories by which the message of the Resurrection would be told. We can perceive certain embellishments in the growth of the tradition. We can perceive also the tendencies and motives of the evangelists as they edit the material into their own frames. But between the Resurrection narratives and the other Gospel narratives there are two significant differences. (a) Inevitably there is a special difficulty in the order and geographical plan of the stories. From the very nature of the case we would expect it to be difficult for the Christian teachers to conserve order and plan in their stories of the appearances of the risen Jesus to groups of people at different places and times. (b) On the other hand the story of the Resurrection was, together with the story of the Passion, a central part of the teaching of the Apostles from the beginning. It was part of the core of the Gospel. If therefore there are embellishments, we remember also that the stories would be handed down with a very special regard for the testimony of eye-witnesses and the authority of Apostles.

THE TRADITIONS BEHIND THE NARRATIVES

As we read the narratives we can observe within them some of the forms of story-telling which were used by the early teachers of the Resurrection. There is the brief sentence telling the good news: "The Lord is risen indeed, and hath appeared to Simon"

(Luke xxiv. 34). There is the story that tells of an appearance of Jesus, told vividly so as to make it plain that Jesus truly was seen and that no mistake was made; an instance is the story of how Jesus shewed His hands and His feet to the disciples and ate a piece of broiled fish before them (Luke xxiv. 36–43). There were also stories telling of the bewilderment and dejection of the disciples and of the way in which it gradually came home to them that Jesus was alive; an instance is the story of the walk to Emmaus (Luke xxiv. 13–35). There were also stories of the teaching given by the risen Jesus, told so as to shew the purpose of the Resurrection and its lessons for the disciples then and for the members of the Church in days to come (cf. Matt. xxviii. 16–20; Luke xxiv. 44–49; John xxi. 1–14). There was also the story of the visit of the women to the tomb and their discovery that it was empty (Mark xvi. 1–8). In all these ways the early Christian teachers would hand down the message of the Resurrection.

These stories, at first told orally, are now known to us through their presence in the narratives of the Gospels. Two questions arise: What signs of embellishment in the traditions are noticeable? What signs are there on the other hand that a genuinely primitive perspective has been retained?

(a) The possibilities of embellishment in the tradition will be apparent at once to a reader who will examine in turn the accounts of the visit of the women to the tomb in Mark and in Matthew. In Mark the miracle is implied but not described. The story is told in utter simplicity. The women arrive wondering who will move the stone so that they may enter. They see that the stone is no longer there. They enter. The tomb is empty. A young man in a white robe tells them that Jesus is not there, and bids them tell the disciples that He will go before them into Galilee. They flee in fear, and tell no one. The reticence of the story tells us of the great event which has come to pass. How great a contrast is seen in Matthew's narrative. In place of the quiet implication of a miracle there is an elaborate description. There was a great earthquake; an angel of the Lord descended and rolled away the stone; his appearance was like lightning, and the soldiers on guard trembled and became as dead men. Such is an editor's embroidery of his source; and if elaboration of the tradition took place in the written stage it is reasonable to think that it took place in the oral stage too.

Other illustrations could be given of the ways in which the traditions became modified in the decades between the events themselves and the writing of the several Gospels. It would be possible for details or sayings connected with one story to be transferred to another story, or for the geographical setting of a story to become confused. Interesting elaborations of the tradition are noticeable in the descriptions of the burial of Jesus and of the character of Joseph of Arimathaea; we can trace in the Gospels a growing tendency to dwell upon the discipleship of Joseph and to treat him as one who is within the true fold. There is also a narrative in which many of the most conservative scholars have been ready to admit the likelihood of a legendary element. This is the story of the guard at the tomb in Matt. xxvii. 62–66; xxviii. 11–15: it contains a number of distinct improbabilities, and it is akin to a cycle of stories used (though not often) by Matthew, which arouse a suspicion that they present Christian midrash rather than history.

(*b*) Yet the presence of embellishments such as these makes it all the more impressive that the stories retain so many signs of a truly primitive perspective.

In his work *Die Formgeschichte des Evangeliums,* a searching examination of the growth of the traditions behind the Gospels, Dr. Martin Dibelius expressed the view that the Emmaus story "has been preserved in an almost pure form," and that the story of the visit of the women to the tomb is in Mark's version "in its pure form," except for the message about Galilee which he regards as an insertion made so as to link the story with other stories.[1] This judgment is not surprising. Both these stories give the impression that they are taking us behind the formal apologetic of the Church and are shewing us the original bewilderment and half-awareness of the disciples and of the women. In both of these stories there is the atmosphere less of demonstration and proof than of the growing awareness of a miracle unexpected and hard to comprehend. There could scarcely be less of the conventional methods of miracle-story-telling: the disciples are made aware of the great event only as Jesus

[1] English trans. (1934 edition), pp. 190 ff.

reveals Himself to them in the Scriptures, in personal converse and finally in the breaking of the bread. It is important also to notice the allusions within the Emmaus story to other parts of the traditions, to an appearance to Peter (Luke xxiv. 34) and to the news brought by the women (xxiv. 22–24), allusions made in a manner so different from that of the narrator of evidence who is striving to prove his case.

Such are the traditions that we find behind the narratives in the Gospels. Some of them are embellished, and some are strikingly undeveloped. That we should expect to be able to weave the stories into a chronological and geographical plan seems inconceivable. But if we eschew the quest for an external unity between the stories, we can the more perceive the inward unity that belongs to them. They are, with very few exceptions, at one in the *manner* of their testimony; and this is a manner which it is very hard to attribute to anything else except the spiritually subtle nature of the event itself. They are at one in that which they affirm, both by cross-reference and by direct description: the appearances of Jesus and the discovery of the empty tomb. Moreover they are at one also with the primitive Apostolic preaching that Christ was buried and was raised again on the third day, and with the primitive revolution whereby the first day of the week replaced the sabbath as " the day which the Lord hath made."

THE FRAMEWORKS OF THE EVANGELISTS

Each evangelist draws upon the traditions which he knows, and builds the stories into a framework in accordance with his own special purpose.

In the case of *Mark* the true text, as we now possess it, ends at xvi. 8:

" And they went out, and fled from the tomb; for trembling and astonishment had come upon them: and they said nothing to anyone; for they were afraid." [1]

[1] The section " Mark " xvi. 9–20, familiar as the conclusion of the Gospel in Authorized Version and Revised Version, is now generally recognized not to be Mark's work but an early compilation, written so as to make the story more complete. The contrast in style between this section and Mark's own narrative is obvious; and the section fits the preceding story very clumsily.

It has been the widespread opinion of modern scholars (including
Hort, Swete and Burkitt) that this verse cannot be the point at
which Mark intended to conclude his Gospel; that the book was
mutilated at a very early date; that there existed a concluding section which is now lost; and that this section very likely included
an account of an appearance of Jesus to Peter in Galilee in fulfilment of the message from the tomb. (It is thought unlikely that
Matthew made use of the lost ending of Mark; but a possible connection has been suggested between the lost ending of Mark and
the fishing scene in Galilee recorded in John xxi and the description in the Apocryphal " Gospel of Peter " of the disciples returning to Galilee after the Passion to resume their former work.) The
general trend of modern commentators has been to deny that these
words can possibly be the deliberate ending to a sentence, a story,
or a Gospel.

On the other hand some powerful arguments from recent writers
have to be reckoned with, on the side of the view that Mark may
really have planned to end his Gospel just at this very point. Literary parallels have been found to shew the possibility of sentences
that end with γάρ. It is also pointed out that the abruptness is in
keeping with Mark's style of writing. Throughout his Gospel he
has recorded the awe and bewilderment caused by the words and
deeds of the Son of God. What would be more characteristic of
him than to end his story by telling of the awe and bewilderment
caused by the news that Christ was risen? The women were seeking Jesus the Nazarene, the dead body of the Crucified: but, says
the voice at the tomb, the disciples will see Him, glorified, in Galilee. That is the end. What more should Mark say? for by his reticence he tells us so much of the indescribable mystery of the
Resurrection.[1]

If probability still lies with the view that there is a " lost ending," the view that the true ending is at the words " for they were
afraid " deserves more consideration than it usually receives. But if
there be a " lost ending " we cannot infer with any certainty what

[1] The view that Mark intended to end at xvi. 8 is set forth by J. M. Creed
in *Journal of Theological Studies*, January, 1930, and by R. H. Lightfoot in
Locality and Doctrine in the Gospels, chaps. i–iii. On the other side see W. L.
Knox in *Harvard Theological Review*, January, 1942.

it contained. It is idle to affirm that it *must* have contained this or
that story. As we shall see, the deductions sometimes drawn from
the message to the disciples are most hazardous.

Matthew (*a*) follows Mark in his account of the empty tomb,
with a good deal of editorial embroidery (xxviii. 1–7). (*b*) He adds
the story of the soldiers guarding the tomb (xxvii. 62–66; xxviii.
11–15) in the interests of apologetic against a slander that the disciples stole the body. (*c*) He inserts a brief section to tell of the
movements of the women from the point where Mark's abrupt ending leaves them. They recovered from their panic and went on their
way to tell the disciples: Jesus appeared to them, and they worshipped Him (xxviii. 8–10). (*d*) Then Matthew concludes with a
scene in Galilee. Here Jesus appears to the eleven, and apparently
to other disciples, at a mountain which the Lord appointed; and
He gives a final missionary charge (xxviii. 16–20). Matthew records no appearances to the disciples in Jerusalem. Here, as elsewhere, the only historical frame that he possesses is that which
Mark provides; and Mark here provides less than he might have
wished. But Matthew has all that he needs for the climax of his
own Gospel. The royal Messiah, claiming all authority in heaven
and on earth, once more teaches His disciples with authority upon
a Mount. He commissions them as Apostles in a universal Church
that replaces the old Israel, and He promises that His presence will
be with them unto the end of the age.

Luke also follows Mark in his story of the empty tomb (xxiv. 1–
7) with, however, a number of interesting divergences. These divergences may be due to the use of another source besides Mark. But
the most important divergence seems to be due to editing. In place
of the message of the young man:

" Go, tell his disciples and Peter, He goeth before you into Galilee;
there shall ye see him, as he said unto you,"

Luke records these words:

" Remember how he spake unto you, when he was yet in Galilee, saying that the Son of Man must be delivered up into the hands of sinful
men, and be crucified, and the third day rise again."

No doubt Luke edited the message in this way on account of the fact that he did not intend to record appearances in Galilee; though some would urge that Luke was preserving another tradition about the form of the message.

Luke's subsequent narratives are all peculiar to his Gospel, and the events are set in and near Jerusalem. (*a*) First, *some* of the women who were at the tomb bring the news to the eleven and to all the rest; but the news seems to the disciples to be idle talk (xxiv. 8–11). (*b*) Then, according to some MSS., Peter visits the tomb to confirm the news for himself (xxiv. 12, omitted by Codex Bezae). (*c*) There follows the Emmaus story, perhaps the most beautiful and arresting of them all. Jesus joins on the road from Jerusalem two dejected disciples who have heard of the story of the women but have learnt nothing that convinces them of the Resurrection. Unrecognized, Jesus unfolds to them the Scriptures concerning the necessity of the Cross and the Resurrection. The walk ends at Emmaus, where Jesus is recognized when he blesses and breaks bread with the two disciples: but as soon as He is recognized, He disappears. The two disciples return at once to Jerusalem and find the eleven who are saying, "The Lord is risen indeed, and hath appeared to Simon" (xxiv. 13–35).[1] (*d*) Then Luke records an appearance of Jesus to the disciples, then and there assembled on Easter evening. He invites them to touch Him, and He eats in their presence (xxiv. 36–43). (*e*) A discourse follows, concerning the fulfilment of prophecy, the mission of the Church and the coming gift of power from on high (xxiv. 44–49). (*f*) Finally, Jesus leads the disciples over against Bethany, blesses them and is parted from them. (The more probable text says simply "he was parted," ἀπέστη: a doubtful text includes the words "and was carried up into heaven," ἀνελήφθη. It is in Acts that the one explicit description of the Ascension occurs: "He was taken up, and a cloud received him out of their sight," Acts i. 9.)

Luke records no appearances in Galilee; and on a first impression his narrative suggests that there was no room for any visit of

---

[1] There is a noteworthy variant reading in Luke xxiv. 34, λεγόντες for λεγόντας, which ascribes the words, "The Lord is risen indeed," not to the eleven, but to the two who had come from Emmaus.

the disciples to Galilee. Event *seems* to follow event in rapid succession from the walk to Emmaus to the parting at Bethany. But. (*a*) vagueness in chronology is one of Luke's characteristics as a writer; and we do not know that he means the contents of his last chapter to be in a direct and rapid sequence. If he does mean it to be so, then the parting would take place late at night, which seems improbable. May there not be a break before the discourse at verse 44, or before the walk towards Bethany at verse 50? (*b*) In the opening verses of Acts, Luke seems to correct any impression he may have left that the events all happened on the one day, for he tells us that the period of the appearances lasted "during forty days." It is wrong therefore to infer that Luke's narrative excludes the possibility that there were, in fact, appearances in Galilee. Nor is Luke's own omission of any Galilean tradition difficult to explain. It is upon Jerusalem that his thoughts are centred. His theme is the going-up of Jesus to Jerusalem to die, the redemption wrought in Jerusalem, the continuity of the divine purpose through the events in Jerusalem, the mission of the Church from Jerusalem, the advance of the Gospel from Jerusalem to Rome. That is Luke's theme; he is absorbed in it; he telescopes his story in accordance with it; he omits what would be a diversion from it.

John is at pains to blend together factors in the tradition — both historical and doctrinal — which hitherto have been presented somewhat apart. Historically, he shews that there was a link between the evidence of the women at the tomb and the evidence of the Apostles in Jerusalem — namely, the visit of Peter and John to the tomb to verify the women's story. He shews also that he knows and values traditions both of Jerusalem and of Galilee. Doctrinally, he shews how great is the importance both of the mysterious and of the bodily aspects of the Resurrection of Jesus. He blends the vivid evidence of sight and touch with contrary lessons on believing without touch (xx. 17) and without sight (xx. 29).

His narrative begins with a visit not of a group of women but of Mary Magdalene alone to the tomb. It was dark. She found the tomb empty, and told the disciples (xx. 1–2). There follows the visit of Peter and John to the tomb to confirm the news (xx. 3–10).

Meanwhile Jesus appears to Mary Magdalene by the tomb and gives her the command not to cling to Him but to go and tell the disciples that He is ascending to the Father (xx. 11–18). On the same day at evening Jesus appears to the eleven in Jerusalem, shews them His hands and His side, bestows the gift of Holy Spirit upon them and sends them forth even as the Father sent Him (xx. 19–23). A week later there comes the episode of doubting Thomas (xx. 24–29), and some words which sum up the purpose of the Gospel. An Epilogue follows (possibly from another hand) to tell of an appearance of Jesus to some of the disciples fishing in Galilee (xxi).

In all this John is drawing out a theological interpretation of the Resurrection. In the next chapter of this book the reader will be asked to study this theological interpretation, and to notice how John shews the relation between the Resurrection stories and the great themes of his Gospel. But John is no less concerned to emphasize the importance of history; and if the new material which he introduces is in some ways hard to harmonize with the earlier accounts, in others ways it corroborates their story and supplies some convincing links to it. John's story of Mary Magdalene is not incompatible with Mark's story of the women as a group. John's story of Peter and John running to the tomb confirms hints given in the Emmaus story of Luke. John's story of the appearance to the eleven confirms both Luke and Paul. The Epilogue confirms a Galilean tradition.

Such are the ways in which the four evangelists build the traditions which they use into the frameworks which we know. The plan and purpose of each is intelligible, both in what he includes and in what he omits. It is a fascinating study to attempt to harmonize what the evangelists tell us and to essay a reconstruction of the events in an ordered scheme of time and place. Up to a point the attempt may be successful, but a limit to the success is always reached. That this is so need not disturb us, for the right question for the historian who is aware of the nature of the Gospels and their composition is not, Can a harmony be constructed? How utterly suspicious we ought to be, if here alone in the whole range of the Gospel narratives a neat harmony could be provided! No, the right questions are: Can we account for the plan adopted by each evangelist? Do the narratives include primitive traditions? Do these traditions concur with one another in their testimony to the main event? Are these traditions corroborated by our other evidence about the primitive preaching of the Apostles? It does not seem to be too confident for us to affirm that the answer to each of the questions is yes.

GALILEE AND JERUSALEM

It would none the less be disturbing if the narratives included a discrepancy so great as to impugn their credibility. What then of the biggest discrepancy that has been alleged — the conflict between the tradition of an appearance in Galilee found in Matthew and the tradition of appearances in Jerusalem found in Luke? This problem has been regarded as a central crux.

The Galilean tradition has had some firm adherents, who have believed it to be the earliest and the best and the key to the understanding of the whole development of the traditions concerning the Resurrection. Dr. Lake in *The Historical Evidence of the Resurrection of Jesus Christ* (1907) and Mr. Gardner-Smith in *The Narratives of the Resurrection* (1926) have presented this view on the basis of the most thorough attempts to unravel the traditions.

Why Galilee? (*a*) It is urged that Mark, our earliest document, clearly points towards an appearance in Galilee as the climax of its own story. No other climax, it is said, could have been intended after the message xvi. 7: "He goeth before you into Galilee." (*b*) Then it is urged that the disciples were in Galilee already. Lake argued that they had fled away home at the time of the Crucifixion and had sought their former way of life, disillusioned (an extreme inference from Mark xiv. 50, "they all left him, and fled"). Gardner-Smith criticized this view, pointed out that it is unlikely that the disciples would have left the city during the feast, and preferred a tradition found in the Apocryphal "Gospel of Peter": that the disciples fled back to Galilee only when the feast was over. This Apocryphal work is no doubt gnostic, tendentious and unreliable, but it may none the less preserve portions of early traditions. For after a passage describing the visit of the women to the tomb (a

passage which draws freely upon the Marcan and Matthaean rec-
ords-or traditions) " pseudo-Peter " continues:

> " Now it was the last day of unleavened bread, and many went out
> returning to their homes since the feast was over. But we, the twelve
> disciples of the Lord, were weeping and grieving: and each one,
> mourning for that which was come to pass, departed to his own home.
> But I, Simon Peter, and Andrew my brother took our nets and went
> away to the sea. And Levi, the son of Alphaeus was with us, whom the
> Lord . . ." (The rest is lost.)

Here is a story of the return of the disciples to Galilee and to their
old life. Lake held that it is based upon the lost end of Mark;
Gardner-Smith, that it is based rather upon the cycle of traditions
from which the lost end of Mark arose. It fits the picture presented
by the fishing-scene in John xxi. " Can there be any other explanation than that he is following an earlier tradition which the other
evangelists have deserted? " (c) There is indeed a further plea for
the Galilean tradition. It is far easier to explain how stories of appearances in Galilee might come to be transferred to Jerusalem, the
subsequent centre of the Church, than it is to explain how the Galilean tradition arose if the appearances were in Jerusalem.

So speak the " Galileans." In their view the disciples were in
Galilee, and Jesus appeared to them there. They subsequently returned to Jerusalem (where *later* appearances may have occurred).
Then a tradition grew which transposed to Jerusalem the stories of
the first appearances, partly perhaps with the motive of bringing
the evidence of the disciples into closer proximity with the story of
the women at the tomb, and partly because Jerusalem had become
the centre of the life of the Church. As we have seen, a chief corol-
lary of the Galilean theory is that there is a gap between the disciples and the women, and the women's testimony could not be
verified by the disciples.

But the Galilean theory is vulnerable. It demands an extreme
scepticism concerning the traditions which Luke records, especially
the Emmaus story with its naïve and seemingly primitive cross-
references to the traditions about Peter and the women. It called
forth the alternative hypothesis of Dr. Burkitt, that Peter set out
for Galilee on receiving the message from the tomb, but Jesus ap-

peared to him on his journey and bade him return to Jerusalem. But the real weakness of the theory is that it rests primarily upon a conjecture as to the contents of the lost ending of Mark, and it is utterly hazardous to affirm what this lost ending *must* have contained. It is not certain that the message at the tomb necessarily demands a first appearance in Galilee as its sequel. The message recalls the words of Jesus before the Passion:

"All ye shall be offended: for it is written, I will smite the shepherd and the sheep shall be scattered abroad. Howbeit, after I am raised up, I will go before you into Galilee." (Mark xiv. 27–28.)

The imagery is that of a shepherd. Jesus had led the disciples from Galilee to Jerusalem, προάγων, "going before them" (x. 32). And after the Resurrection He will go before them like a shepherd once more, leading them into Galilee. Thus the message at the tomb,

"He goeth before you into Galilee,"

may well mean not that Jesus will forestall the disciples there, but that He will direct them thither from another place. An appearance first in Jerusalem is not excluded. How indeed were the women to deliver the message to the disciples unless they were near at hand in Jerusalem?

It is probable that the Galilean theory, in its extreme form, will go the way of many theories that have for a time dominated the discussion of historical problems. It is noteworthy that its chief supporter came to admit a faltering in his allegiance to it. In his latest writing on the subject [1] Lake shewed far less confidence. "More or less corrupted forms of such a tradition are to be found in Matt. xxviii. 16–20, in John xxi. and in the Gospel of Peter. They are, relatively speaking, unimportant; the theory of a Galilean tradition really stands or falls with the interpretation of Mark xiv. 28 and xvi. 7" (p. 8). "Thus though Professor Burkitt's suggestion seems at least sufficiently attractive to make me waver in my allegiance to the Galilean hypothesis, I am not wholly convinced that he is right" (p. 14).

For are we faced simply with the neat alternative: Galilee *or* Jerusalem? Is it not reasonable to suppose that there may have

[1] *The Beginnings of Christianity,* vol. v, 1933.

been appearances in both localities? It may well be that, whereas
Luke is right in describing an appearance to the eleven in Jerusalem on Easter Day and in taking Jerusalem to be the main centre,
there were also appearances in Galilee. Perhaps others in Galilee besides the eleven were permitted to see Jesus (cf. "the five hundred
brethren" mentioned by Paul); perhaps Jesus directed the eleven
thither for the purpose of an appearance vocational in its object and
linked with the mission to the Gentiles.

It seems, finally, to be the greatest mistake to take the record of
the message at the tomb as a kind of clue to the course of events
and a key to the reconstruction of the story. It is astonishing that
scholars have built so much upon these words; for they seem to be
the very point in the tradition where certainty is least possible to
attain. Who spoke the words? What exactly did they mean? What
does the evangelist understand them to mean? These are the last
questions about which we can ever speak with sure knowledge.
Perhaps the message about Galilee, and the saying of Jesus before
the Passion to which it looks back, had a meaning symbolical rather
than geographical and referred less to a place of meeting or jour-
neying than to a Victory and a Mission that would follow the disaster of the Cross. Who knows?

THE TOMB

To the empty tomb witness is borne by the narrative of Mark, by
references within the Emmaus story in Luke, and by the tradition
in John. It is possible that John's story of the visit of Mary Magdalene goes back to a tradition as early as the tradition about the
women recorded in Mark. It is certain that we have the testimony
of the earliest Gospel, and of cross-references in a Lucan tradition.
Are traditions, thus attested in the Gospels and congruous with the
primitive preaching, to be discredited, apart from *a priori* considerations?

The scope for scepticism about Mark's story is enlarged if the
Galilean theory be held. For the theory creates a gap between the
experiences of the women at the tomb and the experiences of the
disciples who saw Jesus, and — Lake contended — gives room for
the possibility that the women's story, unchecked by the disciples,

contained misunderstanding of what really happened. Perhaps they went to the wrong tomb, and a young man directed them to the right one, saying, " He is not here, behold the place where they laid him," or (as Codex Bezae has it), " Behold there his place," ἴδετε ἐκει τόπον αὐτοῦ. Thus a terrifying experience and a misunderstanding formed the basis of the Marcan story.

This hypothesis depends to a considerable extent upon the Galilean theory, which invites — as we have seen — many doubts. It depends also upon a rejection of the evidence that the disciples verified the women's report. Is it conceivable that the disciples would have heard of the empty tomb without going to see for themselves? And is it conceivable that they could have preached that Jesus " was buried and was raised again " without any interest in the grave?

Apart from scepticism about Mark's account (a scepticism in which, as Lake himself has said, presuppositions have a decisive place) there remains the question why no evidence for the empty tomb is cited in the documents earlier than the Gospels. (a) As regards Paul's omission in 1 Cor. xv, Lake has supplied an answer: " Was there any reason why St. Paul should have supplied these details had he known them? Surely not. He was not trying to convince the Corinthians that the Lord was risen: he was reminding them that he had already convinced them." (b) As regards the accounts that we possess of the primitive Gospel in the Epistles and the Acts, the omission of references to the evidence about the tomb is *intelligible*. The accounts are brief, and dwell upon the Gospel itself rather than upon the apologetic evidence used to support it. The Gospel was that Christ died, was buried, was raised and appeared; it implies the empty tomb. But the most prominent part of the evidence was the appearances: for it was the appearances that brought to the Apostles not only evidence but more than evidence in the thrilling consciousness of Christ Himself, glorified and victorious.

" He appeared to Cephas, then to the twelve."

Those were the experiences that mattered intensely to the Apostles, as evidence and as far more. But for the generations to come there was need for greater recourse to that part of the evidence that was not bound up with the particular experiences of the disciples and that spoke plainly of the event that lay behind. It is this evidence which the evangelists set out when they include the narratives of the empty tomb; and in so doing they make complete for all time their witness to the Gospel:

> " How that Christ *died* for our sins according to the scriptures;
> and that he was *buried,*
> and that he hath been *raised* on the third day according to the scrip-
>   tures:
> and that he *appeared. . .*"

Chapter Six

THE THEOLOGY OF THE GOSPEL NARRATIVES

THE study of the historical problems presented by the narratives of the Resurrection ought never to be separated from the study of the theological themes of the narratives. For the narratives are the climax of four books written so as to present the Gospel of God. Each evangelist has his own emphasis upon certain aspects of the Gospel and his own way of expressing them; and the themes prominent in the stories of the Resurrection are bound up with the themes of each Gospel as a whole. Just as each evangelist has his own angle of approach to the " Gospel of Jesus Christ the Son of God," so each has his own special insight into the message that " Christ was raised again on the third day according to the Scriptures."

MARK

We have already noticed the probability that the true conclusion of Mark's Gospel is lost. But it is unfortunate that preoccupation with the fragmentariness of Mark's present ending has sometimes blinded us to the great theological significance of what does survive. Mark xvi. 1–8, the story of the coming of the women to the tomb, is a story in itself, such as might be told in the oral teaching of the early Christians. Its profound teaching is the climax of the recurring themes of the book.

The breathless abruptness of these verses is in keeping with a breathless abruptness which appears again and again in the Marcan Gospel. Abruptly, without preparation or introduction or note of date or background, the story begins: " The beginning of the Gospel of Jesus Christ the Son of God . . . was John who baptized in the wilderness and preached the baptism of repentance unto the remission of sins." God is intervening in history; his Reign is breaking into the world. Presently the preaching of Jesus has begun: " The time is fulfilled, and the kingdom of God is at hand: repent ye, and believe in the Gospel." The event is bewildering. The note of bewilderment recurs. The words and deeds of Jesus seem to lead the disciples from perplexity to perplexity. " They were amazed." " They became sore afraid." " They understood not the saying and were afraid to ask him." " And they were in the way going up to Jerusalem; and Jesus was going before them: and they were amazed; and they that followed were afraid." " All ye shall be offended." The words with which the present concluding section ends are in keeping with the atmosphere of the whole story: " They went out and fled from the tomb: for trembling and astonishment had come upon them: and they said nothing to anyone; for they were afraid."

Now the bewilderment that is so characteristic of Mark's narratives is most apparent in connection with the theme of the suffering of Christ and the glory that lay beyond it. The theme is central both in the sayings of Jesus and in the movement of the narrative.

(*a*) At Caesarea Philippi Jesus declares that He must die. " The Son of Man must suffer." The teaching is again and again renewed. " The Son of Man shall be delivered unto the chief priests and the scribes; and they shall condemn him to death, and they shall deliver him unto the Gentiles, and they shall mock him and shall spit on him, and shall scourge him, and shall kill him." " Verily the Son of Man came not to be ministered unto but to minister and to give his life a ransom for many." Inexorably, by a bewildering divine necessity, the story moves from Galilee to Jerusalem, from the scene of messianic power and blessing to the scene of death. The death is died in utter loneliness. The only recorded word from the Cross is the cry of dereliction. In lonely darkness Jesus dies; and Pilate grants the corpse to Joseph of Arimathaea, who buries it in a tomb. The humiliation of the Servant of the LORD is complete: nothing but the corpse remains, to visit and to care for.

(*b*) But beyond the humiliation there is the victory predicted. In the predictions use is made, as we saw, of a variety of images. Jesus speaks of the coming of the Kingdom of God with power, of the banquet new with the disciples in the Kingdom of God, of a rising again of the shepherd of the flock, and of the coming of the Son of Man in glory. Asked by Caiaphas in the Sanhedrin whether He is the Christ, Jesus answers:

" I am; and ye shall see the Son of Man sitting at the right hand of power, and coming with the clouds of heaven." (xiv. 62.)

It seems wrong to infer from these words that Jesus is speaking of a coming in the far distant future. Luke may be interpreting the meaning correctly when he adds the words " from henceforth." Jesus is using imagery drawn from the Book of Daniel: the imagery tells of the triumph and Reign of the Son of Man, and that triumph will not be delayed. Just now the Messiah is humiliated, struck and spat upon: He shall be seen reigning and victorious. To this victorious coming, beyond the Cross, Jesus is now directing Caiaphas as He had in the past directed the disciples. His Reign will come: and those whom He has made ready will *see*.

With this theme of suffering and glory in his mind the reader of Mark's Gospel passes on to what is now the concluding section.

" And when the sabbath was past, Mary Magdalene, and Mary the mother of James, and Salome, bought spices that they might come and anoint him. And very early on the first day of the week, they come to the tomb when the sun was risen. And they were saying among themselves, Who shall roll away the stone from the door of the tomb? and looking up, they see that the stone is rolled back: for it was exceeding great. And entering into the tomb, they saw a young man sitting on the right side, arrayed in a white robe; and they were amazed. And he saith unto them, Be not amazed: ye seek Jesus, the Nazarene, which hath been crucified; he is risen; he is not here: behold the place where they laid him! But go, tell his disciples and Peter, He goeth before you into Galilee; there shall ye see him, as he said unto you. And they went out, and fled from the tomb; for trembling and astonishment had come upon them: and they said nothing to any one; for they were afraid." (xvi. 1–8.)

The ending may be lost: but the episode in itself is complete. Mark's Gospel is built up from short sections, each containing a separate story that might be told. Here is a story that proclaims the Resurrection, and links it with the theme of humiliation and glory. How often has Mark told a story containing an approach to Jesus and a Word in answer to those who approach! Here it is only the dead body that the women are approaching. But the word spoken to them turns their thoughts away from the dead body of " Jesus, the Nazarene, which hath been crucified " to the coming in glory. He is not here. The day is come. Go, tell the disciples that they will *see Him*. It is a thought of unspeakable awe. They will *see Him*. The women are silent and afraid.

But silence and fear have their own message. They tell, more than words can, of the overwhelming reality of the Resurrection. " It is clear," says Dr. R. H. Lightfoot, "that the silence, fear, trembling and amazement . . . must have had a great role to play within the early Church." [1] By silence the women tell us what no words can tell us. The Resurrection is not as other events in history. It is in truth the Parousia. It is the coming into the world of the life of the world to come.

MATTHEW

In Matthew the simplicity of Mark's story disappears in the presence of some new motives drawn from the needs of Christian apologetics. For Matthew, conscious of the continuity of the works of God in Israel and in Christ, shews that the Resurrection has the familiar signs of a *Biblical* miracle. He adds the references to the earthquake, the angel of the Lord descending and rolling away the stone, the soldiers on guard becoming like dead men. But the language is not merely portentous. It does not suffice to explain it by the hackneyed phrase that Matthew " heightens the miraculous." The point is that he uses the miracle-language of the Old Testament, and in doing so he says in effect, " It was God who wrought this; the God of Israel, now as of old, came to bring deliverance with mighty hand and outstretched arm."

But the most distinctive part of Matthew's narrative is the concluding episode in Galilee. What Galilee means to Matthew is made clear from an early reference to it in his Gospel.

> " The land of Zebulon and the land of Naphtali
> Toward the sea, beyond Jordan,
> Galilee of the Gentiles.
> The people which sat in darkness
> Saw a great light,
> And to them which sat in the region and shadow of death
> To them did light spring up." (iv. 15–16. Cf. Isa. ix. 1–2.)

Galilee is a symbol of the borders of the Gentile world. Into this world and into every part of the region and shadow of death will

[1] *Locality and Doctrine,* p. 33. If Dr. Lightfoot does not carry conviction in his contention that Mark ended his Gospel at xvi. 8, he has done the great service of drawing attention to the theological teaching of this section in itself as well as of the other Resurrection narratives.

the Gospel of God now be proclaimed. In the story-form of a the-
ophany Matthew describes the appearance of Jesus. It is in Galilee,
with the missionary associations of the name. It is upon a mountain, for Jesus is the lawgiver, the Moses of the new people of God.
But more still, He is the royal Messiah claiming all authority in
heaven and on earth; and in the right of His royal sovereignty He
commissions the Church to go into all the world, to teach and to
baptize. He will be with them; for the Gospel that began with the
revelation of, "Immanuel, God with us," ends with the promise,
"Lo I am with you."

He will be with them "unto the end of the world." Here is a
difference of emphasis between Mark and Matthew. Mark views
the Resurrection as itself the coming of the end: the Son of Man
has returned, the age-to-come is breaking in. Matthew rather looks
ahead to the Parousia that still lies in the future when he writes.
The mission to the nations must first take place, and then the Lord
will come again. This difference of emphasis often confronts the
reader of the New Testament, and it cannot be removed or ex-
plained away. The tension is inescapable. The day is come: yet the
day is still to come. The new world has broken in: yet the history
of this world continues. It continues, however, with the sovereignty
of the Messiah, in whom is "all power in heaven and on earth,"
resting upon it.

LUKE

Luke's narratives of the Resurrection diverge from Mark to a
greater extent than do Matthew's, both in literary sources and in
theological themes. If Mark shews us the Resurrection as the breaking into history of a transcendental act of God, Luke shews rather
the place of the Resurrection within that process of history wherein
the purpose of God is unfolded.

For whereas Mark describes both the Passion and the message
of the Resurrection as it were from near at hand, each event being
terrible, staggering and unintelligible, Luke tells the story as it were
from a point further away, whence the events can be seen in their
intelligible place in the divine scheme of history. All was at first
mysterious; but now, Luke seems to say, all possesses a plan that we

can know and understand. The plan belongs to God, and it is unfolded in the whole series of acts in the divine drama: the preparation, the birth, the childhood, the baptism, the ministry, the Passion, the Resurrection, the promise of the Father, the journey of the
Gospel to all the world. Ought not men to realize how inevitable
each step in the plan has been?

" Behoved it not the Christ to suffer these things, and to enter into
his glory? " (xxiv. 26.)
" Thus it is written, that the Christ should suffer and rise again from
the dead the third day: and that repentance and remission of sins should
be preached in his name unto all nations beginning from Jerusalem."
(xxiv. 46–47.)

What was at the first impact miraculous and unintelligible has become, without ceasing to be miraculous, truly " natural " and intelligible. Hence Luke suggests in his narratives that the Resurrection
ought to have been expected, known and understood.

" Why seek ye the living among the dead? " (xxiv. 5.)
" Remember how he spake unto you." (xxiv. 6.)
" O foolish men, and slow of heart to believe in all that the prophets
have spoken! " (xxiv. 25.)

For Luke history and theology are one; and, if he shews us less
than does Mark of the Resurrection as a supra-historical coming of
the Day of the LORD, he draws out instead the important truth that
in the Resurrection one epoch of history, human and divine, reaches
its climax and another epoch has its beginning. He teaches the
truths upon which Westcott was to lay great emphasis: " what was
before miraculous is now natural." " The Resurrection is the central
point of history, primarily of religious history, and then of civil history of which that is the soul." [1]
If therefore Mark's rugged story leaves the reader awestruck,
Luke's sensitive and human narrative brings the Resurrection home
to mind and heart and conscience. He leads his readers to reflect
upon its relation to God, to Christ, to history, to themselves. He
draws together Cross and Resurrection, with a hint of the Johannine Cross-glory theme. Above all, he shews that the Resurrection

[1] *The Gospel of the Resurrection*, p. 6.

does not touch the world at a tangent. It is attested by bodily evidences: "handle me and see, for a spirit hath not flesh and bones as ye see me having." It belongs to the historical order. It reaches down to the thought and feeling of men and women; it kindles their understanding, and it evokes their worship.

For it is in *worship* that Luke's Gospel ends, as it begins. In the beginning Zacharias is in the temple worshipping in the order of his priestly course. At the conclusion, the disciples are in the temple worshipping and blessing God. The scene is the same: but the meaning of worship has been transformed by the Resurrection.

(*a*) It was in the breaking of the bread that the self-revelation of Jesus at Emmaus took place. Till then, the two disciples had not recognized Him. Was this meal the Eucharist? The phrase used is a regular term for the Eucharist (cf. Acts xx. 7), and the minds of Luke's Christian readers would turn inevitably to what has been called "the sacred feast wherein Christ is received, the memory of the Passion is renewed, the mind is filled with grace, and a pledge of glory to come is given unto us." If we cannot be sure of the precise character of the meal and action at Emmaus we can notice this significant parallelism: Jesus in the blessing and breaking of the bread in the Upper Room unfolded the meaning of His Passion, Jesus in the blessing and breaking of the bread at Emmaus unfolded to two disciples the fact of His Resurrection. For the early Christians the breaking of the bread was a central link both with the Passion and the Resurrection; and in the Eucharistic rite the people of Christ still shew forth His death and feed upon His life, and Calvary and Easter are perpetuated in the life of the Church.

(*b*) Finally, Jesus leads the Apostles from Jerusalem to a place over against Bethany; and He lifts up His hands and blesses them and is parted from them. Their response to this last visible act is *to worship Jesus* and, returning to Jerusalem, *to bless God*. Henceforth the worship of Jesus and the praise of God are inseparably blended. Without any weakening of the the monotheism of their fathers the disciples in Jerusalem continued to worship Jesus, risen and exalted at the right hand of God. They expressed their devotion by calling Him Lord, and by applying to Him the imagery of "the right hand of God" from Psa. cx. The earliest known

credal formula is, " Jesus is Lord." *Lex orandi lex credendi*. Within
the primitive worship of Jesus by the disciples in Jerusalem the
whole rich development of the doctrine of His Person in the Apostolic age is implicitly contained. For to worship Jesus is to affirm
that all that is true of God is true of Him.

JOHN

In the Fourth Gospel the narratives of the Resurrection, to a
greater degree than the narratives in the other Gospels, reflect the
special themes of the evangelist.

The central theme of the Fourth Gospel, as we saw earlier, is
Life. The words and works of the Christ are a manifestation of
Life, and they extend to the whole range of human needs, spiritual
and bodily alike. The healing of the sick and impotent, the feeding of the hungry, the giving of sight to the blind, the raising of
Lazarus from death, are all signs of the life-giving mission of the
Son of God. The Life is the life of the age-to-come, the " aeonian "
life, realized already in the present age. It is received by believing
on Christ and by feeding on Him. He is Himself the Life. To possess Life is to know the Father and the Son.

Thus is Life manifested. But, as with the Kingdom of God in the
Synoptic narratives, so with the Life in John's narrative, the full
manifestation must await the Passion. The haunting words " not
yet " recur in the story. " Mine hour is not yet come." " My time is
not yet at hand." " Jesus was not yet glorified." For the Life is in
its essence a life that is given, laid-down, surrendered; and its character is wrought out and bestowed by the historical death and Resurrection of Jesus.

" Therefore doth the Father love me, because I lay down my life, that
I may take it again. No one taketh it away from me, but I lay it down
of myself. I have power to lay it down and I have power to take it
again. This commandment received I from the Father." (x. 17–18.)

The story therefore moves towards the death in Jerusalem. The
death and resurrection of Lazarus is a preliminary parable of the
great events. The corn of wheat must fall to the earth and die (xii.
24). The "hour" comes. Jesus dies on the Cross, while the passover lambs are being slain for sacrifice.

The death and the Resurrection, wherein the Gospel of Life is wrought out, are described by John in close relation one to another. As we saw, the note of victory resounds through the story of the Passion. Even in death there is life-giving-power, as is symbolized by the flowing of blood and water from the side of Jesus pierced by the spear of the soldier. Blood means life: water means cleansing. Both have been the themes of the words and works of Jesus throughout the Gospel; and both are now released freely for mankind through the Passion. But if there is Life present in death, there is also the note of death still to be heard in the midst of Life. For the marks of Calvary remain; and it is with wounded hands and side that the risen Jesus gives His peace to the disciples.

Here is Life eternal — revealed, wrought out, bestowed. The "not yet" that has cast its shadow across the story is no more. For "that hour" came on Calvary (xix. 27), and "that day" came at Easter (xx. 19). And now by the gift of the Paraclete the fruits of life are made available for men.

It is with these theological themes in mind that John writes his narratives of the Resurrection. He views the events of Easter as the climax of these themes and as the fulfilment of the promises made at the Supper. But while he writes as an interpreting theologian he is at pains to shew that here as elsewhere the theology is rooted in history. Nor is his history far removed from that of the Synoptists. Whether he had the narratives of the Synoptists before him (as many modern scholars believe) or whether he used independent traditions (as Mr. Gardner-Smith has powerfully argued), his material is in many ways *akin* to that used by the earlier evangelists. Akin to *Mark's* story of the women at the tomb is John's story of Mary Magdalene at the tomb. Akin to *Matthew's* closing scene in Galilee is John's deliberate use of a Galilean tradition with a missionary motive; for the episode of the fishing on the lake seems full of the symbolism of the Church's mission to catch fish on the seas of the heathen world. Akin to *Luke* is John's record of the appearance of Jesus to the eleven in Jerusalem. It is in essence the same history that forms John's basis. But he sees the history in the fuller light of the Church's knowledge of Him who is the Way, the Truth, the Life.

It is when John's narratives are contrasted with Luke's that his view of the relation between theology and history becomes most apparent.

Like Luke, John insists upon the historical character of the Resurrection and upon the evidence of touch and sight. (*a*) Luke had alluded to a visit of some disciples to the tomb to verify the story told by the women. According to some MSS. he also recorded explicitly a visit of Peter who ran to the tomb, saw the linen clothes by themselves, and departed wondering. John describes this event more fully. It was, he says, the beloved disciple who, with Peter, ran to the tomb. The beloved disciple reached the tomb first, stooped and looked in, but did not enter. Peter then arrived, entered and saw. But it was the beloved disciple who both saw and believed, convinced by the sight of the linen lying deprived of its use and yet in perfect order. The evidence of sight was convincing. (*b*) So too was the evidence of sight convincing when Jesus on the evening of Easter day shewed the disciples His hands and His side (cf. Luke xxiv. 39, "his hands and his feet") and they rejoiced to see Him (cf. Luke xxiv. 41). (*c*) So too was the evidence of sight convincing in the case of Thomas. Here Jesus offered the use of the further evidence of touch. Incredulous, Thomas had said that he would never believe until he had touched the wounds of Jesus. Jesus invited him to have the evidence which he sought. But it was not needed: without touching, Thomas saw and believed. None the less, those who have not seen and yet have believed are blessed.

For in contrast to Luke's emphasis upon evidence and history is John's insistence that evidence and history, though they matter supremely, cannot of themselves be intelligible or reveal God. The action of the Holy Spirit is needed to enable men to perceive the meaning of history. This is a recurring theme of the Fourth Gospel. Men must look through and beyond the facts of history to the Truth which history discloses; and they cannot do this without the aid of the Spirit. Flesh is of inescapable importance: the Word was made flesh: he who would know God must face the deeds of Jesus in the flesh: he must eat the flesh of the Son of Man and drink His blood. But of itself the flesh profiteth nothing: it is the spirit that quickeneth.

Such being his teaching, when John reaches the narratives of the Resurrection he is at one with Luke in emphasizing the importance of the visible and tangible evidences. But he is also insistent, as Luke is not, on turning the mind of the reader to the invisible realities which give the events their meaning.

Among these invisible realities are *the Father* and *the Spirit*. He who would understand the Resurrection must learn that it is the road whereby Jesus goes to the Father; and that only through the new creation wrought by the Spirit can men know the risen Christ. "Touch me not; for I am not yet ascended unto the Father." " Jesus breathed on them and said, Receive ye the Holy Spirit."

THE FATHER

Throughout His early life Jesus is going to the Father. Though He is one with the Father from all eternity He has been made one with mankind, and He journeys to the Father along the road of human life and death. If sometimes the word used is ἀναβαίνω, to " go up " or " ascend," more often it is simply ὑπάγω or πορεύομαι, the ordinary words for a journey. " Yet a little while I am with you, and I go unto him that sent me " (vii. 33). The unbelieving Jews cannot follow Him upon the journey. To them the way is self-barred: " Ye shall seek me, and shall not find me; and where I am, ye cannot come " (vii. 34). But the disciples will be enabled, in the end, to follow Him: " where I am, there shall also my servant be " (xii. 26). " I go . . . that where I am, there ye may be also " (xiv. 3). " Father, . . . I will that, where I am, they also may be with me, that they may behold my glory " (xvii. 24). But they cannot follow Him now: as yet, He must go alone upon a solitary journey, separated from them as He leaves the world.

The departure of Jesus throws the disciples into desolation. But in His discourse at the Supper He tells them of its necessity, and of its coming fruits. It is expedient. It will enable the coming of an entirely new order in which they will share. For He will come again to them (xiv. 3). Both He and His Father will make their abode with those who love Him and keep His words (xiv. 23). They will be enabled to do works greater than those which He has done (xiv. 12). The Paraclete will help them to recollect and to under-

stand what He has said (xiv. 26), and He will take of the things
of Jesus and declare them to the disciples (xvi. 14). They will see
Jesus (xvi. 16). Their joy will overflow (xvi. 22). Their access to
the Father will be such that there need be no limit to the boldness
of their petitions (xvi. 23). No longer will Jesus speak to them in
riddles, He will tell them plainly of the Father (xvi. 25). All this
will be the fruit of His lonely journey to the Father. Let there be
no clinging to Jesus. He has shared hitherto in the mode of their
earthly existence: He goes away that through tribulation He may
lead them to share in His new life, to the Father's glory. These
things will happen " in *that day* " (xvi. 26).

" Arise let us go hence." Jesus goes out to tread the last stages of
the road to the Father. The Passion and the Resurrection were that
road: but they did not of themselves complete it. Easter morning
dawned; Mary saw Jesus; and yet there was still a further step to
be trod. For when Mary wished to cling to Him by the tomb He
said to her,

"Touch me not; for I am not yet ascended unto the Father."

She must not cling to Him, desiring His presence after the manner
of the former days when He shared in this earth's ways of touch.
The old ways are about to give place to new. Jesus is on His way
up to the Father; and, when the journey is perfected, then there
will be touch between Him and those who are His, after a new
manner. Therefore He says: Do not touch me now, but

" go to my brethren, and say to them, I am going up unto my Father
and your Father, my God and your God."

The ascent will be accomplished forthwith. There need be no more
delay. The " not yet " will pass away. " That day," dawning already, will be realized. The Father, to whom Jesus is going, is the
Father of the disciples also. Yet there is a difference: He says not
" our Father," but " my Father and your Father ": His sonship is
from all eternity, theirs is bestowed and derived from His.

THE HOLY SPIRIT

The journey to the Father was completed on Easter Day. Then followed on " that day " at evening the gift of Holy Spirit to the disciples; and the gift has been made possible by the completion of the journey. Far back in the story John has said that the gift of Holy Spirit is made possible only by the Passion and exaltation of Jesus (vii. 39). For Holy Spirit is given so as to reproduce in the disciples "the things of Jesus," namely, the Life-through-death which is the essence of His life. " When therefore it was evening on that day, the first day of the week . . . Jesus came and stood in the midst." He had spoken at the Supper of " that day," and now that day is come. He speaks peace unto them. They are filled with joy. He shews unto them His hands and His side.

" Jesus therefore said to them again, Peace be unto you: as the Father hath sent me, even so send I you. And when he had said this, he breathed on them, and saith unto them, Receive ye the Holy Ghost: whose soever sins ye forgive, they are forgiven unto them; whose soever sins ye retain, they are retained." (xx. 21–23.)

Here is an act of *new creation*. The breath of Jesus recalls, " The LORD God formed man out of the dust of the ground and breathed into his nostrils the breath of life, and man became a living soul " (Gen. ii. 7). Paul says: " The last Adam became a life-giving spirit " (1 Cor. xv. 45). There have perhaps been hints of a new creation already in John's narrative: the voice of the Lord in the garden. Here too, consequent upon the new creation, is the *Apostolic mission*. It is akin to the mission of Jesus from the Father, for " as thou didst send me into the world, even so sent I them into the world " (xvii. 18). The end of the mission is the release of mankind from sin, that through the disciples the mercy and judgment wrought by the Passion and Resurrection may be brought to bear upon human lives. Thus the disciples will forgive sins and retain them. This commission is given to the whole Church. It includes the specific ministry of absolution, it includes (perhaps more directly) the baptism with water and the Spirit. It comprises the entire office of the Church to bring to mankind the cleansing made possible by the Cross.

It is clear that John wishes his readers to understand that the Ascension took place on Easter Day. This is in contrast with the account by Luke, where the Ascension is described (Acts i. 9) as happening at the close of the series of appearances during forty days. The contradiction seems puzzling. The present writer would make this suggestion. Perhaps Luke and John have different happenings in mind. John is, in xx. 17, alluding to (for he could never describe) the journey of Jesus to the Father's glory, a going to the Father which though it involves historical events is essentially beyond history. Luke is describing in a concrete picture an event whereby Jesus gave to the disciples a visible assurance that the appearances were ended. There seems no inconsistency between the truth which John is teaching and the event which Luke is recording.

It is harder to understand the "contradiction" between the story of the gift of the Spirit on Easter Day as John records it and the story of Pentecost as Luke records it. But here the possibility that there was a twofold gift need not be excluded. The Holy Spirit overshadowed the manhood of Jesus both at His conception and at His baptism. Subsequently the Holy Spirit endows the people of Christ both in baptism and in the laying-on-of-hands. Similarly a twofold action may have occurred in the original redemptive events: on Easter Day, a bestowal of the breath of the new life; at Pentecost, an outpouring for the execution of those tasks which the new life involved.

John is eager to shew that when once the day is come, then fulfilment and realization follow quickly. It is clear from the New Testament as a whole that the Resurrection implies the breaking-into-history of the age-to-come. But as we have seen, the evangelists treat the story of the Resurrection in rather different ways in relation to this eschatological theme. *Mark* seems to tell of the Resurrection as the Parousia: the day of the Son of Man. *Matthew* thinks rather of the worldwide task that still awaits the Church before the Parousia, which is still in the future. *Luke* brings the Resurrection more closely to the continuous movement of history of which Jesus Christ is the Lord. *John*, like Mark, dwells upon the realization of the end. To a greater extent than any other writer he shews that eternal life is come: Easter is the day of fulfilment: the things pre-dicted at the Supper are here.

But, for John, there is also a consummation yet to come. Eternal life is here; the victory has been won. But still the disciples must toil all night upon the lake; and one will be girded and carried whither he would not to a martyr's death, and another may tarry until the Lord shall come. But, whether they die or whether they tarry, what is it? For to those who believe in the Resurrection of Christ it is always the " last hour."

Chapter Seven

THE RESURRECTION AND THE CHURCH

I

A BOOK whose subject is the Resurrection of Christ inevitably includes a treatment of the Church. We cannot separate " Christ the firstfruits " and " they that are Christ's," or (as we might well translate) "they that belong to the Messiah " (1 Cor. xv. 23). The word " Christ " itself implies the community over which the Messiah reigns. Nowhere has the relation of Church and Christ been better summed up than in the words of Émile Mersch in his book *Le Corps Mystique du Christ:* " *Les Évangiles n'en parlent pas directement; directement ils ne parlent que de Jésus. Mais précisément le Jésus dont ils parlent n'est pas un Jésus tout limité et tout fermé en lui-même.*" [1]

Some modern writers are puzzled by what appears to them to be a scarcity of teaching given by Jesus Christ concerning the Church, and they conclude that the Church therefore cannot be one of the important elements in Christianity. The same method of argument would lead to the conclusion that the Holy Spirit or the Resurrection itself has an unimportant place in Christianity; for how few are the sayings of Jesus, in the first three Gospels, concerning either of these themes! But a wrong approach is apparent here. If Jesus came to teach a Gospel, He came also to *be,* in His whole life and death and Resurrection and Pentecost, a Gospel: some of the most significant parts of His mission lie beyond His own words as Rabbi or teacher. So with the Church: Jesus did not found a Church by giving a set of instructions as if it were a kind of society for the followers of a teacher. The Church existed already; it was Israel. Jesus summed up the mission of Israel in His own person as Son and Servant. He gathered a remnant around Him, and became Himself the centre and the stem of a new Israel constituted by His

---

[1] " The Gospels do not speak of it directly; directly they speak only of Jesus. But precisely the Jesus of whom they speak is not a Jesus wholly limited and wholly shut up within himself." Page 25.

Resurrection from death. It is in *Him,* and especially in His Resurrection, that the basis of the Church appears. In this, as in all else, Christianity is an Easter faith.

None the less, the most distinct seeds of the Church can be noted in the teaching of Jesus, deliberately and patiently sown. The Messiah addressed His message to Israel: summoning Israel to repent. But as the nation as a whole was unresponsive He gathered around Him a remnant as the nucleus of an Israel to be. Gladly would He have gathered all Jerusalem's children as a hen gathers her brood under her wings (Matt. xxiii. 37), but they would not. He gathers instead the " little flock " of the disciples (Luke xii. 32). In every stratum of the literary sources of the Gospels we find sayings of Jesus about this theme. He appoints twelve " that they might be with him, and that he might send them forth " (Mark iii. 14). That they are twelve in number is specially significant, for Jesus is reconstituting the Israel of God symbolized by the twelve tribes (cf. Matt. xix. 28 = Luke xxii. 30). To the twelve Jesus declares on the night before the Passion the new covenant in His blood (Mark xiv. 24); and a covenant implies a people of God with whom it is made. Once more an Israel is to be set free by a mighty act of God, to serve Him and to be His people.

But the realization of all this lies in the future. The little flock was scattered when the blow fell upon its shepherd; they forsook Him and fled. He died alone. But He died as Israel's true representative, Himself the remnant of Israel, the true vine. And He was raised from death to be the head of a new Israel formed from those of every race and nation, who receive His gift of forgiveness and by faith and baptism make His death their own and become united to His risen life. The confession of the early Christians is, " Jesus is Lord," a confession springing from the belief that God raised Him from death and exalted Him. They make this confession as members of His ecclesia, and they are able to do so only by the aid of the Spirit of the risen Jesus (1 Cor. xii. 3; Rom. x. 8–9). They are baptized into His death and are made sharers in His Resurrection. Such is the origin and the meaning of the Church.

In two important sayings recorded in the Gospels the connection between the Church and the Resurrection is apparent.

(*a*) The first is the saying before the Passion about the smiting of the shepherd and the scattering of the sheep. The imagery of the shepherd in the New Testament is used more than once with the Resurrection in mind.

" It is written, I will smite the shepherd, and the sheep shall be scattered abroad. Howbeit, after I am raised up I will go before you into Galilee." (Mark xiv. 27–28.)

We may compare the shepherd-sayings in the Fourth Gospel, where too the shepherd dies for the flock and rises from death.

" And other sheep I have, which are not of this fold; them also I must bring, and they shall hear my voice: and they shall become one flock, one shepherd. Therefore doth my Father love me, because I lay down my life, that I may take it again." (John x. 16–17.)

Of old, God had " brought his people up out of the sea with the shepherd of his flock " (Isa. lxiii. 11). Now God raised the shepherd from death to unite the flock and to draw together many sheep. The theme recurs in the Epistle to the Hebrews:

" Now the God of peace, who brought again from the dead the great shepherd of the sheep with the blood of the eternal covenant, even our Lord Jesus, make you perfect in every good thing to do his will, working in us that which is well-pleasing in his sight." (Heb. xiii. 20–21.)

Without the Resurrection the flock is scattered and perishing.

(*b*) The second saying, which specially draws out the truth about the Church and the Resurrection and indeed sums it up, is at the close of the narrative of the cleansing of the temple in the Fourth Gospel.

" The Jews therefore answered and said unto him, What sign shewest thou unto us, seeing that thou doest these things? Jesus answered and said unto them, Destroy this temple, and in three days I will raise it up. The Jews therefore said, Forty and six years was this temple in building and wilt thou raise it up in three days? But he spake of the temple of his body. When therefore he was raised from the dead, his disciples remembered that he spake this: and they believed the scripture, and the word which Jesus had said." (John ii. 18–22.)

The theme is not only Johannine. It is clear from earlier documents that Jesus was accused of threatening to destroy the temple made

with hands and to replace it in three days by a temple made without hands (Mark xiv. 58; xv. 29). It is also recorded that He said
that a rejected stone would become the head of the corner in a new
building (Mark xii. 10). Here in the Fourth Gospel the story of
the cleansing of the temple and the words which follow sum up
the ending of the old order and the coming of the new. As Hoskyns pointed out, the word λύω is used both of the destruction of a
building and the dissolution of human life: here it indicates both
the death of the body of Jesus and the destruction of the system
which centred in the temple and its worship. In its place there will
be raised up " the temple of his body ": a temple in which Christ's
people will be the stones, a body in which Christ's people will be
the members. Judaism will be replaced by the risen Christ and the
Christians united to Him. They will be both the temple of God (cf.
1 Cor. iii. 16–17; Eph. ii. 21; 1 Peter ii. 5) and the body of Christ
(cf. 1 Cor. xii. 27; Eph. i. 22–23). These great Apostolic doctrines
have their roots in the ministry of Jesus. Without the Church His
mission is incomplete, but without the Resurrection the Church is
an idle name.

2

It is clear from the Gospels that our Lord is, in Mersch's words,
" pas un Jésus tout limité et tout fermé en lui-même "; and the same
is clear from the Epistles. The members of the new Church are so
closely united to the risen Christ that His life is described by Paul
as including theirs.

"For the love of Christ constraineth us; because we thus judge that
one died for all, therefore all died; and he died for all, that they which
live should no longer live unto themselves, but unto him who for their
sakes died and rose again. Wherefore we henceforth know no man after
the flesh: even though we have known Christ after the flesh, yet now we
know him so no more." (2 Cor. v. 14–16.)

Dying to their own self-centredness, the Christians enter a new
life wherein the centre is not themselves but the risen Christ. No
longer do they think of Christ only in terms of His existence in
history as an isolated figure: for they think of Him as risen and
contemporary and embracing His people as a very part of His own

life. It is this that lies behind the description of the Christians as "the Body of Christ."

It is uncertain how the phrase "the Body of Christ" came into existence as a description of the Church. One suggestion is that its origin is derived from the imagery of the Eucharist wherein the Christians are one body by partaking of the body of Christ.[1] Another suggestion is that the phrase is derived from contemporary Stoic uses of the word *soma*.[2] But it is clear that whatever the origin of the verbal form may be, the truth that it expresses is created by the Resurrection of Christ and the impact of the Resurrection upon the first Christians. The emphasis in the phrase "Body of Christ" is upon the word *of Christ*. The Christians are *His* Body, the sphere of the action of *His* risen life.

From the day of his conversion Paul is made aware of a true solidarity between the risen Christ and the disciples. "Saul, Saul, why persecutest thou *me*?" He knows that Christ is one with His persecuted followers and suffers with them. Hence it is to no solitary Christ that Paul is converted, but to a Christ whose disciples are indeed His "Body." Some incidental references in the Epistles shew the link between the risen Christ and the Christians.

"The body is not for fornication, but for the Lord; and the Lord for the body: and God both raised the Lord, and will raise up us through his power. Know ye not that your bodies are members of Christ?" (1 Cor. vi. 13–15.)

Here Paul is speaking of the human bodies of Christian people, united to the risen Lord so as to be indeed *His* members. Compare and contrast these words:

"Wherefore, my brethren, ye also were made dead to the law, through the body of Christ: that ye should be joined to another, even to him that was raised from the dead, that we might bring forth fruit unto God." (Rom. vii. 4.)

Here the death of the body of Christ upon the Cross is the means whereby the Christians have been "joined" to Christ raised from death.

[1] Cf. Rawlinson in *Mysterium Christi*, pp. 225 ff.
[2] Cf. W. L. Knox, *S. Paul and the Church of the Gentiles*, pp. 160 ff.

These passages are but casual references. For this very reason they have great significance, for they disclose a truth which is in the Apostle's mind concerning the Resurrection and the Church. The truth is drawn out fully in some other expository passages. There is first the comparison between Christ and the Christians and *a* body:

"For as the body is one, and hath many members, and all the members of the body being many are one body; so also in Christ." (1 Cor. xii. 12.)

Then there is the direct *description* of the Christians as *His* Body:

"Now ye are the body of Christ, and severally members thereof." (1 Cor. xii. 27.)

Finally there is the sublime summary in the Epistle to the Ephesians. Here the description of the exaltation of Christ in the heavenly places, supreme over all, is followed by the daring assertion that He is incomplete without the Church which is both His Body and His fulness. Paul prays that God may lead the Christians to a realization of the exceeding greatness of His power, wrought in Christ,

"when he raised him from the dead, and made him to sit at his right hand in the heavenly places . . . and he put all things in subjection under his feet, and gave him to be head over all things to the church which is his body, the fulness of him that filleth all in all." (Eph. i. 20–23.)

The exalted Christ is incomplete without the Church. It is through the Church that He lives and works. The essence of the Church is not the members who belong to it but the Christ from whom its life is derived. It is He, and not they, that provides the Church's definition.

But the foundation of the Church upon the Resurrection implies for it a constant relation to the Passion also. It is by baptism into the death of Christ that we are made His members, and it is by a continually renewed relation to His death that our membership is sustained.

The New Testament shews how the Christian life thus began and thus continued. The convert reaches out by faith from himself to Christ who died for him, renouncing the life-unto-self. He plunges beneath the waters of baptism as one who dies, and he emerges into a new life in Christ who rose again. " Are ye ignorant, that all we who were baptized into Christ Jesus were baptized into his death? " (Rom. vi. 3). But the convert's relation to the Cross does not cease there. The living Christ, to whom he now belongs, is still Christ the Crucified One; and the Christian advances in " the fellowship of his sufferings, being conformed unto his death " (Phil. iii. 19). If once for all he has " died with Christ " (Col. iii. 3), he is not exempt from the subsequent command, " Mortify therefore your members which are upon the earth " (Col. iii. 5). He is ever near to the Cross in his own conflict with sin; in his bearing of sorrow, pain and humiliation when they come to him; in his bearing of the pains of others; in his increasing knowledge of what Calvary meant and means. But in all this he is discovering that the risen life of Jesus belongs to him, and with it great rejoicing. Awhile perhaps it may be that the Cross is more apparent to him, and the risen life may seem to be hidden. But one day the secret that is already present will be made manifest, and in the Resurrection that awaits him after death he will see the risen Christ in whose life, though hidden, he has already shared.

Cross and Resurrection are the ground of the Church's origin, the secret of the Church's contemporary being, the goal of the Church's final self-realization on behalf of the human race. The Word and the Sacraments in the midst of the Church make known to its members continually what is their origin, their secret and their goal. For the *Word* is the Word of the Cross, whereby the Church is made, renewed and judged. The *Eucharist* is the proclaiming of the Lord's death until His coming again; the setting forth before God and man of the whole drama of His life, death, Resurrection and Parousia; and the feeding of His people with His broken body and outpoured blood. The Eucharist looks back to the events of the Gospel; it realizes those events in the present hour; it anticipates the final consummation: " the Body of our Lord Jesus Christ which was given for thee preserve thy body and soul unto everlasting life."

3

The treasure is in earthen vessels; and herein lies the paradox of the Church as it is known in history. On the one hand it contains a divine life and is constituted by that divine life; on the other hand its members are sinful and entangled in the world. The paradox is not new. The Church was never otherwise. The rather romantic tendency of the writer of Acts does not prevent him from describing the deceit of Ananias and Sapphira, and the bickering of the widows about the dole. Paul's realism about the moral failures of the Christians of Corinth does not prevent him from asserting that Christ is in them, wisdom and righteousness and sanctification, and that they are indeed His Body. At once the Church contains the hidden life of Christ and a host of sinful contradictions. " Who is blind, but my servant? "

This paradox provides the historian of the Church with his biggest problems and the good man who studies the contemporary Church in any age with his biggest perplexity. Conscious of the hindrance to Christianity which the paradox affords, Christians have often been led to conclude that the Church cannot after all be an important element in essential Christianity and that real Christianity can be presented without much reference to it. This conclusion is in its turn difficult because it violates the evidence of the New Testament that there is a very close connection between the Gospel and the Church, evidence which recent critical study has tended to enhance. But there have been other ways of escape; and Christians have sought to escape from the paradox of the Church by violent and lopsided doctrines.

(a) One attempted solution has been to regard the true Church as the society of the morally pure and perfect. " Out with the weak and out with those who lapsed under persecution. Out with the harlots and the fornicators. Out with those who fail to reach a certain measurable standard of moral obedience! " This solution has been attempted by many Puritan movements both in early and later centuries. It does violence to the true meaning of the Church. For the holiness of the Church is the holiness of the Spirit whereby the members are made holy. To use visible standards of morality as a test of membership is to transfer the merit and glory from Christ to the members themselves, and to set forth the Church as a society of the moral rather than a family of the redeemed. By this procedure fornication may be expelled, but pride and self-righteousness may eat their way within.

(b) Another solution has been to equate the sovereignty of God and the sovereignty of the visible Church upon earth, so as to identify the visible Church with the Kingdom of God itself. This solution has been attended by disastrous results. It violates the distinction apparent in the New Testament between the Kingdom and the Church. For the Kingdom means primarily not the realm but the Reign or sovereignty of God: and of this Reign, which comes by the way of the Cross, the Church is the servant and the herald. The Kingdom is brought to men through the Church and is found within it: but it always transcends the Church. Attempts to solve the problem of the Church by thus exaggerating its meaning have led to equally violent and one-sided reactions.

(c) Yet another solution is familiar, born of reaction against the last. This is to view the true Church as properly invisible and ideal, laid up in heaven, and to regard the empirical Church upon earth as being not really the true Church. This solution includes the belief that a right understanding of the spiritual and heavenly nature of the Church will lead to an indifference to its visible order and its sacramental continuity. This solution likewise contradicts the nature of New Testament Christianity. For the visible Body with its God-given sacraments and its God-given ministry does matter. The Church belongs to history as well as to heaven, to flesh as well as to spirit. It bears witness to the historical Incarnation of God. It is " sent " historically by Jesus Christ even as He was " sent " by the Father. It links men with the Cross and the Resurrection as historical events. Men truly know the Church of heaven if they are humble enough to bear the pains and paradoxes of the visible Church upon earth.

Each of these attempts to make the Church less paradoxical involves a false short-cut and a denial of truth. For the New Testament will not ease the paradox for us: it allows us to overlook neither the truth that the Church *is* the Body of Christ nor the existence of Christians who crucify the Son of God afresh and put him to a perpetual shame. But the New Testament suggests that the way is to accept the paradox, not with complaisance nor with a sense of grievance but with the light of the Cross and Resurrection upon it. The man who knows, from the Cross, his own need is not ashamed to put himself beside the other members of the Church whose need is like his own; and to discover amid the contradictions of the Church's members the risen life of Christ which is the divine answer to his need as to theirs.

4

It is, however, not only in the New Testament that the Biblical meaning of the Church is disclosed. For just as the Resurrection sent the Apostles back to the Old Testament in their understanding of Jesus Christ, so it sends us back to the Old Testament to find there some permanent truths about the Church in its relation to God and to the world. As Augustine said, *" Obscurius dixerunt prophetae de Christo quam de Ecclesia"* (in Psa. xxx).

The Church of Israel was called by God not to glorify itself but to make Him known to the nation. It possessed an imperishability, not on account of any merits of its members but on account of the faithfulness of God who wills to use Israel for the redemption of mankind. When Israel fails, the judgment of God falls and punishment follows: yet there is a remnant whom God uses as the stump from which a new and better tree may grow. God does not find the Israelites of any particular generation to be indispensable: He is not pledged to them, if they are unfaithful to Him; He can sweep them aside, and from the stones of a heathen world He can raise up new ones who will serve Him better. But Israel continues imperishable, even if its true mission be represented by a very small number or by the lonely Christ, who bears the destiny of Israel to Calvary and to the grave.

For the God of Israel is the God who judges and raises up. His people come to learn of Him and to make Him known not by the even tenor of a steady spiritual growth, but through crises of judgment and resurrection. Great deliverances and times of spirit-

ual prosperity are followed by the disasters born of pride and complacency: humiliation follows, and in the day of humiliation God
raises up His servants and prophets. What is true of the old Israel
is true also of the new. Centuries of achievement lead on to stag-
nation and self-sufficiency, and the God who raised up Moses, Amos,
Jeremiah, Ezra raises up Benedict, Francis, Wesley, Keble. The
Church is judged when it gives the glory to itself: it is renewed
only by accepting the judgment and by being raised again to seek
the glory of God in the service of mankind.

But if the comparison between the old Israel and the new is
important, it is no less important to notice where the contrast lies.
It lies most chiefly in the fact that whereas the old Israel was sustained by repeated actions of God in raising her up, the new Israel
has behind it and within it the one, final, decisive Passion and
Resurrection of Christ. Her mission is to make His Passion and
Resurrection known, so that mankind may learn in the midst of
every historical crisis both the judgment and the mercy which the
Passion and Resurrection bring. And she fulfils her mission only
by being brought herself again and again beneath that judgment
and mercy which she teaches to mankind. " Rejoice not against me,
O mine enemy: when I fall, I shall arise; when I sit in darkness,
the Lord shall be a light unto me. I will bear the indignation of the
Lord, because I have sinned against him; until he plead my cause,
and execute judgment for me: he will bring me forth to the light,
and I shall behold his righteousness " (Micah vii. 8–9).

Chapter Eight

THE RESURRECTION OF THE DEAD

THE belief in " the resurrection of the body " has been a stumbling-block both in the ancient and in the modern world. In the beginning, no doctrine could have been better chosen for exciting ridicule in Athens and disbelief in Corinth. In these latter days, it has been almost an axiom of liberal theology that the clause needs either removing or else interpreting as equivalent to the immortality of the soul. Yet to have succumbed to the objectors, either in the old world or the new, would have been a disaster. It would have blunted the cutting-edge of the Gospel and removed a doctrine which sums up the genius of Christianity in its belief about man and the world. Today, with the recovery of a truly Biblical perspective and with the abandonment of a rigid antithesis between spirit and matter, the wheel has turned; and it does not seem strange or surprising to read this confession made by Dr. Niebuhr:

" These closing words of the Apostolic Creed, in which the Christian hope of the fulfilment of life is expressed, were, as I remember it, an offence and a stumbling-block to young theologians at the time when my generation graduated from the theological seminaries. Those of us who were expected to express our Christian faith in terms of the Apostolic Creed at the occasion of our ordination had long and searching discussions on the problem presented by the Creed, particularly by this last phrase. We were not certain that we could honestly express our faith in such a formula. If we were finally prevailed upon to do so, it was usually with a patronising air towards the Christian past, with which we desired to express a sense of unity even if the price was the suppression of our moral and theological scruples over its rendering of the Christian faith.

" The twenty years which divide that time from this have brought great changes in theological thought, though I am not certain that many of my contemporaries are not still of the same mind in which they were then. Yet some of us have been persuaded to take the stone which we then rejected and to make it the head of the corner. In other words there is no part of the Apostolic Creed which, in our present opinion, expresses the whole genius of the Christian faith more neatly than just that despised phrase, ' I believe in the Resurrection of the body.' " [1]

[1] *Beyond Tragedy,* pp. 289–290. Charles Scribner's Sons.

I

While traditional Christianity insists upon distinguishing the revealed doctrine of Resurrection from a philosophical belief in the immortality of the soul, it regards the latter not as untrue and irrelevant
so much as incomplete, distressingly dull and missing the gift of the
Gospel. There are grounds, both philosophical and psychological
and religious, for believing that the soul survives death; though the
life of a soul without the body is a conception which it is difficult to
imagine. It is *incomplete;* because the self is far more than the
soul, and the self without bodily expression can hardly be the complete self. It is *dull;* because it implies the prolongation of man's
finite existence for everlasting years. In contrast both with the in-
completeness and the dullness of the immortality of the soul Christianity teaches a future state (not as of right but as of God's gift)
wherein the soul is not unclothed but clothed upon by a bodily expression, and wherein the finite human life is raised so as to share,
without losing its finiteness, in the infinite life of Christ Himself.

The Christian Gospel was not first addressed to people who had
no belief in a future state. Greeks were familiar with a philosophical doctrine of immortality. Jews believed in the resurrrection of
the body. Sometimes this was thought of as a resuscitation of human relics and a reconstruction of human existence after the fashion
of the present life. Sometimes it was thought of as a transformation of dead bodies into an utterly new state of glory and spirituali-
zation. But nowhere, either for Greek or for Jew, was belief in the
future life vivid, immediate, central and triumphant. Nowhere did
the belief combine a conscious nearness of the world to come with
a moral exalting of life in this present world. This was what Christianity brought. Its doctrine was not a flight to another world that
left this world behind, nor was it a longing for another world that
would come when the history of this world was ended. It was the
very near certainty of another world, with which the Christians
were already linked and into which the life of this world would be
raised up.

For the Christian belief about the future state centred in Jesus
Christ. He had been seen and loved in this life; and He had been

seen and loved also as one who had conquered death. He had become vividly known as the Lord both of the living and of the dead;
and the conviction of His people concerning the future life rested
upon their conviction about Him in whose life they shared. It was
an intense and triumphant conviction that where He was there also
would His people be. It found utterance in ringing words. " He
hath brought life and immortality to light through the Gospel."
" Fear not; I am the first and the last, and the living one; and I
was dead, and behold I am alive for evermore, and I have the keys
of death and of Hades." " Awake, thou that sleepest and arise from
the dead, and Christ shall shine upon thee."

Concerning the character of the life to come our Lord Himself
says little. He reveals the God who rules that life and is Himself
its centre, for it is a life unto God. It is not by speculations or by
detailed revelation that men may win an understanding of the future state, but by conformity to the God who rules it and by knowledge of Jesus Christ who is the way to it. For He is not only the
way to it, but Himself the very life of those who enter it. The central fact about the life of the Resurrection is that it is " in Christ."
Some will share in that life by conscious faith in Christ, unless they
betray that faith through their own lives. Others who have never
known Him may share in it if, after the Parable of the Sheep and
Goats, they have unconsciously ministered to Him. " In Christ " —
whether by conscious faith or by a relationship that is at first unconscious — men shall be made alive.

Yet there is some explicit teaching concerning the nature of the
Resurrection. By one dialogue and by one act Jesus Christ revealed
that twofold aspect of the life to come which was to be summed up
in the words " the resurrection of the body."

(a) Questioned by the Sadducees as to a point of casuistry concerning domestic relationships and their counterpart in the Resurrection, Jesus said that in the Resurrection " they neither marry nor
are given in marriage; but are as angels in heaven " (Mark xii. 25).
He said in effect that the Jewish beliefs which imported the conditions of this life into the Resurrection were wrong. The dead are
transformed, so as to be like angels with bodies like " garments of
light and glory." He added that the ground of belief in the future

life is seen in the Scriptures, where God is the God of the dead patriarchs: they live because they belong to God who is "not the God of the dead but of the living."

(*b*) But though the future life is to be a life transformed far beyond imagination and far beyond flesh and blood, men are indeed *raised*. "As touching the dead that they are raised," says Jesus. There is identity and continuity. And this is shewn in the act of the Lord's own Resurrection. While there was the glorifying of His body to which the narratives testify, there was also the continuity of the whole manhood, body and spirit, raised from death. The Son of God took upon Him the whole of human nature (often in the New Testament the word "flesh" is so used) in order that the whole might be raised in glory.

2

Nothing is more impressive in the Apostolic writers than their refusal to exclude the body from its relevance to the moral issues of their faith and from the final destiny of the Christians. The Hellenistic environment of the Church almost cried out to it to assert a "spiritual" salvation, whereby men might escape from the prison of the body into a destiny from which all the transitory things of physical nature were excluded. But the Christians clung to the belief that the body had been divinely created and divinely redeemed. "Waiting for the adoption, to wit the redemption of our body": nothing less than that was their longing. They yearned "not to be unclothed, but clothed upon, that mortality might be swallowed up of life" (2 Cor. v. 4).

It is Paul who gives the most incisive expression to this belief. Food and digestion may belong to this earth, but the body belongs to Christ.

"Meats for the belly, and the belly for meats; but God shall bring to nought both it and them. But the body is not for fornication, but for the Lord: and the Lord for the body; and God both raised the Lord, and will raise up us through his power." (1 Cor. vi. 13–14.)

The body has its place in the great design of redemption through the Resurrection of Christ.

"If Christ is in you, the body is dead because of sin: but the spirit is life because of righteousness. But if the Spirit of him that raised up Jesus from the dead dwelleth in you, he that raised up Christ Jesus from the dead shall quicken also your mortal bodies through his Spirit that dwelleth in you." (Rom. viii. 10–11.)

Paul here says that the body of a Christian is indeed still liable to death owing to his share in the sinful race. But the essential being ("spirit" seems here so used) of a Christian is made alive because it belongs to the new life of righteousness. Is this essential being, however, divorced from the body? No, because the Father who raised up Jesus will extend His life-giving action to the bodies of the Christians through the indwelling Spirit. The work of the Spirit in us prepares our bodies for the day when the Resurrection will accomplish in them all that God intends.

This consummation will be brought about at the Lord's return.

"For our citizenship is in heaven; from whence also we wait for a Saviour, the Lord Jesus Christ: who shall fashion anew the body of our humiliation, that it may be conformed to the body of his glory, according to the working whereby he is able even to subject all things unto himself." (Phil. iii. 20–21.)

It is possible that when he says "the body of his glory" Paul is thinking of the exalted Jesus whom he saw at his conversion, whence the words "glory" and "light" came to have for him a special meaning (cf. "the glory of God in the face of Jesus Christ," 2 Cor. iv. 6).

It is, however, in the fifteenth chapter of 1 Corinthians that the grand exposition of the doctrine occurs. Paul is here dealing with a crisis in the faith of some of his converts in Corinth. They are denying the resurrection of the dead. Paul recalls his own teaching concerning the Resurrection of Christ, which the Corinthians had accepted. How impossible is their position now: for if Christians who have died do not rise again, then Christ cannot have been raised; the preaching of the Apostles has been worthless; the Christians must still be living in sin like the heathen, for it was the Resurrection of Christ alone that set them free. By denying the resurrection of the Christians they are denying the fact and the efficacy of the Resurrection of Christ. " But now hath Christ been raised from the dead, the firstfruits of them that are asleep. For since by man came death, by man came also the resurrection of the dead. For as in Adam all die, so also in Christ shall all be made alive " (xv. 20–22). The Resurrection of Christ is the prelude to the resurrection of the Christians. Whether Paul is here teaching a universal resurrection is not certain, for the concluding words just quoted are perhaps rightly taken by Moffatt as meaning " all the members of the Christian community." No safe conclusion can here be drawn concerning the question of universalism; Paul is asserting that the Resurrection is the beginning of a new order of life in which men may share: " Christ the firstfruits; then they that are Christ's at his coming " (xv. 23).

But how are the dead raised? and with what manner of body do they come? This is the crucial question for the Corinthians, and for all who are puzzled by the Gospel. Paul's answer (xv. 36–49) may thus be paraphrased. He points his readers to an analogy from nature. " Fool, do you not realize that in the everyday processes of the cornfield, there is an illustration of the secret about the Resurrection? You sow a seed; and you reap not a seed but something utterly unlike it yet truly derived from it, for the variety of forms and bodies in God's universe is quite limitless. Here then is your analogy for the resurrection of the dead. The body comes into the world (this, rather than the burial of a corpse, seems to be the meaning of ' it is sown ') liable to death, and it is raised immortal:

> what is sown is mortal,
>   what rises is immortal:
> sown inglorious,
>   it rises in glory:
> sown in weakness,
>   it rises in power:
> sown an animate body,
>   it rises a spiritual body.

Adam was merely one into whom the breath of life had been breathed by God: Christ is one who Himself bestows life on others. Adam belonged to earth and to earth's limitations: Christ is heavenly, and comes from heaven. We have already experienced the life that is akin to the earthly Adam; and we are going to experience the life that is akin to the heavenly Christ."

Thus Paul tries to explain how the dead are raised. At this point he passes from the dead and speaks of " us " who will still be alive at the Parousia. " We shall not all sleep: i.e., we shall not all die; but we shall all be changed," transformed into the new and glorious life of the body when this " mortal shall have put on immortality." But it is with the dead that Paul's discussion is chiefly concerned, though no doubt they would be a minority. By the help of the analogy from nature he has affirmed a double truth. (a) The resurrection body will be utterly unlike the present body: indeed he says that " flesh and blood cannot inherit the kingdom of heaven." It is hard to imagine Paul ascribing to the risen body such actions as the eating of a piece of broiled fish. (b) Yet there is continuity. " Sown an animate body, it rises a spiritual body," or, as may be more correct: " there is sown an animate body, there rises a spiritual body." There is identity, as between seed and corn. It is a false inference, drawn by some, that the words " it is sown in corruption " mean that Christ's body perished in the grave and that the resurrection body is entirely new and unrelated to the past, for " it is sown " seems to refer not to burial but to the entry of the body into its existence in this world.

The analogy used by Paul serves to help his exposition: but it has its limits. Paul employs it for what it was worth; but he is equally insistent that the Resurrection involves a transcendental action of God which outruns human analogies and human understanding. " God giveth . . . as he wills." " I tell you a mystery." " Thanks be to God which giveth us the victory." It was less by the reasoned deductions from the analogy of nature than by belief in God's own unimaginable action that Paul's doctrine came into being; and its ground and its credibility rest upon the fact that Jesus Christ, the firstfruits, died and was buried and was raised and glorified. Similarly when Paul writes of a " spiritual body " the contrast is not between a body " formed out of matter " and a body " formed out of spirit "; it is between a body as we know it now and a body that has become the perfect instrument of the Holy Spirit, between a body that is conditioned by our present limitations and a body wherein the victory of Christ has done its perfect work. Some words of the late Fr. P. N. Waggett, S.S.J.E., may be quoted:

"The resurrection of the body may sometimes be called the 'physical resurrection,' but the phrase is likely to discredit the fact it points to. The Resurrection is a victory of spirit in the region where death now rules. We are not asked to believe in a reconstruction of the body after the fashion which belongs to the reign of death, but to believe that the death of the body as well as that of the spirit meets its conquerer in Christ. The death we see is a real event, as real on its lower level of importance as the sin which is its counterpart in the spirit. And this real event of death, so serious, so tyrannous, so much unworthy to be the conclusion of the body's story, finds its cure in Christ. This cure lies in the victory of Christ over bodily death in His own person, and will be accomplished in His members by the extension of the same victory. 'God both raised the Lord, and will raise us through His power.'" [1]

It is believed by some scholars that in 2 Cor. v Paul shews an altered view, and has abandoned the doctrine of 1 Cor. xv in favour of a belief that is virtually the same as a Hellenistic doctrine of the immortality of the soul. This would imply an abandonment of the identity insisted upon in the former Epistle, and would be consistent with the decay of the body of Jesus in the tomb and the endowment of His spirit with a new body rather than the glorifying of the old. The discussion of the passage involves a lengthy treatment of exegetical problems; and rather than embark upon it here, the writer would refer his readers to the most recent examinations of the question, and would state the conclusions to which he himself has been led. These are: that in 2 Cor. v. 2–4 Paul refers not to the fate of those who have died but to the fate of those who will be alive at the Parousia; that when the passage is so read the resemblances to 1 Cor. xv are impressive; that the argument for variations in Paul's belief has been unwarrantably exaggerated. The belief in the Resurrection of the body is, at a later date, found forcibly expressed both in Romans and in Philippians, which belie the notion that Paul abandoned his belief. [2]

The belief involves a far-reaching insight into the implications

---

[1] Paper on "*The Resurrection*" in *The Holy Eucharist with Other Occasional Papers*, p. 199.

[2] W. L. Knox on *S. Paul and the Church of the Gentiles*, pp. 135–145, argues that 2 Cor. v. 1–10 marks a change in Paul's belief under the influence of Hellenistic thought. But the similarity of belief in 1 Cor. xv and 2 Cor. v. 1–10 is convincingly shewn by L. S. Thornton in *The Common Life in the Body of Christ*, pp. 284–286.

of the Gospel. Paul refuses to acquiesce in a contemporary Jewish conception of a resurrection after the pattern of carnal life as we know it. He equally refuses to succumb to a rigid divorce between spirit and matter, soul and body. He will not limit the word " body " to the body as we know it. Perhaps his familiarity with the phrase " the body of Christ," which bore various meanings and yet expressed a personal identity, prepared him to feel his way towards a belief that the continuity of a body lies in its continuous relation to a person rather than in an identity of material particles. Be that as it may, his doctrine reaches far beyond the cleverness of the human mind or the pattern of human analogies: its source is in the Apostle's belief in God who created and redeemed both mankind and the material world, and in the event of the Gospel whereby Jesus Christ died and was buried and was raised again on the third day.

3

The interpretation of Paul's doctrine in subsequent Christian thought forms a rather complicated chapter in history. As in Judaism there were those who thought of the resurrection of the dead in terms of the body as we know it in this world, and those who emphasized its transformation; so in the Christian Church there have been those who taught the resurrection with the crudity that Paul deliberately avoided, and those who have entered into Paul's own insight. But it would be too simple to say merely that one school was right and the other wrong. Those who adhered to a " crude " view were sometimes bearing witness to a Christian view of the body as against a " spirituality " which threatened the whole Christian conception of man and the world. Already before the first century was out there were those who insisted that, alike in His earthly ministry and in His Resurrection, Christ was merely a phantom; and against such teaching we find Ignatius of Antioch (c. 112) insisting that, in both stages, Christ was both spirit and flesh. In the second century, Gnostics sought to tear Christianity from its historical roots, to divorce the God who is spirit from the God who created the material world, and to present Jesus Christ as one who redeems us from matter and flesh as from evil things.

It was in face of these dangers that Christians asserted their belief in the resurrection of the flesh or of the body.

As regards the Creeds the main facts are as follows. The Western baptismal creeds, including the Apostles' Creed, almost without exception professed belief in the *resurrection of the flesh*. This also appears in some early Eastern creeds, such as the Creed of Jerusalem as given by St. Cyril. But from the middle of the fourth century the prevailing form in the East was the *resurrection of the dead*. This was the form that found its way into the longer " Nicene " Creed, and thus became the authorized doctrine of the Universal Church. The phrase is Scriptural, and it avoids the possibility of a crude interpretation more readily than does the phrase " resurrection of the flesh." In the Church of England at the Reformation the " Nicene " Creed remained: " I look for the Resurrection of the dead." As to the Apostles' Creed, in the form used at Morning and Evening Prayer the word " flesh " was altered by Cranmer into " body," but in the form used in holy baptism the original phrase " resurrection of the flesh " was retained.

(*a*) What has been called the " cruder " belief comes first into view. The phrase " resurrection of the flesh " was apparently known in Rome before the end of the first century (cf. Clement; 1 Cor. xxvi. 3). It was unscriptural. It could easily be used to imply a conception far removed from that of Paul, and it was in fact often so used. An instance often cited is that of Tertullian who insisted that no part of the present constituents of the body will be lost in the resurrection, " not even a hair or an eye or a tooth." Had not Christ said that all the hairs of our head are numbered? " The flesh will arise, itself whole and entire " (*resurget caro, et quidem omnis, et quidem ipsa, et quidem integra*). In fairness to Tertullian it should be said that some of his other teaching greatly mitigates the crudity of these words; and the motive that prompted this teaching must be understood. But crudity there was, here and in other Latin writers; and there ensued, both within the Latin Church and subsequently within the Reformation Confessions, a presentation of the resurrection which so interpreted the continuity of the body as to miss that view of the continuity which Paul had taught. For centuries many Christians have had a mental picture of the material particles of dead bodies being reassembled, and of the bodies rising from their graves at the last day. But this is a belief which the Creed does not compel and which Paul's teaching does not encourage.

(b) On the other hand there was another tradition. The phrase " resurrection of the flesh " did not necessarily involve a crude belief. For in Biblical Greek the word " flesh " often bore the meaning, unknown in classical Greek, of " human nature " (cf. " all flesh shall see the salvation of God," " the Word was made flesh "). But this Biblical meaning was not always, nor indeed more often, intended; and it was probably the crude possibilities of the word " flesh " that led Eastern Christians to prefer the expressions " resurrection of the body " and " resurrection of the dead." This brings us to the great teachers who insisted that the body in its true meaning cannot be understood in terms of its contemporary component particles.

The greatest teacher of this kind was Origen, the Alexandrine scholar of the third century. He held that the matter by which bodies exist is characterized by constant mutation. Wood is turned into fire, fire into smoke, smoke into air; a human body is like a river, for as the water departs and the river remains, so the particles composing a body depart and the body remains. In the resurrection there will not be the solidity of the flesh, the liquid blood, the sinews, the structure of the limbs: yet the body will be there. Here we see with eyes, hear with ears and act with our hands. There " we shall be all sight, all hearing and all activity." " A certain principle lies within the body, from which, since it perishes not, the body is raised up in incorruption."

There is a modern ring in Origen's teaching. Westcott wrote of it: " There is no point in which his insight is more conspicuous; by keeping strictly to the Apostolic language he anticipated results which we have hardly yet secured. He saw that it is the spirit which moulds the frame through which it is manifested; that the body is the same not by any material continuity, but by the permanence of that which gives the law, the ' ratio,' he calls it, of its constitution. No exigencies of controversy, it must be remembered, brought Origen to his conclusion. It was, in his judgment, the clear teaching of St. Paul." Origen's view never died out. Though he was bitterly attacked by Jerome, his belief was in accord with " the resurrection of the dead " as the Nicene faith was to affirm it. In the ancient Church his teaching had some great adherents, including Chrysostom in his commentaries and Gregory of Nyssa in his *Soul and Resurrection*. In the modern era no disciple of Origen has been more ardent than Westcott himself, who links both Paul and Origen with those modern tendencies in thought which they anticipated.

For in truth the trend of modern science and philosophy seems to have features which confirm the credibility of the Pauline doctrine. The thought of a few decades ago was sometimes marked by a rigid contrast between spirit and matter, between personality and physical organism; and there are theologians who still hail this thought as if it were the last word of modernity. But today there is in physics the tendency to regard material objects as the organization of energy in particular forms, and to hold that the persistence of a body lies not in the immutability of its physical constituents but in their continued organization in accordance with the principle of the body's self-identity. Again, in the study of personality there is a reluctance to exclude the body from the essential self; in every act of consciousness the body plays its part as well as the mind. It is no doubt possible to shew that the mind may continue without the body, but it is impossible to conceive of a true life of the self without bodily expression. Indeed, the outlook of modern thought gives no encouragement to a sharp distinction between spirit and matter or to a belief in a spiritual life that can be diametrically contrasted with the bodily life. Rather does it seem to encourage us to beware of setting limits to the possibility of a bodily life that is both continuous and yet utterly different.

For science and theology concur in reminding us that our present experience of a body cannot set the limits to what a body may be. The New Testament speaks of the fleshly presence of Christ on earth as His body, of the Church as His body, and of the Eucharistic gift as His body. These phrases do not imply identity of material; but they are more than metaphors, and they tell of a true identity in that each is the organ of Christ's own activity. It is indeed only thus that the continuous identity of *any* body can rightly be defined. In the case of the body of the resurrection, what eludes our knowledge and understanding is the manner of the transition between the present and the future states. Moreover there is this further point: the body here and the body hereafter are related not only to the self of the individual Christian, but also to the Christ to whom the Christian is united and in whose life the Christian will truly share. The relation between ourselves and *His* risen body may be closer than we can imagine, for it is in *His* risen and glorious body that we ourselves shall be made complete.

To abandon the use of the word " body " in connection with the resurrection of the dead would indeed remove certain difficulties. But it would introduce difficulties no less great, and it would involve us in the poverty and materialism of limiting the word " body " to the body as we know it in its earthly and frustrated state. To cling to the words " the resurrection of the body " is to affirm that in our present bodies there is the law of a bodily life beyond our dreams, when the Spirit of Him who raised up Jesus Christ has done His perfect work in us.

4

The rejected stone may yet become the headstone of the corner. For it sums up the Christian view of the world. As Niebuhr has said in the Gifford Lectures for 1939 it " embodies the very genius of the Christian idea of the historical." [1]

Man, nature and history have their solution not within themselves but within a divine Kingdom that transcends them. This divine Kingdom cannot be realized as a climax of human progress upon the plane of history, nor yet as a movement of mankind to an immortality that belongs to it by right. It will be realized by God's act in " raising up " mankind and delivering it from the contradictions which neither history nor immortality can solve. Yet this divine Kingdom will not be far removed from nature and history; for in it both nature and history will be " clothed upon " and fulfilled.

" *Non eripit mortalia,*
Qui regna dat caelestia."

[1] *The Nature and Destiny of Man,* vol. ii, p. 305.

It is thus in the resurrection of the dead that the goal of the individual and the goal of the redeemed society find their perfect coincidence. The individual cannot reach his goal except in union with those who shall share with Him in the love of God and in the Body of Christ. The traditional picture of a final resurrection and of spirits waiting (though in a conscious and growing activity) for their bodies at the last day, tells of the truth that the perfecting of the individual is reached only in the perfecting of all. Thus the thought of my resurrection is inseparable from the thought of the resurrection of all the members of Christ.

The resurrection of the body is something which the mind of man cannot conceive, just as the mind of man cannot conceive a purely spiritual immortality. But whereas a bodiless immortality is inconceivable because it seems to make the future life maimed and meaningless, the resurrection of the body is inconceivable because it suggests a richness of life, in the blending of old and new, that defies human thought. The insight of a Paul, an Origen or a Westcott may assist our belief, and the analogies that lie near at hand may shew the rationality of the belief; but the point is soon reached when the Apostolic words confront us, " Behold I tell you a mystery. . . . Death is swallowed up in victory."

But the mystery springs from the infinite love of God, the creator and redeemer of mankind and of the world. Because His love is infinite it hath not entered into the heart of man to conceive the good things that He has prepared for them that love Him. But, because He is creator as well as redeemer, those good things will be fashioned not only from what is new but also from what is old. Nature will not be discarded, in order that men's souls alone may be salvaged and saved. The life of nature here and the life of the body which links us to nature will not be as a ladder, whereon we may climb to heaven and fling it aside when the ascent is finished. Rather will all that God has made have its place and its counterpart in the new heaven and the new earth. " Immortality " will be put on; but " this mortal " will find there its clothing and its home.

Chapter Nine

CONCLUSION

I

To LEARN the meaning of the Resurrection," wrote Westcott, " is the task not of one age only but of all." Just as the evangelists apprehended and presented different aspects of its meaning, so have the various epochs in the history of the Christian Church. There has yet to be written a great book telling of what the Resurrection has meant in the thought, doctrine and worship of Christians down the ages.

It was the news of Jesus and the Resurrection that first won the ancient world. In the Church of the Fathers it was specially the East that held the Resurrection in its central place. The Greek theologians seldom isolated the Cross; and the atonement meant to them the victory of the Resurrection, whereby nature rejoices in a new creation and whereby mankind may share in the risen life of Christ and so become partakers of the divine nature. Similarly the worship of the Eastern Church has clung to the Resurrection in a way that the West, both Latin and Reformed, has strangely missed. For if in the West we are wont to think of ourselves as worshipping upon earth and of Christ coming down to us in the Eucharist, the East has never forgotten that the bread and the wine and the worshippers and earth itself are lifted up to heaven where Christ is. To attend the liturgy of the Eastern Church is to perceive and to feel how far the West has missed the realization that the first truth in Christian worship is that as Christians we have been raised together in the heavenly places with Christ.

It would be absurd to say that the West lost sight of the Resurrection, for every saintly life and every achievement of Christian thinking bears witness to it. Yet there have been phases in the West when the Cross was isolated and seen without the light of Easter upon it. The tendency can be traced in art, where the crucifix with the figure of the dead Christ upon it replaced the earlier

" Majestas " crucifix with Christ crowned, robed and victorious. It can be traced in doctrine, where the sacrifice of the atoning death has often been separated from the victory of the atoning Resurrection. It can be traced in worship, where the commemoration of Calvary in the liturgy has replaced the commemoration of the whole drama of God's redemption. In all this, sweeping generalizations are out of place. It is often inevitable for Christians to fix their gaze solely upon " Jesus Christ and him crucified," to know nothing save the Cross; and when they do so they are indeed near to the Resurrection. None the less there has sometimes been a concentration upon the Cross that is less than Pauline, and there is a germ of truth in Westcott's words: " It has been indeed disastrous for our whole view of the Gospel that a late age placed upon the Cross the figure of the dead Christ, and that we have retained it there." [1]

Today we have behind us a century in which there has been teaching upon the Resurrection as great as any in the long centuries since the Apostolic age. In England two great teachers made it their central theme. One was Richard Meux Benson, of Cowley, who penetrates farther than perhaps any other writer into the necessity of seeing the Passion with the light of Easter upon it and of understanding the Resurrection only in terms of faith in the Crucified. " How entirely the Passion is seen simply through the lustrous halo of the Resurrection in S. Paul." [2] " Our victory can only be the victory of the dead." [3]

The other was Westcott. The more it has seemed that some of the tendencies since his day have proved one-sided and unfruitful, the more does the greatness of his work stand out. His theme was the place of the Resurrection as the climax of creation no less than of redemption. With his thinking moulded by the study of the Johannine writings Westcott presented the Resurrection both as the fulfilment of the processes of nature and history and as the miraculous entrance of a new divine order into both. On the one hand " we see in the risen Christ the end for which man was made, and the

[1] *The Revelation of the Risen Lord*, p. xxvii.
[2] *Spiritual Letters*, p. 54.
[3] *Ibid.*, p. 115.

assurance that the end is within reach. The Resurrection, if we may so speak, shews us the change which would have passed over the earthly life of man, if sin had not brought in death." [1] On the other hand " there was a tendency towards the central truth of history but there was no tendency to produce it." [2] " It is either a miracle or an illusion. . . . It claims to be the opening of a new life to the world. It cannot then be rightly contemplated by comparing it with the events of common history." [3] Both the historical and the transcendental, both the humanism of the Gospel and its supernatural character, are authenticated by the Resurrection. " Paganism proclaims the grandeur of man: Judaism the supremacy of God. Christianity accepts the antithesis and vindicates by the message of the Resurrection the grandeur of man in and through God." [4]

2

The eighty years that have passed since Westcott wrote those words have seen the most violent movements in events and in theology. In events there has been the great expansion of humane and scientific progress, and subsequently the catastrophe of two great wars. In theology there has been first the heyday of the liberal school, and subsequently the rediscovery of the supernatural and transcendental aspects of the Biblical revelation.

The liberal movement in theology advanced very sure of itself. It had roots in some of the great Christian affirmations, and a kinship with the Christian humanism both of Alexandria and of the Renaissance. It knew that the world was made by God, and that in Him was life, and the life was the light of men. It was able to shew how the processes of evolution in nature and of history in man were a gradual unfolding of the Spirit of God the creator. It related creation with evolution, revelation with historical development. God is present in time and in change, as the created world with man as its crown struggles forward towards its goal.

But in the latter days of liberal theology it became increasingly apparent that a great omission was being made. Over-zealous in its alliance with contemporary ideas of progress and contemporary

[1] *The Revelation of the Risen Lord,* p. xxxiv.   [3] *Ibid.,* p. 52.
[2] *The Gospel of the Resurrection,* p. 72   [4] *Ibid.,* p. 210.

hopes of a divine Kingdom to be realized by a steady growth within history, liberal theology neglected the truths that God is transcendent and that His supreme revelation is an intervention from above and the beginning of a new creation. Hence it was easy to present the Resurrection as the disclosure of the hope of mankind's ascent to God through a spiritual immortality. It was less easy to grasp that it is the victory of God over sin and death. The event that is the supreme symbol of the transcendence of the living God was turned into a symbol of His presence within the advance of humanity, and little more.

It was in reaction from liberal theology that Karl Barth and his school uttered afresh the message of God's otherness and sovereignty and His mighty act in the Resurrection, as the war of 1914–1918 was drawing to its close. The Resurrection was central in the message of Barth; and he recalled Christians whose minds were full of man's religion, man's experiences and man's progress, to the Act of the living God which confronts a race helpless to save itself. " *Jesus Christ our Lord.* This is the Gospel and the meaning of history. In this name two worlds meet, two planes intersect, the one known and the other unknown. . . . Jesus has been *declared to be the Son of God with power according to the Holy Spirit through His resurrection from the dead.* In this declaration and appointment — which are beyond historical definition — lies the true significance of Jesus. Jesus as the Christ, as the Messiah, is the End of History; and He can be comprehended only as a Paradox, as Victory, as Primal History. . . . The Resurrection is the revelation; the disclosing of Jesus as the Christ; the appearing of God; the apprehending of God in Jesus. . . . In the Resurrection the new world of the Holy Spirit touches the old world of the flesh, but touches it as a tangent touches a circle, that is, without touching it." [1] It may be hard to assent to all Barth's propositions, but it is harder still to deny that he has stirred Christians in every land and tradition to face once more the transcendental and catastrophic themes of the New Testament.

It is, however, in the Barthians' treatment of history that our appreciation is likely to be mingled with dissent. They rightly affirm

[1] Barth, *Epistle to the Romans,* Eng. trans., pp. 29–30.

that the Resurrection is more than a historical event, and that it is impossible to demonstrate it by evidential proofs apart from faith in God. They rightly remind us that the empty tomb of itself was not and could never be the cause of Christian belief in the Resurrection. But they sometimes go further still and appear to deny that the examination of historical evidence had in the Apostolic age, and can have today, *any* part in the Resurrection faith.[1] Here it is hard to follow. It seems utterly true that the Resurrection " is as invisible, as unthinkable, as the Incarnation," [2] that " Easter is not an historical event to be reported," that " the Apostles' witness is based upon the fact that they received a revelation "; we can agree, and be grateful for the reminder. But does it follow that the evidence, including that of the empty tomb, had no place at all? Rather than accept this paradoxical treatment both of history and of the place of reason in the receiving of revelation, it seems wiser to draw back and to attempt the harder task of holding together both the serious treatment of historical evidence and the belief in the living God of the Bible. Is it possible to learn from the shaking that Barth has given to us, and yet to return and to use what Westcott had taught us?

3

It is the message of the Bible, in all its richness, that the people of our generation need. It is insufficient and misleading to present the Old Testament as the story of the growth of man's ideas about God, without the primacy of the greater theme of God's own acts and God's own utterances in the events of Israel's history that makes the Old Testament what it is. It is equally misleading to present the Gospel as the conception of God taught by Jesus, without due reference to the mighty act of God Himself in the Passion and Resurrection. Read in its own light, the Bible has the Resurrection as its key. Its God is the God who raised up Jesus Christ from the dead, and in so doing vindicated His word in the Old Testament and in the Cross of Christ. It is only in virtue of the Resurrection that the Bible is one, and that the message of the Bible is coherent and true.

[1] Cf. Brunner, *The Mediator*, pp. 573–579.   [2] *Ibid.*, p. 573.

But though the revelation in the Bible is unique and breaks into the world from above, it is not " wholly other." For the God who there reveals Himself is also the God who created the world. Therefore the theme of the Gospel, Life-through-death, does not come as wholly strange to the world. Rather is it like a pattern already woven into nature and into the life of man. Though it is blurred by human sinfulness the pattern is not obliterated; and throughout all life there runs, however faintly perceived, a law of living through dying, a law whose presence testifies that man is made in the image of God. The Gospel of the glory of God in the face of Jesus Christ is both strange to mankind and yet nearer to mankind than the breath which they breathe. For the truth in Him is also the truth in them:

> " Und so lang Du das nicht hast
> Dieses Stirb und Werde
> Bist Du nur ein trueber Gast
> Auf dieser dunklen Erde."

NOTE (A): THE ASCENSION

THE Creeds distinguish two separate events, the Resurrection and the Ascension. In so far as it is only Luke who describes the latter event Christian tradition derives its conception of the event from Luke's narratives. In Luke xxiv. 50–52 Jesus blessed the disciples " and was parted from them." The words " and was carried up into heaven " are textually doubtful, and it cannot be affirmed with certainty that the " Ascension " is mentioned in these verses. But in Acts i. 9, the reference to the Ascension is clear; at the close of the forty days Jesus " was taken up and a cloud received him from out of their sight." The narrative has resemblances to the story of the ascension of Elijah. Besides this narrative, there are in the New Testament many references to Jesus " going to heaven " or " being exalted " or passing " to the right hand of God " or " ascending." It is generally believed that these phrases refer to an event distinct from the Resurrection and identical with that described in Acts i. 9.

It is possible, however, that the Apostolic writers often made little or no separation between the Resurrection and the exaltation to heaven, and that where a distinction is made it may be due in part to the existence of two kinds of imagery: (*a*) the raising of Jesus from death, (*b*) the entrance of Jesus into the heavenly Lordship foretold in Psa. cx. Jesus was no longer among the dead, for God had raised Him. Jesus was no longer sharing in the limitations of His earthly life, for all sovereignty in heaven now was His. Both facts may be embraced in the confession " Jesus is Lord "; and both facts, with no clear division between them, may be included in such references to the glorifying of Jesus as Rom. viii. 34; Phil. ii. 9; Col. iii. 1; Eph. i. 20; 1 Tim. iii. 16; Acts ii. 33; 1 Peter i. 21; iii. 21–22. It may similarly be the intention of Mark and Matthew in their narratives to connect the Resurrection and the exaltation. For Mark, the risen Christ is the Son of Man in glory. For Matthew, the risen Christ is the possessor of all authority in heaven and on earth.

Yet the tradition in Luke concerning the Ascension as a distinct event cannot be dismissed. There is nothing incredible in an event whereby Jesus assured the disciples that the appearances were ended and that His sovereignty and His presence must henceforth be sought in new ways. But as to the glory of Jesus Christ it is impossible for us to say wherein the Ascension added to the glory which the Resurrection had already brought. A precise distinction is beyond human scrutiny. So far as we can know, the Resurrection was the glorifying of the manhood of Jesus Christ; and the event of the Ascension, which Luke describes, taught a truth to the disciples but added no greater glory to the Lord.

It is true that the Apostles believed in a three-storeyed universe, and would think of the exaltation of Jesus as a journey through the skies to a local heaven. Yet the abandonment of their astronomy does not involve the modification of their essential doctrine; for more than one passage in the New Testament makes it clear that they realized that the exaltation of Jesus implied a sovereignty and an omnipresence that transcend astronomy altogether.

In an important essay, " Jesus the Lord," in the volume entitled *Mysterium Christi* (1930) Dr. Hermann Sasse pointed out that although the Resurrection and the exaltation are hardly to be separated as historical events they are to be distinguished as theological truths. It was one thing to assert that Jesus Christ was no longer held fast by death. It was another thing to confess that He shares in the eternity, omnipresence and omnipotence of God. All this was implied in the confession " Jesus is Lord," and only " in the Holy Spirit " could the confession be made (cf. 1 Cor. xii. 3).

NOTE (B): APPEARANCE AND VISION

In his essay upon the Resurrection in *Essays Catholic and Critical* (1926) Dr. E. G. Selwyn suggested that the appearances of the risen Lord may be regarded as visions akin to those experienced by Christian mystics. His view is very different from the vision-theories discussed in Chapter IV of this book, for he attaches the greatest importance to the event of the Resurrection, attested by the empty tomb, before and behind the appearances of the risen Lord. But he makes it clear that, if we believe that the glorified Lord passed to a new and mysterious mode of existence, there may not be a great deal of difference between temporary accommodations to the former mode of existence (Westcott's view) and visions granted to the disciples. Whether Dr. Selwyn's own interpretation is convincing or not it is plainly congruous with the Gospel and the Creed. Indeed his discussion brings into very clear relief the distinctive importance of the two foundations — " He was raised " and " He appeared."

INDEX OF SUBJECTS

Acts of Apostles, 12–13, 27–28
Appearance of risen Lord, 42–43, 50–52, 69–74, 124
Ascension, 66, 85–88, 122–124

Baptism, 31, 97
Body, Resurrection of, 32, 35, 47–49, 106–117

Church, 30–31, 87–89, 91–101
Creeds, 21, 112
Crucifixion, 18–20, 82–84, 97, 118

Death, 22–24, 35, 104–106

Empty tomb, 43–45, 52–56, 63, 72–74, 124
Eucharist, 81, 97

Form-criticism, 14–16

God, the living, 10, 28–29, 55–56, 121
Gospel, 10–13
Gospels, 14–17, 56–69
    Matthew, 65, 78–79
    Mark, 63–65, 75–78
    Luke, 65–67, 79–82
    John, 15–17, 20, 67–69, 82–89

History and theology, 35–38, 53–58, 79–80, 83–85, 119–121
Holy Spirit, 16–17, 30–32, 87–89, 124

Immortality, 35–36, 104–106, 115–116

Miracle, 36–38
Modernism, 50–56, 113–115, 119

New Creation, 30–33, 36–38, 55, 87

Old Testament, 21–28, 100–101

Paul: doctrine, 27–33, 94–97, 106–111
    evidence, 41–45
"Peter," Gospel of, 64, 69–70
Preaching of Apostles, 12–16, 21–22, 42–45

Vision theories, 50–58, 73–74, 124

INDEX OF NAMES

Augustine, 100

Barth, K., 120
Benson, R. M., 118
Brunner, E., 121
Burkitt, F. C., 64, 70

Cadoux, C. J., 56
Chrysostom, 48, 114
Creed, J. M., 64
Cyril of Jerusalem, 112

Dibelius, M., 62

Gardner-Smith, P., 69–70, 83
Gregory of Nyssa, 114

Holland, H. S., 9, 25
Hoskyns, E. C., 9, 94
Hort, F. J. A., 30, 64

Keim, Th., 50
Knox, W. L., 64, 95, 110

Lake, K., 44, 52–53, 69–71

Lightfoot, R. H., 64, 78
Luce, H. K., 54–55

Mersch, E., 91, 94
Montefiore, C., 50

Niebuhr, R., 103, 115

Origen, 113–114

Renan, E., 50

Sasse, H., 123
Selwyn, E. G., 124
Sparrow-Simpson, 42
Strauss, 50
Streeter, B. H., 51–52
Swete, H. B., 64

Tertullian, 112
Thornton, L. S., 31, 110

Waggett, P. N., 109–110
Westcott, B. F., 36–37, 48, 80, 116–118

The First to Follow
The Apostles of Jesus

John R. Claypool

Edited by
Ann Wilkinson Claypool

MOREHOUSE PUBLISHING

An imprint of Church Publishing Incorporated
Harrisburg – New York

Unless otherwise noted, the Scripture quotations contained herein are from the New Revised Standard Version Bible, copyright © 1989 by the Division of Christian Education of the National Council of Churches of Christ in the U.S.A. Used by permission. All rights reserved.

Morehouse Publishing, 4775 Linglestown Road, Harrisburg, PA 17112

Morehouse Publishing, 445 Fifth Avenue, New York, NY 10016

Morehouse Publishing is an imprint of Church Publishing Incorporated.

Cover art: Giotto di Bondone (1266–1336). *Washing of the feet*. Fresco. Scrovegni Chapel, Padua, Italy. Credit: Scala/Art Resource.

Cover design by Jennifer Glosser

Library of Congress Cataloging-in-Publication Data
Claypool, John.
   The first to follow : the apostles of Jesus / John R. Claypool ; edited by Ann Claypool.
      p. cm.
   Includes bibliographical references.
   ISBN 978-0-8192-2296-1 (casebound w/o jacket)   1. Apostles.
I. Claypool, Ann. II. Title.
BS2440.C53 2008
226'.0922—dc22

                              2008000363

Printed in the United States of America

08 09 10 11 12 13   10 9 8 7 6 5 4 3 2 1

Contents

Preface ix

Introduction 1

Andrew, The First Disciple 5

Simon Peter, A Man of Extremes 19

Philip, The Careful Realist 37

Nathanael, Without Deceit 53

Thomas, A Truth Seeker 63

Simon and Matthew, Unlikely Companions 81

Thaddaeus, Three Names and One Question 91

Judas, The Traitor 102

James and James, The Greater and Lesser 117

John, The Disciple Whom Jesus Loved 130

Sources 147

In grateful memory
of
dearly beloved John

Preface

T his book evolved from a study of the twelve apostles that my husband, John, presented at Saint Luke's Episcopal Church in the fall of 1992, and that was the only time that he gave all twelve of these presentations about the original disciples. He did have the occasion to lecture on Peter, John, Thomas, and Judas at The Furman Pastors' School in South Carolina, in 1998, and at The Chautauqua Institute in New York, in 2000, where he added talks on Andrew, Matthew, and Simon, also. These teachings on the apostles helped me to understand and identify each of them better than I ever had before. Their individual personalities came alive to me as I gained a greater appreciation of the challenges they faced and the ways they were affected by Jesus. The series was so enlightening to me that I encouraged John to put it in book form for the benefit of many more people than the limited groups with whom he had been able to share it personally. Sadly, he did not have the opportunity to do so.

In June of 2003, John was diagnosed as having a form of cancer called multiple myeloma, and our lives were "caught up in a medical vortex," as he described it. He underwent a stem cell transplant in March 2004, and we were ecstatic when we learned that it had been successful. Naturally, we hoped he would remain free of cancer, but the disease reoccurred and he needed a second stem cell transplant by June 2005. Worse yet, he experienced serious complications from the second stem cell transplant that he had not suffered during the first one. By the grace of God and John's incredible courage, he made it through many grueling weeks in the hospital, and we were full of hope and joy when he came home cancer-free again. Only one week later, an abdominal aortic aneurysm ended his life on earth, after two years of bravely battling cancer. Within a six-month period, my mother had died; John and I had watched the television coverage of Hurricane Katrina, in horror, as it devastated my hometown of New Orleans and overwhelmed my family and friends living there; then just days later, John passed away on September 3, 2005. My world was turned upside down, and learning to live without him was the most difficult thing I have ever had to do.

Soon after his passing, John's long-time friend and former editor, Cynthia Shattuck, offered me the opportunity to put more of his work in writing, by transcribing and editing his audio recordings for a manuscript to be published by Church Publishing Incorporated. I was still experiencing an enormous amount of grief when we talked about such a task, but I remember thinking that she and her colleagues were giving me a rare chance to honor John's memory in a very special way. I felt close to him as I listened to his recorded voice and converted his spoken words into a manuscript to be published. I had helped John type and edit the last eight of the eleven books that he wrote and, in that process, had many telephone conversations with his publishers and editors to save him some time and effort. He was extremely loving and generous, and I thoroughly enjoyed working with him. I am thankful for the opportunity to share more of his work through this book, in hopes that his words will be a gift to many readers.

I appreciate immensely those friends whose interest, encouragement, and help made this book possible. I am indebted especially to Keith Miller, Barbara Brown Taylor, George Wirth, Hardy Clemons, Alan Culpepper, William Hull, Fisher Humphries, Russell Levenson, Nancy Ford, Cathy Randall, Macon Riddle, Allen Samford, Carleton Sokol, Brooke Wallace, Carole and Howard Hovde, Dorie and Pat King, and Judy and Guy Parker. I am truly blessed by my family's support and understanding during my long periods of preoccupation with this project, especially our children and grandchildren, Rowan and John Claypool VI, C. T. and Ashley Williams, Laura Williams and Marty Vanderploeg. Most of all, I am grateful to Cynthia Shattuck, Ryan Masteller, and Church Publishing Incorporated for their confidence in me and for all they have done to bring *The First to Follow* to fruition. My personal thanks go to Cynthia for not only doing the hard work of editing, in order to produce something worthy of being published, but also for her friendship and encouragement through much of the emotional roller coaster of grief.

Last, but definitely not least, I have special gratitude for John's dear sister and her husband, Marie and Bob Piper, who read every draft of every chapter, corrected many mistakes, and made brilliant editing suggestions to improve the clarity and flow of the manuscript before I sent it to Cynthia. They helped me research the references, as well, and the three of us shared a strong commitment to honoring the memory of "our" John by making this book a reality. Their help was invaluable, and working with them on this project was an unexpected gift that deepened the loving family bond we already shared. Our collaboration was one of many blessings that I received in the process of bringing about this book, and I hope that you will be blessed by reading it.

Ann Wilkinson Claypool

Introduction

One of the first things that Jesus did in his ministry was to reach out to twelve individuals and draw them into a circle of close companionship with him. This book is about those twelve apostles, their relationships with Jesus and each other, and what the dynamics of that community can mean for us today. It is obvious from the gospels that Jesus was deeply connected to other people; Saint Augustine said that Jesus loved each person he ever met as if there were no one else in all the world to love, and he loved all as he loved each. I have never known which aspect of Jesus is more incredible, his capacity for individual affection or the amazing inclusiveness of his love.

Jesus not only loved others, but also let people know that he wanted them in his life as much as they wanted him in theirs. I think that this mutuality gives us the best image of how God wants to relate to us. I believe that we can understand more fully what the Holy One is doing in our own life and time by looking at the disciples whom Jesus selected and at how their relationships with him developed. I will concentrate on aspects of personality and biography as we study the lives of the apostles, in the belief that one of the best ways to understand ourselves is through stories about other people. We can learn great truths by studying Jesus and his disciples. The apostles are the link between Jesus and the kingdom of God. They are the very foundation of the church, and it is important to look through the prism of their experiences at what we can learn about how Jesus did his work.

Jesus began his ministry alone, but it soon became a communal movement as he called followers to his side, not only because he sensed their potential in helping to build the kingdom of God but also because they were so curious about what he was doing. After he told a particularly intriguing story about the parable of the sower, some of the listeners came to him and asked Jesus to tell them more about the parables. It was to those who showed the greatest curiosity about what he was teaching that he gave the most of himself, saying, "To you has been given the secret of the kingdom of God" (Mark 4:11). One of my wisest seminary professors told his classes, "You need to distinguish between the people who really want to hear what you have to say and those who are not interested. It is important to remember that you cannot bless them all." I think he was right on the point that the key to effective ministry is to answer readiness rather than to press reluctance. As we read Scripture, we clearly see that Jesus was answering readiness in others, rather than pressing those who were less inclined toward him. He sought those who showed the greatest interest, and drew them into a close, intimate relationship. As we look at the first disciples that Jesus called and consider ourselves as part of that enlarging circle, I hope we gain a deeper sense of our own spirituality and how Christ would like to relate to us.

One of the things that will become increasingly obvious when we study the apostles is that Jesus did not wait for people to be perfect in order to call them into the circle of God's love. It is important theologically where you place perfection in the great saga of our experience. If perfection were something we had to have before God would accept and help us, then there would be no hope for any of us. The Baptist preacher Carlisle Marney always said that it is too late to worry about innocence. Eventually, all we have left is a guilty self and the need to know what to do with it. Perfection is not a prerequisite of divine inter-action, but the goal toward which we strive. Although we cannot fully embody it in this life, it is that omega point by which we measure our progress.

Extreme perfectionism is one of the highest forms of self-abuse. It is a dangerous misconception held by many through-out the Christian church that we have to be perfect before God will have anything to do with us. Since we are all flawed, per-fectionism leads to the unbecoming pretense of being better than others, in order to hide our human failings and feelings of inadequacy. Trying to hide who we really are separates us from an authentic relationship with God. I believe that a true understanding of the Christian vision holds that we are accept-able to our gracious and merciful Lord just as we are, with all of our imperfections. As I look at these disciples Jesus chose, it is clear that there is hope for every one of us, for they were far from perfect.

At the end of the fifth chapter of Matthew is that well known Scripture verse that has caused many people deep anguish: "Be perfect, therefore, as your heavenly Father is perfect" (Matthew 5:48). I cannot count the number of people who have asked me, "How in the world could I ever be perfect? What does it mean when I fail?" In the ancient Greek of the gospels, the spelling of the imperative and the future tenses is exactly alike. Therefore, I believe that the better translation is, "You *shall* be perfect," as this way of putting it offers the promise that God is always at work drawing you and me toward wholeness and completion.

Walter Brueggemann, a scholar of the Old Testament, tells his students that if "The Story" does not connect with our own stories, then studying the Bible is only a spectator sport. The great gift of Scripture is its capacity to inform, illumine, and encourage the writing of your own story. As I write about these twelve individuals who lived long ago, my concern is more personal and contemporary than it is historical. They were the first to follow Jesus, and we are called to follow, too. I hope to show that the same Jesus, who taught and blessed those first disciples, still has the power and desire to teach and bless every one of us.

Andrew
The First Disciple

In 1901 and 1902, the American psychologist and philosopher, William James, was invited to give the Gifford Lectures on natural religion at the University of Edinburgh, which grew into his famous book *The Varieties of Religious Experience*. There he presented literally hundreds of descriptions of ways that human beings have experienced religious conversion. James is known for the distinction he drew between people who are "once-born" and those who are "twice-born." The once-born find it much easier to respond to God and to give themselves in love and obedience because of their personality structure, disposition, and experiences early in life. In contrast, the twice-born have more conflicted religious experiences, perhaps because of their tempestuous personalities or difficult things that have happened to them. These are people who have experiences like Paul's on the road to Damascus, and are likely to exclaim, "Once I was blind and now I see! Once I was dead and now I'm alive!" Some of us may wish for such a sweeping spiritual change in our lives, but James sees value in both experiences. Neither is automatic or effortless. A religious experience is highly personal and participatory, occurring when something in us freely responds to that mysterious reality that we dare to call the Holy One.

I remember hearing an old preacher say, "If you could get religion and not know it, then you could lose it and not miss it." You have to be involved. The once-born cross the stream at the narrowest point, while the twice-born may have to cross an ocean. Christ is the Lord of all kinds of experiences. Disciples in the twice-born category would include John, who became the "beloved disciple," after having been a "son of thunder" in his youth; and Matthew, the tax collector, and Simon, the Zealot, who began at opposite poles of ideologies and personalities but were so transformed by Jesus that they became intimate companions. Many of the disciples in the twice-born category had decisive experiences that markedly changed their lives, whereas Andrew seemed spiritually inclined from the beginning. He brought to Jesus a mature spirit and open nature, characteristic of those James called once-born. He moved from strength to strength, and Jesus simply helped to enhance who Andrew was already, without the striking changes that we find in the journeys of the twice-born. There is no set pattern or singular way that God works in our lives but rather a vast keyboard on which he plays. All of us are recipients of the mysterious, ingenious mercy of the Holy One, and it may be that your walk with God has been that steady unfolding of strength to strength, from step to step. Andrew's reliable character was very much the same throughout his life.

Andrew was one of three pairs of brothers that became part of the intimate circle of Jesus' disciples. It is interesting that six of the twelve gathered around Jesus had another brother who was also a disciple. These brothers were James and John, Andrew and Simon Peter, and Matthew and James. Andrew was a fisherman by trade, from a little town called Bethsaida, on the northeast corner of the Sea of Galilee. He went to Capernaum, on the northwestern side of the lake, where tradition says that he and Simon Peter worked for James and John's father, Zebedee, in his thriving fishing business. Andrew is mentioned in Matthew, Mark and Luke, but it is only in John that we find any information about what kind of person he was, and how he grew in his friendship with Jesus.

The first glimpse we have of Andrew is in the company of John the Baptist, whose ministry touched Andrew's soul and prepared him for Jesus. Many believe he was the first disciple to be attracted to Jesus and to say yes to following him. John the Baptist reminded his listeners often that he was not the Messiah himself, but the one who prepared the way for the Messiah. He would tell them that he baptized with water, but the One to come would baptize them with the Holy Spirit, the energy and power of God. John the Baptist had a sense of expectancy that something was about to happen that would change everything. Andrew was with him one day when Jesus came into John's line of vision. As soon as John saw his cousin, Jesus, he pointed to him and said, "Here is the Lamb of God who takes away the sin of the world" (John 1:29). It was his first acknowledgment that here was the One about whom he had spoken for so long.

I imagine that Andrew and all those who were gathered there with John the Baptist were astounded by his words and, particularly, by the image that he chose: the Lamb of God. You see, for a thousand years, the Israelites had been looking for a lion of God to come as the Messiah. They were not looking for a lamb. They expected another King David, who would drive out the Romans from their sacred soil and extend the political power of Jerusalem, but that was not God's intention for the chosen people. God had a different plan in mind when he called the descendants of Abraham to be his chosen ones (Genesis 22:17). The same generous impulse that moved God to create, also moved him to bless what he had created.

When you stop and think about it, if the goal is to bless and to re-establish trusting, loving relationships between God and those who have turned away from him, then a lamb willing to endure suffering is what you need. You cannot bludgeon people into being good, nor force seeds of love to grow with a sledge-hammer. If you want to evoke love and call people out of evil back to goodness, you need someone who is willing to accept and endure the ravages of evil without imitating and returning evil. The Lamb of God is far better equipped to restore creation to its loving maker than a king who comes with a sword. When it comes to changing evil into good, nothing is more powerful than the spectacle of innocent suffering. Yet, the unexpected metaphor of a lamb was likely to have been confusing, and even shocking, to Andrew.

Jesus and Andrew had both grown up in the northern part of Palestine called Galilee, which was not a very large area. Andrew could have easily known Jesus when he worked in the shop of his father, Joseph, as a young carpenter's apprentice from the insignificant hill town of Nazareth. Andrew was probably surprised that a fellow from his hometown area turned out to be the one whom God had chosen to do the messianic work. Many of us think that anybody who shares the same humble beginnings as ours cannot be particularly special. Time and again we see this tendency to underestimate the people we have always known. The Wright brothers grew up in Dayton, Ohio and built their flying machine in their bicycle shop. After they had made their successful flight from Kitty Hawk, North Carolina, word of it got back to the newspaper editor in Dayton, who said: "I don't believe it! I don't think human beings will ever fly. That is not something they were meant to do. That's what the birds are supposed to do, and if human beings ever do fly, it won't be anybody from Dayton." That just seems to be the way we provincial folk are. Andrew might also have said to himself, "Should a messiah of any kind come, be he lamb or lion, he won't be from that nondescript town of Nazareth!" The amazing thing to me is that, even though Jesus was far different from what Andrew could have expected, he was willing to let reality come to him on its own terms. Jesus, the Lamb of God, was not at all what Andrew had anticipated, yet he stayed open and receptive to him.

Andrew was with John the Baptist again when John saw Jesus the next day and said to the crowd for the second time, "Look, here is the Lamb of God." On this occasion, Andrew and another disciple followed Jesus and asked him where he was staying. Jesus replied with wonderful simplicity, "Come and see" (John 1:39).

He invited Andrew and his friend to spend time with him and, in that time together, something astonishing occurred: Andrew saw in Jesus the very presence of God himself, come to do the work of Messiah. Andrew was willing to allow reality to break through his vastly different expectations and registered it fully. Thus he discovered in Jesus not just another good man making his way to God, but the good God himself who had chosen to make his way to humankind. It is the deepest core of my convictions that Jesus gives a face to the mystery of God, and on that face there is the smile of unconditional love. It is the mystery of incarnation and the great central truth of the Christian faith that, for us and our salvation, God chose to become what we are, so that we could see more clearly what God is. It is an overwhelming discovery that the One who walks the pages of the New Testament is God, in a form that we can understand. We humans rarely see the world as it is because of the tendency to paint the windows of our perceptions with personal desires and expectations. Pretty soon, we are doing business with the images that we have constructed and confusing them with reality. In contrast, as Jesus revealed himself and Andrew remained open to him, they made a remarkable connection.

As I understand evangelism, it is really gift giving. It is not high-pressure salesmanship or twisting somebody's arm, but more like one beggar telling another beggar where he has found bread. Andrew's very first reaction to having seen the heart of God in Jesus was to go share this discovery with his brother, Simon Peter. He told him, "We have found the Messiah" (John 1:41). This first act of passing on what he found meaningful and of value gives us insight into his nature. It was a sign of Andrew's great maturity and emotional health. He was living out what it means to be made in the image of God. Authentic goodness is self-diffusive, meaning that when something good happens, you want to share it rather than keep it for yourself. My most vivid memory of wanting to share good news with everyone occurred in August 1945, when word came that the Japanese had surrendered and World War II was finally over. I was at a family reunion in Mississippi, and we all got in cars to drive around town, honk our horns, and share the jubilation as the church bells rang. Sharing our joy made the occasion even more thrilling.

There's a saying often repeated in Twelve-Step programs— we are as sick as our secrets and as healthy as our sharing. The things that we keep inside, where no one can see and no light can shine, are the things that can make us ill in many ways. We need to acknowledge problems in order to find solutions, and the things we are willing to share can be healed through the light of exposure. There is a generosity in sharing that continues to bless. As soon as Andrew experienced what he had found in Jesus, he was eager to share it with his brother. Andrew knew that Simon Peter was more dynamic, more outgoing, and more of a leader than he was. He had probably spent his whole life being introduced as Simon Peter's younger brother, the one who always played second fiddle. Andrew could have been possessive of his relationship with Jesus, as a way of being special, but he was not that kind of person. He was bound to have known that if he told his brother the amazing news of Jesus, Simon Peter would join in, become closer to Jesus than Andrew, and become a leader of the group. This would mean that Andrew's place in that company of Jesus' followers would be diminished because Simon Peter simply had a more dominant personality, but that did not deter him from sharing his secret.

Simon Peter was more flawed and complicated than Andrew, a classic twice-born personality in William James's typology. Yet, very soon after the group of the twelve was formed, Simon Peter did become a leader and one of Jesus' three closest confidants, along with James and John. Andrew had been the first apostle to follow Jesus, but was not recorded as ever being first in anything else. The beautiful thing is that he did not seem resentful or bothered by that at all. He must have had the kind of self-acceptance that trusted he was a gift of God exactly as he was, and that freed him to accept others just as they were. He did not live his life trying to outdo Simon Peter or anyone else, but was content to take gratefully what he had been given from the hand of God, without envy of what others had been given. The experience of envy is a sign of insecurity. If we are secure in our own uniqueness and can think of ourselves as blessed by God exactly as we are, then we can celebrate freely the gifts of others. Our lives are each a matchless gift from God, with different limits and special qualities that are all expressions of his love.

I have referred often to a crucial moment in my own spiritual development when I was about thirty-four years old. I went to a Kiwanis Club in downtown Louisville, Kentucky, to hear a personnel manager of a large national firm speak about his philosophy of management. The most memorable thing that he said was that, when new recruits joined his team, the first thing he wanted to determine about them was whether they were intent on *being* something, or *doing* something. He said:

> People who are intent on being something don't have their ego needs met, so they are always trying to use the job to promote themselves. At one level, they might want to do what needs to be done to solve a problem but, at a deeper level, they are more concerned about how they can use occasions to come out ahead and advance up the career ladder. People like that are not likely to take risks or make sacrifices, so they are a real liability to any company. The higher they go, the more costly their decisions become, in their own self-interest, and the worse it is for the whole enterprise. My task is to identify and weed out those people as quickly as I can. In contrast, the people who want to *do* something are more secure and self-confident. They believe that the way that they are is good, and they don't try to use their job to enhance their status. When a problem arises, they simply ask what needs to be done and are willing to do it without worrying about getting the credit. They have the kind of judgment that the company needs at the highest levels.

I had never heard that distinction before, and I confess to you that this speaker held up a mirror to my own condition. As I heard those two types of personality described, I realized in ways I could not deny that, all my life, I had been trying to *be* something because of a crippling sense that I was not good enough as I was. I was trying to get something from outside of myself that would make me feel better on the inside. It was a startling insight that I had been so busy trying to get something from my work for myself that I did not give myself unreservedly to any task. This realization broke new ground and prepared me for what happened next.

At a private meeting of fellow clergy a few weeks later, someone said to me, "John, if you and I could ever hear the Gospel deep in our gut, we could fully believe the astonishing affirmation: 'You are the light of the world.' Jesus did not say that you have to be number one to get light, or out-achieve everybody else to earn light. He said that, by the grace of God's creation, you *are* the light of the world. If we could ever feel that truth in the depth of our souls, then we could truly let our light shine. We could give freely what has been given to us and know that the glory belongs rightly to the God who created us all." That was a pivotal, life-changing moment for me, as I comprehended that I was *already* the light of the world, not by virtue of what I had made of myself, but because of what God had made of me. I did not have to compete, compare, or try to do better than everybody else, but could simply give of myself, out of the grace of my own creation.

I believe that Andrew possessed genuine spiritual maturity and self-acceptance. He would have been high on the list of the personnel manager in Louisville, because he was more intent on what he needed to *do* than on what he would *be*. He was willing to take the amazing news about Jesus and share it with Simon Peter, in spite of knowing that doing so would mean that he would be elbowed out of the limelight. He was secure enough to remain in the background with more concern for the common good than for his own welfare alone. That is a high and worthy goal for every one of us, and it is within reach when we trust that we are the light of the world. We are what we are by the grace of God, and we do what we do out of what we have been given, not what we have earned through our own efforts.

The next time we see Andrew, he was with Jesus and the other disciples in a wilderness area when they came upon a huge group of people. Jesus began to teach them and heal those who needed healing. As the day wore on and the sun began to set, restlessness moved through this crowd of more than five thousand. The disciples became anxious and as much as said to Jesus, "Don't you think we ought to dismiss this group? They are getting hungry and people get unruly when they don't have enough food. We might have a riot on our hands. Let's disburse this crowd and send them to the nearest villages to get something to eat." I can easily understand why the disciples would have fears about this crowd because the evangelists recorded that there were five thousand men there, not counting the women and the children. In spite of this huge number of people, Jesus told his disciples, "You give them something to eat." He calmly approached the whole situation by asking, "How many loaves have you? Go and see." Well, feeding this enormous mass of people was something the disciples had not even considered. They were focused on the problem of scarcity, and it had never occurred to them that there might be resources available within the present situation.

Interestingly enough, Andrew was the only one of the twelve who responded to Jesus' request. Instead of being immobilized by fear, he began to go through the crowd to find out how much food they had, then came back to Jesus to say, "There is a lad here who has five barley loaves and two fish." Andrew added that the small amount the boy had did not seem like much in a gathering that large (John 6:9). However, the disciples had been asked to "go and see" what was available, and I think Andrew had been around Jesus long enough to believe there are always possibilities with Christ. You probably know the rest of this story as well as I do. Jesus took what was there and gave thanks, lifting his eyes to heaven and thanking God for what they already had. Through his gratitude, what little they had multiplied until it became enough to feed the whole crowd. Although we cannot be sure of how this happened, some think that others there were hiding food under their robes and were moved to share what they had brought by the generous example of the boy. Others believe Jesus miraculously multiplied the loaves and fishes himself. What is clear is that the gospel says something very powerful here about the creative potential of being grateful for what we have, even when it does not seem to be much. This is the one miracle story that was recorded in all four of the gospels, which indicates how powerfully every gospel writer was moved by it.

We would do well to follow Andrew's example and enjoy what we have in gratitude and generosity, instead of lamenting that it is not more. When we realize that what seems quite small has the power to multiply in the hands of Jesus, nothing is too little to be put to some kind of redemptive use. If we focus on the half-fullness of life, give thanks for that, and use it creatively, we can start a marvelous chain reaction. Jesus can do anything with just about everything. Adopting a sense of hopelessness can lead to giving up, and I believe that despair is presumptuous because we don't know enough to predict the future. Just think of the times that you have been surprised by some situation improving that you thought was impossible. Who are we to doubt that anything can happen with the One who can create something out of nothing and raise dead things back to life? On Good Friday, no one expected Easter. Andrew demonstrated great faith in our Lord when he brought him the boy with much less than what was needed. Andrew's trust in the creativity and ingenuity of Christ was not disappointed, and ours won't be either.

The last time we encounter Andrew, some Greek gentiles had approached Philip and asked to speak to Jesus. Philip must have been unsure of what to do in that situation, perhaps because he thought salvation was only for the Jews. Whatever the reason, Philip turned to Andrew, and together they went to tell Jesus about it. Every time we see Andrew in the gospels, he is graciously bringing people to Jesus, knowing how well it will turn out. He brought his brother, Simon Peter, the boy with the loaves and fishes, and the Greek gentiles straight to our Lord.

It is not surprising that this man who was in the habit of introducing others to Jesus went on to preach in many lands. According to tradition, his ministry took him to Cappadocia, Bythynia, Galatia, Byzantium, and north of the Black Sea to Scythia, a place known for its barbarous, rough and savage people. It is also not surprising that Andrew would accept such a challenge in his missionary efforts. Legends tell that he died a martyr in the town of Patras in Greece. Many other disciples are better known in the pantheon of history, but I admire Andrew's generosity, maturity, and his faith in what is possible with Christ. We would all do well to emulate him and keep bringing people to Jesus.

Simon Peter
A Man of Extremes

Simon Peter is the most well known disciple in the canons of Holy Scripture, and more is written about him than any of the other followers of Jesus. His name comes first in all the listings of the apostles because he was the recognized leader of the twelve early in Jesus' ministry. He was always in the foreground taking the initiative, like a right-hand man or chief operating officer. Peter is mentioned in the gospels more than anyone else except Jesus, and stories about him are prominent in the book of Acts, as well as the four gospels. Two epistles bear his name, 1 Peter and 2 Peter, although the first is more likely to reflect his teaching than the second, which was written at least one hundred years after his death.

One of the unique things that we know about Simon Peter is that he was the only disciple who was married. Three of the gospels record that Jesus went to Peter's home and healed his mother-in-law, and he was accompanied on his missionary travels by his wife, Perpetua (1 Corinthians 9:5). The church historian Eusebius recorded that, at the end of their lives Peter was made to watch his wife be crucified before he was. His last words to her were, "Remember the Lord."[1]

Peter was also the leader of the followers of Jesus after the resurrection, in the earliest Christian communities, and it would be tempting to focus only on the climax of his life, as he moved across the pages of Acts with courage, boldness, and wisdom. He was the one who stood up fearlessly on the day of Pentecost and interpreted what was happening; his preaching that day inspired the baptism of "about three-thousand persons" (Acts 2:41). He demonstrated superb leadership repeatedly, and opposition did not intimidate him. When he preached at Pentecost, he was well aware that he ran the risk of being killed as Jesus had been, less than two months earlier. From the descriptions of him in the book of Acts, it would be easy to imagine Simon Peter had the mark of grandeur from the time he was born and had risen straight to the top. However, what is written about him in the gospels reveals his difficult journey to becoming the person described in Acts, and gives us deep insight into the power and persistence of God's grace.

Simon Peter's progress was not even and gradual like the steady movement of an escalator. It was more like a roller coaster, involving huge swings between good news and bad news. What is paramount to me is the way that Jesus continued to work with his imperfections, for it inspires profound hope that the Holy

---

1. Ronald Brownrigg, *The Twelve Apostles* (New York: Macmillan, 1974), 78.

One will not abandon us when we are slow to learn, but will continue to work patiently with us through our problems, sins, and errors. The encouraging message of Simon Peter's life is the incredible truth that Christ keeps calling us to fullness of life.

All four gospels record Simon Peter's first encounter with Jesus, although they differ in details. Matthew, Mark, and Luke refer to Jesus saying that the disciples will become "fishers of men." In John's gospel, Simon Peter's brother Andrew was the first to discover Jesus, and when he brought Simon Peter to Jesus, there seems to have been an immediate connection between them. About two years into Jesus' ministry, it was Peter who identified him as "the Messiah, the Son of the living God." At this juncture, Jesus was wondering if his teaching had gotten through to any human heart. So, he took his disciples to an out-of-the-way place called Caesarea Philippi, and asked them what people said of him. The disciples began to tell him that different people thought that the Son of Man was either John the Baptist, Elijah, Jeremiah, or one of the other prophets come back to life. After all that they had shared together, I can imagine that Jesus took a deep breath before he risked asking, "But who do you say that I am?" It was Simon Peter who uttered the words that are absolutely foundational to the whole Christian enterprise: "You are the Messiah, the Son of the living God." Jesus replied, "Blessed are you, Simon son of Jonah! . . . I tell you, you are Peter, and on this rock I will build my church, and the gates of Hades will not prevail against it" (Matthew 16:16–18). Thus, Simon Peter was the first one to say openly that Jesus was the Christ, the Son of God, and Jesus blessed him mightily for that high moment of recognition that scholars call "The Great Confession."

Simon Peter's new name was a symbol for the fact that Jesus sensed hidden potential in him and was willing to set in motion a process of transformation. Simon was not stable like a rock when he met Jesus. It may have even surprised him to hear Jesus suggest that the name Peter would be a fitting for him. For when Simon first met Jesus, he was a working man—a Galilean fisherman too poor to own a boat. He was mostly a man of much promise, or a "diamond in the rough," as the saying goes. Jesus had extraordinary intuition to envision so quickly the grand person that Simon Peter could become. Sometimes we need light from a borrowed lamp, and are sustained by someone else's faith in us. Our spirits rise and fall, and there are days when we do not feel that we have much worth. Jesus told his new disciples that they would be transformed from catchers of fish for the nourishment of people's bodies to blessing and healing people in ways they could not yet imagine. His prophetic word to Simon Peter was that he would become strong like a rock and serve as the sturdy foundation of his church. Simon Peter must have been strengthened by Jesus' faith in him through his many pitfalls and difficulties.

Simon Peter was obviously a man of extremes, given to swinging from one position to its opposite, with volatile impulsivity. He was full of enthusiasm and vigor, but he frequently went beyond appropriate limits and wisdom. An example of this tendency occurred on the last night of Jesus' life, when Jesus took a towel and began to wash the disciples' feet, a task typically done by servants. When he reached Simon Peter, his disciple said,

"You will never wash my feet," to which Jesus replied, "Unless I wash you, you have no share with me." So what did the man of extremes do? He said, "Lord, not my feet only but also my hands and my head!" This is a typical illustration of how quickly he could reverse his stance completely.

Another memorable incident involving Simon Peter occurred after Jesus told his disciples that he would have go to Jerusalem, suffer at the hands of the chief priests, elders, and scribes, and be killed. He told them that he would be raised from the dead, but he wanted them to understand that the road he must take to redeem the world would be one of suffering.

Simon Peter exclaimed, "God forbid it, Lord! This must never happen to you." It is easy for me to understand why he reacted this way to Jesus' prediction that he would suffer and be killed, because he loved Jesus, and nobody wants a loved one to suffer. Yet, with the same vehemence with which he had just affirmed Simon Peter as the "rock" of his church, Jesus rebuked him: "Get behind me, Satan! You are a stumbling block to me; for you are setting your mind not on divine things but on human things" (Matthew 16:21–23).

That does sound harsh, and it has been suggested that Jesus used the term, "Satan," in responding to Simon Peter because what he said reminded Jesus of the temptations he had faced in the wilderness. No sooner had he been baptized and been called God's beloved son than he was driven into the wilderness and tempted by the spirit of this world offering him alternatives to what God was calling him to do. Jesus may have reacted to Simon Peter in frustration, because he did not want anyone to undermine his resolve to do God's will regardless of the suffering involved.

It is clear from this exchange that the relationship between Jesus and Simon Peter was intense, and there were many ups and downs as Simon Peter learned the hard lessons that Jesus had to teach him. Jesus had a remarkable gift for looking deeper than outward appearances and sensing grand capacities in people that they had not yet discovered themselves. I am fond of the story about a sculptor who was commissioned to create a statue of Abraham Lincoln for the library of a little college in the Midwest. Sculpting is a tedious, time-consuming process, and the sculptor carefully chipped away at the stone, day by day, for many months. He did this work in a studio, where a woman came to sweep up the chips every night, and she enjoyed noticing the progress of his work. After a long time, the statue was almost finished, and the sculptor was surprised to find this woman still at his studio when he arrived one morning. She had stayed all night just to speak to him. She told him, "I think what you have done is absolutely wonderful, and I stayed to tell you that, but I want to ask you something, too. How did you know that Mr. Lincoln was in that stone?" She could not fathom how the sculptor had brought forth the lifelike figure of Abraham Lincoln from a piece of granite.

Simon Peter eventually emerged into an impressive person and leader from what may have seemed similar to a rough-hewn piece of stone. The changes that took place in him over time were anything but simple or easy. He was tragically unaware of much of what was going on within him, as are most of us flawed human beings. He had not taken the inner journey to consciousness of his own personal dynamics, and there were parts of him that he did not recognize or embrace at all. Jesus helped him to stop living in such blind denial.

In his prize-winning book *The Denial of Death*, Earnest Becker made the point that one of our most important human challenges is to orchestrate the vast diversity of our potential in meaningful ways. He compared our personhood to a keyboard, and wrote that most of us are tempted to use only some of the keys that God has placed on the keyboard ignoring the others. Becker used images from the book of Genesis to interpret our human makeup. In that earliest and most primitive account of creation, God formed a human shape out of the dust of the earth, almost like a child might do as he played on the beach. Then God stooped over and breathed his very life into this pile of dust (Genesis 2:7). Becker saw this passage as a profound image of our human composition because we are drawn from the depths of the earth and, thus, kin to all levels of reality: the inorganic, organic, vegetable, and animal. Yet, we are breathed on by the sky, too, and given God-like capacities to remember, create, think, appreciate beauty, and more. So Becker imagined us as a hybrid breed, part animal and part angel, and he stressed the importance of developing and harmonizing the vast range of powers within us.

Years ago, I was on a radio panel in Louisville, Kentucky, called "The Moral Side of The News." Each week on the radio broadcast, four ministers discussed the moral and immoral aspects of some current event. When the local school system offered a very basic course in human sexuality at the junior high school level, there was a firestorm of protest against it. The four of us on this panel were asked to meet one night with a group of protesters called "The Concerned Citizens," in the hope of promoting a spirit of compromise and understanding. I will never forget the event, because we were gathered in a hot high school gym before the days of air conditioning, and the people in the crowd that gathered were very tense. There was particularly strong protest against using the scientifically correct anatomical names for the sexual organs, as had been proposed for the course curriculum. I asked, in complete earnestness, "Mr. Kruger, if you don't want those parts of the body called by their proper names, what *would* you like us to call them?" I remember him getting very red in the face and blurting out, "Do you have to call them anything?" He revealed quite clearly that he did not want to even admit that those parts of the body existed and they were not to be mentioned at all, as far as he was concerned. The huge problem with that approach is that we are not able to control or care for anything we will not acknowledge. This denial of our human nature and physical being can lead only to harm.

There is an amusing story about a proper Boston matron who went to see Phillips Brooks, her rector at Trinity Church in Copley Square, Boston. It was during a period of intense controversy about evolution, in the late nineteenth century, and she said to her rector, "Mr. Brooks, I hope it is not true that human beings are descended from the apes but, if it is true, I hope it does not become widely known!" In other words, if it is true, for God's sake, let's just leave it in the realm of unawareness and not even mention it. I believe Jesus worked tirelessly to call Simon Peter out of similar disowning of powerful parts of his being, and we are called to greater awareness, too.

Simon Peter had much difficulty recognizing his own faults. For example, he could not accept that he was capable of turning his back on Jesus and all that he believed or held precious. When Jesus warned his disciples that they would be tested in ways they had never been tested before, he argued with Jesus, boasting, "Though all become deserters because of you, I will never desert you." He honestly did not realize that he could betray or abandon Jesus. He thought he was much stronger and nobler than he actually was. Although Jesus specifically predicted that he would deny him three times that night, before the cock crowed, Simon Peter insisted, "Even though I must die with you, I will not deny you" (Matthew 26:33–35). Jesus must have looked at him with deep sadness, and thought, "Simon Peter, how out of touch you are with the weak side of your nature."

As we know, Jesus was exactly right, and Simon Peter did the very thing he claimed he could never be guilty of doing. After the last supper, Jesus did what we all need to do in the face of great threat. He prayed to God that he would be given the strength to stand what was ahead and do the Father's will, while his fore-warned disciples slept in unawareness, including Simon Peter. So when the spiritual tornado came, Jesus stood strong and they fell away. In spite of Jesus' words of warning and preparation, the disciples were overwhelmed by fear when the Romans arrested Jesus and took him away.

I think that at all times we humans are acting either out of love, or out of fear. Love is the assurance that there is enough of what we really need. Fear is the suspicion that there is not enough of what we actually need, and there never will be. Each of these realities has the power to cancel out the other. Scripture tells us that love has the power to cast out fear, and we need to remember that fear has the power to cast out love in the same way (1 John 4:18). I am never less loving than when I am most afraid. In the midst of panic, or trauma caused by forces against me, I am likely to be concerned only for myself and how I will survive. When Jesus was taken by force, every one of the eleven remaining disciples fled into the night in terror and self-preservation. (Matthew 26:56). When the moment of testing came, all of them folded and betrayed the most valued, loyal person in their lives. As a friend of mine used to say, "Don't focus all of your condemnation on Judas, because all of them let Jesus down."

In Simon Peter's defense, let it be said that he did follow along at a distance when Jesus was taken to be interrogated at the house of Caiaphas, the high priest. He was in the courtyard, waiting to see what was going to happen, when two maids of the high priest accused him of having been with Jesus. He denied it, saying he did not even know what they meant, and cursed and swore an oath for emphasis. After a while, other bystanders said that his Galilean accent betrayed him and again, he swore, "I do not know the man" (Matthew 26:69–74; Mark 14:66–71; Luke 22:54–60; John 18:16–17, 25–27). When Simon was questioned about his relationship to Jesus, fear overtook him. He had been boastful and overconfident instead of praying for strength with humility, so his fear undid him.

While the courtyard was still reverberating with his words of denial, two terrible things occurred. First, just as Jesus had predicted, the cock began to crow and Simon Peter realized that what Jesus had said to him, just hours before, turned out to be true. He was doing the very act of betrayal that he had sworn he would not do. Then, in Luke's account, Jesus turned to look down at Simon Peter from the room where he had been imprisoned by the guard, and Peter was suddenly aware that Jesus had heard every word of denial and betrayal that he had uttered (Luke 22:61). His heart broke as he realized that, in the midst of the worst thing that had ever happened to Jesus, there came to his ears the sound of the voice of one of his closest friends, and he was claiming he did not even know him. Jesus heard him say that he was not one of his followers and had no connection with him at all. It was dawning on Simon Peter that Jesus had every reason to feel abandoned and defeated at the moment that he was about to give his life for them, without one of his disciples remaining with him and for him. At that point, we are told in three of the gospels that Simon Peter broke down and wept bitterly.

Simon Peter's illusion that he was impervious to temptation is relevant to every one of us. If we think that we could never do something another human being has done, we are in grave danger. Any soldier who has been in battle can tell you that those in combat who do not think they are in danger are in the most danger of all. Simon Peter's denial of his own imperfections led him to betray the best relationship of his life. As fellow human beings, we have no cause to be smug or self-righteous because humans have done all varieties of terrible things. Under certain circumstances, none of us is above sin or failure.

I imagine that the next three days were the worst that Simon Peter had ever experienced. Every time he shut his eyes, he must have remembered the look on Jesus' face after hearing his words of denial. His anguish could have only intensified after Jesus was crucified, nailed to a cross, left to hang there for six agonizing hours until he finally breathed his last, and was laid in the tomb on Friday night. Then, something happened that the disciples had not dared to dream, even though Jesus had told them. Some of the women went to finish the burial preparations for his body on Sunday morning, and they returned with "trembling and astonishment," to tell of their incredible experience of finding the tomb was empty. A young man in a white robe told them that Jesus had risen and, according to Mark's gospel, Jesus sent this word: "Go, tell his disciples and Peter that he is going ahead of you to Galilee; there you will see him, just as he told you" (Mark 16:7).

Why do you think he added, "and Peter"? Remember, Peter had said publicly that he had no connection to Jesus, but Jesus did not reject him in return. To the contrary, he made a special effort to include Simon Peter in the gift of Easter and forgiveness, and revealed another glimpse of his inexhaustible mercy.

At this point in the Easter story, I am always struck by the event of the resurrection as the most mysterious and awesome of all the surprises to be found in Holy Scripture. Imagine that you had a son, brimming with goodness, who went to help a group of people that were desperately in need. Then, those people rejected, tortured, and killed your boy, even though his intention had been only to bless them. Ask yourself if it would ever occur to you, for one moment, to send your son back to the kind of people that treated him that way, even if you did have the power to raise him back to life. It is beyond my comprehension that God would have any heart for our species after we had done the very worst to Jesus. To be honest, I would have given up all hope for humankind.

Thus, in my opinion, the real miracle of Easter is not that God could resurrect Christ Jesus, which is astonishing by itself. The real miracle is that God would have wanted to do so. God's mercy is greater than anything I can begin to imagine, if he could still have hope for humans that are capable of doing to the innocent what we did to the best person that ever lived among us. The staggering miracle of Easter is that God's goodness is finally bigger than our badness, and his power to forgive is greater than our power to sin. Saint Paul showed his understanding of that when he said, "Where sin increased, grace abounded all the more" (Romans 5:20).

The awesome truth is that the total amount of our human destructiveness is just a fraction of the incredible compassion at the heart of God. The basis for all hope is that there is immeasurably more mercy in God than there is evil in us. The true proportions of this reality are portrayed in one of my favorite quotes from *Piers Plowman,* the fourteenth-century allegory: "But all the wickedness in the world which man may do or think is no more to the mercy of God than a live coal dropped in the sea."

This amazing grace runs all through the story of Simon Peter. When he got word that Jesus was alive again, he had to be filled with mixed emotions. I imagine he was astonished and elated, but also terrified because he would have to face those eyes that had looked into his and knew exactly how despicably he had behaved. Yet, in his infinite mercy, God sent Jesus back to "the disciples and Peter."

Simon Peter was there that Easter night when Jesus first appeared to the disciples, and on the following week when Jesus showed Thomas his wounds. But it was not until they were back in Galilee, days later, that Jesus dealt openly and honestly with Simon Peter. He had returned to go fishing, which was his livelihood before Jesus came into his life. The others had come with him, and they caught no fish that night. Jesus was standing on the beach at daybreak, but the disciples did not realize that it was Jesus. He asked if they had caught any fish and, when they said they had not, he told them to cast the net on the right side of the boat. They did what he suggested and caught so many fish that they could barely haul in the heavy net. Suddenly John told Peter, "It is the Lord!" With his typical eagerness, Peter jumped out of the boat into the sea to reach the Risen One there on the shore, even though Jesus knew of his boastfulness and empty resolve better than anybody else (John 21:1–7).

To me the most grace-filled part of this story is that Simon Peter did not receive one iota of harshness or recrimination from Jesus. Instead, Jesus led him very tenderly to face the truth about himself. Three times, once for each denial, Jesus asked him, "Simon, son of John, do you love me more than these?" Jesus' reference to "these" may have included not only the other disciples, but also the boats nearby and his life as a fisherman that they represented. There was none of Simon Peter's old cockiness as he answered three times in the affirmative: "Yes, Lord; you know that I love you." He must have been deeply moved by Jesus' forgiveness.

I believe that forgiveness is more like birth than anything else, because it is God's willingness to give us another chance in life, on the same terms that we were given at birth. What did any of us ever do to get into this world? We did nothing at all. We had no power to earn our way into this life. Birth was a sheer and total gift, and forgiveness is God's gift of innumerable chances to move beyond our faults, not because we deserve to, but because he wants us to know his kind of joy. God is more interested in our future than our past, more concerned about what we can become than what we have been. Wisdom can be born of failure, as we are given every chance to learn from our mistakes, pass them on to the arms of everlasting mercy, and begin again.

To experience forgiveness as Simon Peter did, we have to attribute much less significance to our performance in history and elevate our appreciation of what God does. John the Baptist expressed it well when he was talking about Jesus and said, "He must increase, but I must decrease" (John 3:30). We are saved by grace, and grace alone. What we humans do, or fail to do, is insignificant in comparison to God's gift of life and continual mercy. It is clear that God enabled Peter to learn from his mistakes, for he became the leader of the church in Jerusalem, Samaria, Antioch, and Rome, to name only a few of the places he influenced significantly. The descriptions of Peter in the book of Acts, and the many legends of his great faith that have come to us, present a magnificent testimony to what the forgiveness of God can do.

It is crucial for us to acknowledge our weaknesses, take responsibility for our sins, and confess them honestly without blaming others. Only then can we learn from our mistakes and turn to a hopeful future. Why do you think that many people find it hard to accept grace and forgiveness? I have pondered that question for many years, and the only plausible conclusion I have reached is that the credit and praise belongs completely on God's side of the equation when we receive forgiveness. I have every reason to be thankful, but no reason to be proud. Thus, I think it is hard to accept God's grace because it cuts directly across our egos. Years ago, a psychiatrist told me that excessive guilt is the shadow side of pride, because it is thinking of ourselves more highly than we deserve. If we shift our focus from our own achievements or failures to the powerful grace of God, then the kind of transformation that took place in Simon Peter is possible for every one of us.

I can illustrate an important part of what I have learned from Simon Peter in a story about something that happened to a friend of mine. His young son had eagerly begun kindergarten and, in October of his first year in school, the teacher said to his class, "Would you like to make something with your own hands to give to your folks for Christmas? They will get lots of store-bought gifts, but might prefer something you made yourselves. What do you think of that idea?" My friend's son held up his hand, and said, "My father smokes a pipe, and I'd like to make him an ash tray." So the teacher said that she would help him do that. She gave him some clay, and they shaped it in the form of an ashtray. She asked him his father's favorite color, and he said, "blue," so they colored it blue. She even got a kiln, let the boy put the ashtray he made in it, and they watched as it turned bright, then dark, and then hardened. At every stage of this process, this five-year-old boy's hopes and expectations for Christmas Day increased. He could just imagine his father unwrapping a tie, or some socks, and then opening his present, made by his son's own hands, and being overwhelmed with pride and joy.

The traditional Christmas pageant was performed on the last day before school was dismissed for the Christmas holidays. The school auditorium was packed with parents and grandparents, and soon it was time to go. The little boy went to his classroom to get the carefully wrapped package for his father. He headed back to his parents but in his haste to run down the hall, wave goodbye to his friends, and put on his coat, all at the same time, he suddenly tripped. His precious package flew up in the air and came crashing down on the floor, with the terrible sound of breaking. When the little fellow realized that all the work he had done in the fall and his dreams for Christmas Day were completely dashed, not surprisingly, he began to cry as if his heart had broken.

My friend had been a military officer, and he told me later that he was uncomfortable seeing any male weep in public, especially his own son. So he walked over to his child and said in a brusque manner, "Don't worry, son, don't worry. It doesn't matter, it doesn't make any difference at all." However, his wife brushed him aside, because she was much wiser than he in matters of the heart. She said, "Yes, it does make a difference that something this precious has gotten broken," and he watched as she did two wonderful things. She swept up their child in her arms, and wept with him the tears that are always appropriate when we break the things that are precious. Then, she reached into her purse, took out a handkerchief, and gently wiped the tears from their little boy's eyes, and then from her own eyes. Her husband listened with wonder as he heard her say, "Come on, son, come on. Let's pick up the pieces, take them home, and see what we can make of what is left."

In that touching story you have an image of the alternatives we have in response to those times when the things that are most precious to us have been broken. You can cry as the little boy did, as if one mistake is irreparable and leaves nothing but loss and despair; or you can deny the significance of what has happened, as my friend did, and drain any meaning out of the experience. However, I think that God would want us to respond like that wise mother, descend into the crucible of pain, and weep the tears that are always appropriate when we have broken the blessed things of God. To do less would minimize the impact of any occasion of loss or sin, but then, you can pick up the pieces, take them home, and see what can be made of what is left. Jesus helped Simon Peter pick up the broken pieces of his life and create something very worthwhile out of what was left. Therein lies the basis for hope for the future, in spite of the past.

It is likely that the only reason we have the story of Simon Peter's denials in our gospel canon is that he had the humility to tell it himself. Peter must have shared how his horrid shame was overcome by mercy, when he failed the One who would never fail him. He probably witnessed to others about the endless blessings of Jesus and told how he felt when Jesus sent for him by name, even after he had betrayed him. Imagine Peter getting a far-off look in his eyes and adding, "Someday I'll stand in the judgment hall of God and, in that moment, he will do for me what I failed to do for him in his hour of greatest need. There will come to my ears the sound of my best friend's voice saying, 'Yes, I do know him, Father, he is one of us.' "

Philip
The Careful Realist

Philip was the first person to whom Jesus extended his famous invitation, offering him the most basic form of salvation to be found anywhere: "Follow me." Soon after Jesus met Philip, he made this simple though life-changing proposal: "Come join me and share the rest of your journey with me," and Philip did just that. Such immediate acceptance of a life-altering offer seems out of character for Philip, because later passages in the gospels show him to be a cautious and deliberate man, who was typically slow to make decisions. This essential invitation to the Christian life is worth examining more closely, and the first thing I notice is that Jesus does not call us to him and then send us out into the world to rely on only our own resources. It is most reassuring to realize that the Christian life is not a solitary journey, because Jesus asks us to follow in companionship with him. One of the most amazing aspects of the Christian life is that Jesus accompanies us into the future.

In the Middle Ages, theologians used to talk about the "preve-nient" grace of God. The word, comes from the Latin, *pre*, which means "before," and from *venire*, "to come," and in this sense it refers to the grace that "precedes" us from before the beginning of the world. I have fond memories of my professor of historical theology who would graciously step back and say, "Prevent me," whenever he came to a door with me. This was his humble way of saying, "Go before me." We are blessed immeasurably by the prom-ise of Jesus to go before us wherever he invites us to go. He prom-ises that we will never find ourselves alone because, if we choose to be aware, this One goes with us. This tremendously comforting promise offers us access to a profound dimension of wisdom, and can take away the terrible loneliness of life, as we seek to follow Jesus. It is a promise that I have learned to take very seriously. To be honest with you, there have been moments in my life when this particular promise seemed to become an actual reality.

In 1976, I was invited to give the sermon at the Memorial Church at Harvard University, which is right in the midst of Harvard Square in Cambridge, Massachusetts. I went there with a fair measure of apprehension about doing well and, as I flew to Boston, I happened to read something about this promise of Jesus to go before us and not leave us to face life by ourselves. Later, when I was processing into the church behind a magnifi-cent choir, it appeared to me briefly that a figure in the shape of a shepherd was walking ahead of me, mounting the high pul-pit, and was standing there, as if to say, "When you get to this place, I am right here beside you." This image of the grace of God going before me was enormously reassuring, as are Jesus' words,

"Follow me." He was saying, "I will join you where you are. I will go ahead of you. I will not abandon you." How blessed we are to be invited into such an amazing pilgrimage, accompanied by divine wisdom and energy for the rest of our lives.

To enter into salvation is to become part of an ongoing process that makes it possible to be honest about our present condition without despair, because we have hope that we will develop beyond what we are at the moment. The New Testament speaks of salvation in three different tenses. There are references that say we *are* saved, others that say we are *being* saved, and there are references that say we *will be* saved. This means to me that, when we dare to follow Jesus, we begin an adventure that starts wherever we are but has no end to it. There is always something more. Salvation is a dynamic process, rather than something that remains static or happens all at one time.

The writings of Sister Macrina Wiederkehr have been of great inspiration to me, and in an excerpt from her book *Seasons of Your Heart*, she describes a lovely image from her childhood that seems wonderfully consistent with my vision of this dynamic process of salvation as we follow Jesus. For example, she writes of the memory of her mother kneading dough in preparation for baking:

> Kneading the dough was a little like loving it, she told me. You had to love it just right for it to grow into good bread—not too much, not too little. While she mixed and kneaded the dough, we talked of many things, but when she covered the dough and put it in a warm place to rise,

it was time to be quiet and to wait. For me, it became a sacred, mystery hour, a holy hour, an hour of watching and waiting for the miracle of rising. During that time of waiting, she would always tell me not to frighten the dough. It seems the dough grew best in a silent, peaceful atmosphere. And so if friends came over to play at that time, I would always tell them: "Don't scare the dough!" They would look at me strangely and never quite seem to understand. But I understood.

Today I understand that even more. Are not we a little like the dough? Shouldn't we be kneaded just right so we can rise to full stature? And is it not wise for us to give each other a reasonable amount of space, of time, of quiet in which to grow, to rise? Whenever I make a holy hour I like to compare it to the hour of waiting for the dough to rise. It seems so similar. I sit with the dough of my life, waiting for what is unfinished in me to rise. Once again it is an hour of mystery. A hint of eternity steals through my being as I wait the miracle of rising.[1]

And when the leaven of Jesus is mixed into our lives, our flesh and blood, it makes it possible for us to be called forth and rise to full stature over time. This is what happened for Philip after Jesus said, "Follow me."

Notice that the first thing Philip did was to generously share his discovery of Jesus with Nathanael, his friend from the village

---

1. Macrina Wiederkehr, *Seasons of Your Heart* (New York: HarperCollins, 1991), 58–59.

of Cana. Philip's neighbor, Andrew, from Bethsaida, had the same impulse to share the good news of Jesus when he went directly to tell his brother, Simon Peter, "We have found the Messiah" (John 1:40–41). One of the most consistent themes of my life is my conviction that generosity is the deepest characteristic of God. We see this noble quality of the mystery throughout Holy Scripture. At the bottom of reality is a spirit of generosity, and when you and I are spiritually healthy, we want to share the good things that happen to us and turn them into gifts for somebody else. It is only when we are spiritually unhealthy that we want to keep the good that comes to us for ourselves, instead of sharing it with others. If we clutch what is good in our lives closer to ourselves, then we have let our wills become crossed with the divine principle within us. Sharing generously is the essence of loving intimacy.

One of the best parts of my marriage to Ann is the delight that we both receive in sharing nearly everything. Both of us work and have busy lives, and there is nothing more pleasing to me than to come home at the end of the day to hear her say, "I have so much good news to share with you. I have many things to tell you." Then we share whatever the day has given us, and the gifts of the day become presents to each other. I believe this is a vital part of what it means to be made in the image of God, and when Philip was invited by this Generous One to follow him, he must have felt that this news was much too good to keep for himself, so he shared the gift of Jesus with Nathanael. I think that we are never closer to the primal joy of existence than when we let the flow of grace come into us gratefully, and move out through us generously. It is when our blood stops circulating that our bodies get sick; it is when money is hoarded and does not move through the economy that a financial depression sets in; and it is when bodies of water are stagnant that they cannot sustain much life. These examples suggest to me that the true richness of being made in the image of God can only thrive in a spirit of generosity.

One of my favorite stories is told by Anthony de Mello about a holy man who reached the outskirts of a village one night and settled down under a tree.

The sannyasi had reached the outskirts of the village and settled down under a tree for the night when a villager came running up to him and said, "The stone! The stone! Give me the precious stone!" "What stone?" asked the sannyasi. "Last night the Lord Shiva appeared to me in a dream," said the villager, "and told me that if I went to the outskirts of the village at dusk, I should find sannyasi who would give me a precious stone that would make me rich forever." The sannyasi rummaged in his bag and pulled out a stone. "He probably meant this one," he said, as he handed the stone over to the villager. "I found it on a forest path some days ago. You can certainly have it." The man looked at the stone in wonder. It was a diamond. Probably the largest diamond in the world for it was as large as a man's head. He took the diamond and walked away. All night long he tossed about on his bed, unable to sleep. Next day, at the crack of dawn, he woke the sannyasi and said, "Give me the wealth that makes it possible for you to give this diamond away so easily."[2]

I have often heard it said, "There are no pockets in a shroud"—for death is going to make generous givers of us all. We came into this world with absolutely nothing, receive everything we have in this life, and are going to give back everything at the end of our lives in history. This should give us our best clue as to what is really important in this life.

I imagine Jesus sensed the spirit of generosity in Philip that led him to share his good news with Nathanael, who was skeptical at first: "Can anything good come out of Nazareth?" Philip's response shows that he was wise in the ways of diplomacy; instead of arguing with Nathanael, he had already learned from Jesus the best way to handle situations like this. So he said to Nathanael the very same thing that Jesus said to the two disciples of John the Baptist: "Come and see." He simply invited his friend to experience Jesus for himself. We cannot argue people into the kingdom of God. We love them into the kingdom. We cannot make people into converts through intellectual debate, because that usually evokes resistance and defensiveness. The way to draw people into the circle of Jesus' company is to love them as Jesus did. Such love becomes the magnet that draws people: "And I, when I am lifted up from the earth, will draw all people to myself" (John 12:32). He would

---

2. Anthony de Mello, *The Song of the Bird* (Chicago: Loyola University Press, 1982), 183.

not do this, not by a display of intellectual brilliance, but by that unconditional love that was the essence of who he was and what he did. So Philip didn't say, "Come and listen," nor did he say, "Come and argue." Instead, he invited his friend to come see for himself. It reminds me of Edgar Guest's popular poem, "Sermons We See":

> I'd rather see a sermon than hear one any day;
> I'd rather one should walk with me than merely tell the
>   way. . . .
> I might misunderstand you, and the high advice you give.
> But there's no misunderstanding how you act and how
>   you live.[3]

We have a second glimpse of Philip, when Jesus and the disciples encountered a large group of people in the Galilean wilderness. Jesus had compassion on them, and began to teach them and heal their sick. As the sun was going down, the disciples came to him and said, "Send the crowds away so that they may go into the villages and buy food for themselves" (Matthew 14:15). They did not want to take responsibility for trying to feed that many people, nor risk the problems that might erupt in a restless, hungry crowd. They must have been very surprised when Jesus answered, "They need not go away; you give them something to eat" (Matthew 14:16). Jesus asked Philip how they could buy bread to feed everyone, and John's gospel comments,

---

3. From *Collected Verse of Edgar Guest* (NY: Buccaneer Books, 1976), 599

"He said this to test him, for he himself knew what he was going to do" (John 6: 6).

Philip told Jesus that even if they spent all the money they had, they could not buy enough bread to feed even a little to each person there. Philip's reaction was entirely practical and human, but Jesus may have hoped he would have a sense of greater possibilities because he had witnessed Jesus heal many people, perform amazing miracles, and was there when Jesus turned water into wine at the wedding in Cana. With this in mind, I can make more sense of Jesus singling Philip out to test him, perhaps to raise his consciousness of how much more is possible with Christ than Philip's grasp of the facts led him to assume. Philip was probably the kind of person who would call his limited sense of potential "realistic," and Jesus was calling him to a higher faith in the power of divine energies. Philip had not learned yet that, ultimately, despair is presumptuous, because it is saying something about reality and the future we cannot know. Who can predict what is impossible for the One who can raise the dead to life? Nobody expected Easter.

In Mark's account of this event, Jesus brushed aside Philip's comment and asked, "How many loaves have you? . . . Go and see" (Mark 6:38). It was Andrew who told Jesus that he'd found a boy with five loaves and two fishes, but he admitted that did not seem like much with so large a crowd. Then, I imagine that all twelve of the disciples watched in astonishment as Jesus did three things. First, he took the small amount that was there and gave thanks for it. Instead of wringing his hands, and saying, "Oh dear, we don't have enough, so there is nothing we can do," he took what was there and held it up to God in gratitude. Next, he had the whole crowd sit down, which was remarkably practical, and through the magic of gratitude and divine energy of Jesus, everyone wound up having enough.

I have heard more rational explanations: perhaps others in the crowd were holding back food for themselves under their cloaks, and the boy's generosity inspired them to share what they had, too. Even if that were true, it is still a miracle that enough food was produced to feed everyone. I imagine that the disciples walked away from that event in utter amazement. This is the only miracle described in all four of the gospels, which emphasizes the powerful effect it must have had on the gospel writers. The crucial lessons we can learn from this event are unmistakable. If we are grateful for what we have and have faith that God will bless our efforts to do the best we can with it, then what we have can multiply. We do not have to know how our gratitude and faith work to make such things happen. We may tap into other people's generosity and creativity. We may create a chain effect. Who knows what miracles can come from gratefully doing the best with what we have?

Years ago, I heard about an American missionary who was in China during a time of terrible famine. With his influential contacts in the States, this missionary succeeded in getting a whole shipload of food shipped to China, which he planned to distribute to the people in his region. He was very excited that he had been able to do something to relieve the terrible starvation that was going on around him, so he announced that the food would be distributed at a certain time the next morning. Well, the hunger was so great that the crowd exceeded, by far, the number of people he had expected. There was so much panic that a terrible mob scene broke out as soon as his helpers began to distribute the food. People began to trample each other, and the police had to be summoned. Several people were killed before the day was over, and what had been meant as a gesture of helpfulness, turned into a horrible disaster.

That night the missionary was broken hearted. Too distressed to sleep, he took out his Bible to try to find some consolation in Scripture and came upon the feeding of the five thousand. He was struck by the ingenious strategy that Jesus used, according to all four of the gospel accounts: Jesus had the people sit down. He thought to himself, "Of course, that is the perfect form of crowd control! If I had gotten everybody to sit down, people would not have pushed and trampled each other." He could hardly wait to repeat the process the next day with that one difference of requiring everyone to sit down before any food was distributed. With that one change in the process, the food was passed out to everyone without any problems at all. The missionary was astonished by Jesus' common sense and effectiveness. The missionary marveled, also, at how calmly Jesus handled a seemingly impossible situation, without a hint of discouragement or despair. He simply gave thanks for what he had, and began to do something with it. He was composed and practical, and the end result was that solutions were found beyond anything that Philip could have imagined.

We see Philip for the third time just before the crucifixion. Some men from Greece had heard about Jesus and went to Jerusalem during one of the high feasts. They approached Philip and said, "Sir, we wish to see Jesus" (John 12:20–21). They may have sought out Philip because he was the only apostle who had a Greek name. Philip seemed surprised that these gentiles were making this overture and knew of no precedent or protocol for introducing Greek pagans to Jesus. So, instead of acting decisively himself, Philip asked Andrew what he should tell the Greek men. Andrew was much more confident that Jesus would be interested in anybody that was interested in him. Thus, Andrew took Philip and the Greeks to talk to Jesus.

Philip's hesitancy suggests to me that he was not the kind of person who liked to take responsibility. He was not the kind of bold, clear-cut, can-do kind of leader that Simon Peter or John was, but I give him credit for not acting out of prejudice by turning these Greek strangers away or ignoring them. He may have been an indecisive, hesitant man, but I admire his humble willingness to acknowledge his limits and confer with somebody capable of providing assistance. In other words, he was not too proud to call in some help. No one is capable of doing everything, and people who live out of a clear sense of both their gifts and their limits have a strong advantage. One of the best ways to prevent overload or ineffectiveness is to ask for help when you need it.

I once heard an intriguing sermon on the Parable of the Good Samaritan that took a very different slant on the priest and the Levite from any I had ever heard. They are usually condemned for seeing the man stricken by the side of the road and passing by without doing anything, but this preacher suggested that the priest and the Levite may have just been realistic enough to know that they did not have anything with them that would be helpful to the man in need. Perhaps they were not able to be of assistance, whereas the Samaritan had a donkey with him, and he had oil, ointment, and a cloth with which to apply them. He had what was needed with him, and the priest and the Levite did not, so they went for help, instead. If this was actually what happened, then their leaving was more practical and realistic than it was bad or cruel. The preacher said wisely that we need to be guided by our gifts and capabilities in our responses to people, because we will see enough human brokenness to completely sink a compassionate heart as we go through life. We will be of no help to anyone if we spread ourselves too thin, or try to do things that are beyond our ability.

Years ago, I remember driving somewhere in Louisville and seeing a stalled car on the other side of the street when I reached a stoplight. An older lady was standing beside the car with its hood up. She looked quite dismayed, and it was obvious that something was wrong with her car. I felt compassion for her, as if I were seeing my own mother standing there in that kind of plight. So I did a U-turn, parked behind her car, got out of my car, and asked her, "Are you having trouble?" She answered, "I don't know what's wrong with my car. It's smoking, quit running, and I don't have any idea what to do."

Now the worse thing that could have possibly happened would have been for me to get under that hood and try to fix that car. I knew clearly what I could, and could not, do to help her. So, I told her, "I know of a full service gas station nearby, and I will be glad to go there and get a mechanic to come help you." I asked her if there were any phone calls that I could make for her, and she said that would appreciate my calling to tell her hair stylist that she would be delayed for her appointment because of car trouble. I told her, "Now, that I can do!" I can go to a garage and dial a telephone, but I cannot fix a car. I was letting my limits and my gifts govern the way that I helped a stranded neighbor. It seems to me that, although Philip was not decisive in the face of a request from Greek strangers, he was helpful by going to Andrew, whom he trusted to know what to do. We can learn a good lesson from his example.

The last time we see Philip is in that great passage at the Last Supper, when Jesus was preparing his disciples for what was about to come. He spoke the words you have probably heard at many funerals, "Do not let your hearts be troubled. Believe in God, believe also in me. In my Father's house are many dwelling places. If it were not so, would I have told you that I go to prepare a place for you? And if I go and prepare a place for you, I will come again and will take you to myself, so that where I am, there you may be also. And you know the way to the place where I am going." Here is that same incredible promise that Jesus will never abandon us, that we can count on him. Then Thomas asks, "Lord, we do not know where you are going. How can we know the way?" Thomas is telling Jesus that they were clueless, with no idea of what was going on. So Jesus went on to put it even more clearly, "No one comes to the Father except through me. If you know me, you will know my Father also." Yet, in spite of all Jesus had taught them, and this unmistakable clarification, Philip asked for more: "Lord, show us the Father, and we will be satisfied." Jesus' response must have been filled with genuine frustration and sadness as he asked, "Have I been with you all this time, Philip, and you still do not know me? Whoever has seen me has seen the Father." We may think of Philip as a slow learner to have been with Jesus for three years without understanding that he was in the presence of God, but the idea that the Messiah was both man and God was a radically foreign concept to first-century Jews. We owe Philip a debt of gratitude for his dogged inquisitiveness, because Jesus' response to him has blessed Christians for twenty-one centuries: "Whoever has seen me, has seen the Father" (John 14:1-9).

Jesus was telling them that when they looked into his face, they saw the essence of the Holy One. The unique distinction of the Christian religion is this wonderful gift of the incarnation: the One who inhabited the heavens has assumed the form of a human being and has come to us for our salvation. God became what we are, so that we can understand what God is. The answer that Jesus gave to Philip, "The one who has seen me, has seen the Father," puts the unique central claim of the Christian religion in its very clearest, most powerful form: incarnation, the coming of God in flesh and blood. It is the most incredible act of mercy, and the most redeeming and enlightening of all events. The Eternal chose to enter time and space to become what we are, and this sets Christianity apart. To the question that humans have asked from time immemorial, "What is God like?" John's gospel answers, "God is like Jesus."

In time, these words must have worked their way into Philip's consciousness. It is generally accepted that he became one of the great missionary preachers of Asia, and was martyred for his faith in the Roman-Greek city of Hierapolis in Phrygia. There are many legends about Philip, but there is considerable doubt that any of them are true. The only other mention of him in Scripture is that he was part of the group that met in the upper room in Jerusalem, after Jesus' ascension. There are later references to someone named Philip in Acts, who was one of seven men called to be deacons by the apostles, but many biblical scholars do not think they refer to the apostle (Acts 1:13; 6:3–6).

Philip had a long way to go when he first encountered Jesus, but the invitation to come and follow began a remarkable pilgrimage through which his life was transformed by the grace of Jesus.

Nathanael
Without Deceit

Nathanael's story begins with a mystery. Who is this apostle who appears by name only in the gospel of John and nowhere else? Although in John he is called "Nathanael," another and similar apostle called "Bartholomew" appears in Matthew, Mark, and Luke—but never in John. Because they never appear together in the same gospel, and because both of them are often linked with the apostle Philip, Nathanael, and Bartholomew are probably the same person. Nathanael would have been the first name of this disciple, because in that era it was a common practice to place the word "bar," meaning "son of," *after* the first name, followed by the name of the father. This way of identifying one's father is called a patronymic, so this disciple's patronymic would have been Bar Tolmai, "son of Tomai," from the Anglicized name, Bartholomew.

It is interesting to note that Philip and Bartholomew are always listed together, much like the pairs of brothers who are among Jesus' followers. Philip was the one who brought Nathanael to see Jesus, and these two were linked in earliest church histories and legends as well. It appears that they were best friends, who studied Scripture together, followed John the Baptist together, and became Jesus' disciples together.[1] Nathanael was the first person with whom Philip shared his exciting news of the Messiah. He went straight to his best friend, Nathanael, and told him in breathless excitement, "We have found him about whom Moses . . . and also the prophets wrote, Jesus son of Joseph from Nazareth" (John 1:45).

It seems obvious that Philip knew Nathanael would be interested in news of the long-awaited Messiah and spoke to him of Jesus in terms of Moses and Old Testament prophecies. They must have been pious Jews who were familiar with Scripture and prophecy regarding the Messiah. They were likely to have studied the word of God together on many occasions, hungry for divine truth and full of desire to receive the Messiah. However, in spite of Philip's unequivocal announcement, it is also obvious that Nathanael did not accept Philip's word that Jesus of Nazareth was the long-awaited Messiah. Nathanael's initial reaction is clearly skeptical as he queried Philip, incredulous that the Messiah could possibly come from the nearby village of Nazareth. (John 1:46)

As a careful student of Hebrew Scripture, Nathanael would have known that Nazareth is never mentioned in the Old Testament and, according to the prophet Micah, the Messiah

---

1. John MacArthur, *Twelve Ordinary Men*, (Nashville: Thomas Nelson, 2002), 136–37.

would come out of Bethlehem, "one of the little clans of Judah" (Micah 5:2). Furthermore, Nathanael may have had a more personal reason for his response. We can understand this better by knowing more about the context in which he lived. Cana was a village located eight miles north of Nazareth, in the midst of a cluster of villages north of the Sea of Galilee. Andrew and Peter were from Bethsaida; James and John were from Capernaum, and Cana was Nathanael's hometown. Given how close these small villages were to Nazareth, the people who lived in the area would have known one another. Familiarity breeds contempt, as the saying goes, and Nathanael's inability to imagine a savior from his own neck of the woods might have been simply his bias. The people of Cana may have had a history of rivalry with Nazareth, in much the same way that high school football teams do now. It is even possible that Nathanael and Jesus had known of each other as they were growing up and, as is so often the case with hometown boys, Nathanael felt competitive because he came from a rival-neighboring town. This sincere student of Scripture had his flaws and prejudices, too, which kept him from being able to recognize something genuinely new. It is easy to let the impressions of the past bleed into the present, and there is no more perennial challenge than learning to balance our experiences of the past, awareness of the present, and anticipation of the future.

We are gifted with a capacity for memory that links us to what has already occurred, the capacity for attention to the "here-and-now" moment, and the ability to envision the future to some extent. All three of these abilities are crucial, and we need to guard against letting any one of them dominate our lives. If you had no memory, then what I have written here would be meaningless to you. We could not communicate at all unless you remember what these words mean. On the other hand, it is good to remember the past but not stare at it too long. We all know people who are so focused on regrets about past events in their lives that they begin much of what they say with, "If only. . . ." Others glorify the past, believing that the God of the good old days cannot be trusted for any good new days. Fearful people anticipate the future with anxious dread and pessimism, preventing them from enjoying life at the moment and often allowing their terrible expectations to become self-fulfilling prophecies. Anxious people begin many sentences with the words "What if" and end with any number of "worst-case" scenarios. Ideally, a life well-lived calls us to stay open to the present moment, hold on to lessons from the past, and to avoid future hurtful consequences of our actions—all at the same time. These are tough but worthwhile challenges and, initially, Nathanael was not looking at what might be new and unique about the present moment. Rather, he was allowing his past impression of the folks from Nazareth to blind him to the possibility that Jesus of Nazareth was truly the Messiah.

The Bible begins with the incredible affirmation that God created a universe out of nothing. This means that novelty is always possible. New things can occur, and one cannot always account for present reality in terms of its antecedents. It is a great source of hope to remember that God can bring something into the present that is absolutely different from the way it used to be. If we allow our perceptions from the past to distort the way we view what we see now, we risk missing something new and wonderful that might be happening right before our eyes. I believe that truth is best communicated in story form, because a story that we can visualize is usually more compelling than an abstract concept. For this reason, I have collected many stories over the years, and I love to tell them in order to remind myself of the truths expressed through them. Nathanael rejected an idea perfunctorily because it did not fit with the way he had experienced life before, and two of my favorite stories illustrate some problems with doing that.

The first story is from the philosopher Soren Kierkegaard, and it is about a little Danish traveling circus that went from village to village. The pattern of the circus folks was to arrive at a town in the morning, find a field close to the center of town, and arrange to put up their tent and signs to announce their presence. In those days, there wasn't much happening, so word would spread quickly that the circus was coming. The circus performers would set up the tent and put on their show. Then, after it was over, they would take down the tent, load it in wagons, travel through the night to the next village, and repeat the same process. One night, the circus tent caught on fire about an hour before the performance, when the only member of the troupe who was fully clothed was one of the clowns. Since he was the only one who could go for help immediately, he was dispatched into the village to get some help, and he did it as well as anybody could have done it. He spoke to every citizen he met and told them of the urgent crisis, saying, "Please get your buckets, get water from your wells, and help us put out this fire. We need your assistance and we need it quickly." Unfortunately, there was a serious problem because the people in that village had prior experience with clowns, and they had always seen them as jokesters whose job was to entertain and make people laugh. Consequently, it was as if they heard him with their eyes, because their past ideas of what it means to be a clown kept them from hearing anything new. It was not until they looked at the horizon and saw the flames blazing above the trees that it dawned on them that this was something they had never experienced before. Here was someone dressed as a clown, doing something that no clown they had known had ever done, but by the time they realized he was really asking for help, it was too late.

My grandfather told me the other story on this subject, and he lived in Simpson County, Kentucky, not far from where it occurred. The story was that, in the cold bitter winter of February 1809, a rural mail carrier was making his way through the back woods of Hardin County, Kentucky, when he came across a local citizen who asked the him, "Tell me what's happening out in the big world. We're so cut off back here that we know very little." As you know, there were no televisions, no Internet, no phones, and very few newspapers then. So the mail carrier said, "Well, it looks like we're having trouble with the crown again. We can't seem to get Great Britain off our backs, and we may be in for another war with them. There is talk of a national bank, which would really affect everything, even in rural areas like this. There is a lot going on in the big world out there. What's going on back in these parts?" The local citizen replied, "Shucks, mister, why would you even bother to ask? Nothing ever happens back here. Oh, there was a baby born last night to Nancy Hanks and Tom Lincoln, but shucks, mister, nothing ever happens back here." You probably realize that baby was Abraham Lincoln, but the folks in the story would not have believed that an incredibly significant future president of the United States had just been born in their "neck of the woods." They had forgotten that God creates out of nothing, and people cannot always account for the present from what they know of the past. Staying open to new experiences and surprises is a great asset in being fully human.

When we first saw Nathanael in Scripture, he reacted with prejudice when he was told something that did not square with what he had always thought. He was skeptical that any good thing could come out of Nazareth, but Philip did not argue or become defensive. He simply said, "Come and see," asking Nathanael to experience Jesus for himself. To his credit, Nathanael agreed to see Jesus with Philip, and when Jesus saw him coming from a distance, he said, "Here is truly an Israelite in whom there is no deceit" (John 1:47). Nathanael must have been surprised that, at first glance, Jesus was affirming him as a true son of Abraham, who had no deceit. Synonyms for the word, *deceit* are: guile cunning, slyness, wiliness, craftiness, cleverness, deceptiveness, hypocrisy, and duplicity. Jesus was giving Nathanael a huge compliment by saying that these negative qualities were not part of his character. Notice the sharp contrast between the ways that Jesus and Nathanael encountered each other. Nathanael scoffed at the idea that Jesus could be the Messiah, while Jesus focused on the positive aspects of Nathanael. We all have a choice as we interact with people around us. We can look for their faults or we can focus on their good qualities.

I will always be grateful for the Sunday school teacher I had when I was six years old. I can still remember her special class on the Sunday before Thanksgiving, at the church my family attended in Nashville. As I entered our classroom, the first thing

I noticed was a pitcher on a table in the middle of the room, half full of a red liquid substance. As the class started, our teacher invited us to engage that pitcher and its contents with all of our senses. She suggested that we hold it up to the light to see the different colors of red in it, and let us smell it, taste it, and pick it up to see how heavy it was. We were all involved in concentrating on this pitcher of liquid when our teacher asked a crucial question, "Tell me, is the pitcher half full or half empty?"

Well, there was a little girl in the class who reminded me of Lucy in the "Peanuts" comic strip because her mouth was always wide open. She was the first to answer and call out, "It's half empty, it's half empty." Then a young boy, with all the makings of a pensive philosopher, spoke up and said, "No, I think it is half full." The rest of us continued to struggle to decide if it was half empty or half full, when that inspired facilitator of children's understanding said gently, "The truth is that all of you are right, because both of those things that you have said are technically correct, but it makes a big difference which of those views of reality you focus on most. If you concentrate on what is half empty, you will be discouraged and feel drained, as if everything is going against you, but if you choose to look for what is half full, you will always have something to celebrate and energize you." Then she talked about Thanksgiving and the similar choice to be thankful for what we have, instead of bitter or resentful about what we do not have. On that day, I began to learn the invaluable lesson of the most appropriate response to that which is genuinely ambiguous, in terms that even six-year-olds could understand. Jesus chose the half-full perspective as he looked at Nathanael, and Nathanael chose the half-empty view when he first considered the prospect that Jesus might be the long-awaited Messiah.

Nathanael seemed mystified when he asked Jesus, "How do you know me?" He had to be wondering what prompted Jesus to give him such high praise: "Here is truly an Israelite in whom there is no deceit." Jesus' response to him may seem enigmatic: "I saw you under the fig tree before Philip called you" (John 1:48). To understand more fully what Jesus meant, it helps to know that, in biblical times, "under the fig tree" was a well-known image for a place that somebody would go to think or study quietly. It was a good place for a person who liked to ponder things, because many houses in first-century Palestine were primitive and had only one room, with little space for anything besides a place to sleep and a place to cook. Houses might be hot and smoky from the fires burning to cook meals. They were mainly shelters against the cold at night, affording no privacy, so people were likely to go outside to sit under a tree when they wanted to reflect or meditate. A fig tree was particularly appropriate because its canopy was even wider than the tree was high. Fig trees often grow to be about fifteen feet high, and some of them have limbs that stretch out as far as twenty-five feet, providing shade from the hot sun.

It is possible that Jesus had seen Nathanael in the nearby town of Cana and noticed that he had a contemplative side to him. He may have seen him sitting quietly under a fig tree, and reasoned that he was a diligent man of prayer, with the capacity to look beyond the surface of things. Nathanael may have been skeptical that Philip had really encountered the true Messiah, but this one "without deceit" was genuinely seeking the truth.

Once he was in the presence of Jesus, he surrendered completely, without reserve. He was wonderfully transparent, without any hidden agenda. His honest, open, and spontaneous temperament led him to accept Jesus of Nazareth as the Son of God as quickly as he had doubted him, at first. He exclaimed, "Rabbi, you are the Son of God! You are the King of Israel" and Jesus responded by affirming Nathanael's faith, promising him that he would see even greater things (John 1:49–51).

We are given more detail about Nathanael's call to follow Christ than we have about any other disciple. The only other thing we know of him from Scripture is that he was still with the other disciples after the crucifixion (John 21:2). We can learn more about him from legends and from the writings of Jerome, the foremost biblical scholar of the ancient church and also from references by John Chrysostom, the archbishop of Constantinople. These legends say that Nathanael went on to preach in India, Phrygia, and Armenia, before he died a martyr for having incurred the wrath of a powerful king by converting his brother to Christianity. The Armenian Church claims him as its founder. It is easy for me to imagine that Nathanael became an enthusiastic missionary, whose forthright honesty and scholarly devotion to the word of God attracted and persuaded many others to follow Christ. Our closer look at him has revealed, once again, that God calls ordinary people from insignificant locations, and empowers them to become missionaries who work to transform the world. It is my firm belief that this Holy One continues to call and empower us, too.

Thomas
A Truth Seeker

The Apostle Thomas is a familiar symbol of doubt, just as Judas Iscariot is a symbol of betrayal. It is not unusual to hear people call someone who has been disloyal to them "a Judas," and Thomas is similarly associated with the experience of doubt, even by people who don't know much about the Bible. Many of us have probably used the phrase, "doubting Thomas," because this individual has long been identified with a skeptical relationship to truth. Thomas has received much more than his share of bad press. I have a great affinity for this particular disciple because believing and seeking the truth have been arduous struggles for me, too.

I was initiated into the fellowship of the doubters when I was ten years old and had befriended the young son of a career military officer, whose family had moved into a home near mine in Nashville. One day I was with this new neighbor in my front yard, and I told him that I had to leave because it was time for me to go to church. He responded, "Church! Do you believe in that sort of stuff? My father said that anybody who thinks there is a God is just a plain fool." I had never heard such shocking words in my life, much less in my own front yard. I was truly terrified by the idea of having a real live atheist standing right there in front of me, and I would not have been surprised if the earth had swallowed him up. So I shot back at him in anger, "Well, *my* father thinks there is a God. I think *your* father is the fool," and with that loving Christian witness, I left!

That experience marked the end of innocence for me. Later I began to wonder, "Here is my friend believing what his father believes, and I am doing exactly the same thing, believing what my father believes. How do I know that my father is right and his father is wrong?" I have struggled with that question with relation to truth for more than half a century, so I have a lot in common with Thomas. He inspires a deep sense of kinship in me and I think that Thomas may have understood the truth process better than any of the other disciples. If I were to give a subtitle to this chapter, it would be "Taking up for Thomas." I am not suggesting that Thomas was perfect, but his story can help us understand more about discovering and acknowledging what is true.

Thomas's name appears in the lists of apostles we see in the Gospels of Matthew, Mark, and Luke, but only in John's do we get three glimpses into his character. In the first, word had just come to Jesus that one of his friends, Lazarus, was critically ill. Lazarus's sisters, Martha and Mary, sent for Jesus to come to Bethany, because they knew of his healing power. They pleaded for him to come quickly to save their brother's life. However,

Jesus was all the way on the other side of the Jordan River, and he did not drop everything to rush to Lazarus's side immediately. This is a classic illustration of how Jesus lived from the inside out, and not from the outside in. In other words, he maintained an internal center of control. He was sensitive to the people and events around him and cared deeply about them, but he did not give control of his life to external forces. He lived out of an inner sense of his own uniqueness, through his relationship to the One that he called "Abba Father." In John's gospel Jesus is in the habit of saying that "his hour" or "the hour" has come. It was as if he knew inwardly when it was the right time for him to carry out his purpose, and he trusted his own instincts.

In Stephen Covey's *Seven Habits of Highly Effective People*[1] he warns against letting things that only seem urgent crowd out the things that are truly important to us. For example, it is easy to let a high priority, such as time with our loved ones, get crowded out of our schedules by less important things that seem pressing, such as e-mail, phone calls, or memos requesting quick replies. One of the great dangers we face is letting our primary concerns become tyrannized by what others consider urgent. As Covey defines it, the urgent category usually involves somebody else's agenda. The important category includes what is of the highest value to you. With the information overload increasing from the proliferation of technology, it can be discouraging to calculate the huge amount of time it takes just to review and respond to

---

1. Stephen Covey, *The Seven Habits of Highly Effective People* (New York: Free Press, 1989).

the communications that pour into our lives, many of which we did not want to receive at all.

Jesus did not let what was urgent to others prevent him from doing what was important to him. He stayed true to his own sense of timing and did not get to Bethany until two days later, after Lazarus had already died. Martha was very upset with him for not having hurried there, but Jesus used this occasion as his last opportunity before his crucifixion to reveal that he was the resurrection and the life. In calling Lazarus back from the dead, he did something that simply healing a sick man would not have accomplished.

When the word came to the disciples that Lazarus's sisters had summoned Jesus to Bethany, they were alarmed because Lazarus lived across from the Mount of Olives in Jerusalem, where Jesus had antagonized the Jewish authorities only a few weeks earlier. They had tried to stone him, but he hid and escaped. If Jesus went to Bethany, word of his return would soon get to Jerusalem and he would be in grave danger. They may have thought that he was delaying because he was fearful for himself. However, two days later, Jesus said, "Let us go to Judea again" (John 11:7). His disciples tried to dissuade him, but Jesus was determined to go. It was then that Thomas uttered the first words that we know from him in Scripture. He spoke up in that critical moment and said, "Let us also go, that we may die with him" (John 11:7, 16).

If Jesus had made up his mind to go on this risky mission, Thomas was ready to go with him and demonstrate his loyalty. The faith that Thomas had in Jesus rose above his personal desires and fears. Thomas did not want to go to Bethany, but he accepted that reality often cuts squarely across what we would like to be true. It is important for us to realize that we are not purely rational beings. We are highly emotional creatures with strong desires, needs, and feelings. What we want to be true can become powerful enough to distort our perception of reality.

I have personally experienced this distortion of reality. At five o'clock on a snowy Saturday afternoon on January 10, 1970, my little daughter who had been suffering from leukemia breathed her last breath. When the doctor on the other side of the bed said, "She is gone," I was the most astonished person on the face of this earth. Looking back later, I realized that I had seen all the signs of decline of her health. I had been told clearly that the disease was getting the upper hand and we were losing the battle against leukemia, but I did not want her to die and I was so passionate in this desire that it completely distorted the way I perceived what was happening. So, I was the most surprised person in the world when she stopped breathing. I had not been able to make the heroic choice to adapt my desires to the actual shape of reality. When it comes to knowing the truth, desire is often a greater problem than ignorance. Eventually, we will have to adjust to reality because reality will not adjust to us. Truth is ultimately supreme.

The second episode involving Thomas took place on the night before Jesus was betrayed. Jesus was aware of the darkness that would soon engulf them, and was preparing his disciples for what was about to happen. He wanted them to know that they would need to pray and draw strength from God to get through the ordeal that was coming. He reassured them that what they saw in him was the deepest truth about God and that, in the economy of God, the worst things are never the last things. Then, he said the following words of comfort: "Do not let your hearts be troubled. Believe in God, believe also in me. In my Father's house there are many dwelling places. If it were not so, would I have told you that I go to prepare a place for you? And if I go and prepare a place for you, I will come again and will take you to myself, so that where I am, there you may be also. And you know the way to the place where I am going." It must have been an intense moment, and I imagine the disciples became very distressed as they listened to Jesus. Thomas probably broke a heavy silence when he spoke up and said, "Lord, we do not know where you are going. How can we know the way?" (John 14:1–5).

I am confident that Thomas was not the only disciple wondering what Jesus really meant, but he was the only one willing to acknowledge it. I admire Thomas for admitting his ignorance honestly: he was authentic enough to be truthful and humble enough to ask. Pride can play as much havoc with our perception of the truth as wishful thinking. If we have taken fixed and adamant positions in the past, we may be too proud to admit it, even to ourselves, when new evidence proves us wrong. Also, pride may keep us from asking for information that we need to learn new truths. I remember many situations in which I did not understand what was happening but was ashamed that I might be the only one who did not "get it," so I pretended to know what was going on. By doing this, I remained ignorant and unable to progress beyond a certain level. I remember all too vividly when a teacher at the elementary school I attended said, "Students, we are going to learn long division now." I had no idea what long division was, but it seemed to me that everybody else in the class caught on quickly. I was embarrassed and unwilling to raise my hand and risk facing the ridicule of my classmates, so I let the teacher think I had understood when I had not. Until I was forced to quit hiding my ignorance, I could proceed no further in mathematics. We are reminded in Scripture, "You do not have, because you do not ask" (James 4:2).

It is not enough to ask the right questions, however. We must also listen for answers. There was a young religious seeker who went to Burma and met with a celebrated holy man, known for his profound wisdom. The young man said to him, "I want to ask you some questions because I am in search of the ultimate." Then, the young man bombarded him with questions, interspersed with his own lengthy opinions, and he replied defensively to the holy man's answers. Finally the holy man said, "Let's break our discussion and have tea together," and so they did. When the young man extended his cup, the holy man poured until the cup was full, and kept on pouring until the tea was running over into the saucer and then on down to the floor. The young man exclaimed, "What are you doing?" The holy man answered, "I'm hoping to illustrate to you the way that you are. There is no way for you to learn anything when you are as full of yourself as you are."

Only the humility to listen attentively to what you do not know can create the space for new learning. We are indebted to Thomas for asking his question and listening for Jesus to respond, because it evoked a concise and remarkable statement of the heart of Jesus' teaching: "I am the way, and the truth, and the life. No one comes to the Father except through me. If you know me, you will know my Father also. From now on you do know him and have seen him" (John 14:6–7).

The third and most famous of Thomas's encounters with Jesus is the one that has given rise to Thomas being labeled a doubter. It took place after the resurrection. The worst had happened: Jesus had been treated as brutally as possible and crucified. Then some of the women went to tend to Jesus' corpse on Sunday morning and came back with the shocking news that the tomb was empty. Later, Mary Magdalene lingered, weeping outside the empty tomb, when Jesus appeared to her and asked her to tell his followers that he had ascended to the Father. So she went and told them about this extraordinary experience.

I can only imagine how difficult it must have been for them to wrap their minds around the idea that Jesus had been restored to life. It is difficult for me, even now, to comprehend how the wretched evil that humans had done was not enough to quench God's love for us. The disciples had to have been amazed, especially after two other followers reported that Jesus had walked with them on the road to Emmaus, and they had recognized his unique way of breaking the bread and blessing it. Then, on Easter night, Jesus appeared to the disciples, in the same upper room where they had gathered only days earlier to share their last supper before he was crucified. His risen presence let them see the wounds from the nails in his hands and the place where the spear had gone into his side. Both Luke and John record that he spoke to them and even ate a piece of fish to show that he was really alive.

For some reason, Thomas was not with the other disciples that night, but they told him the mind-boggling news that Jesus was alive and had actually been with them. Thomas could not believe their fantastic claim: "Unless I see the mark of the nails in his hands, and put my finger in the mark of the nails and my hand in his side, I will not believe" (John 20:24–25). This has led to Thomas's reputation as a skeptic and a cynic, but I want to make the case that Thomas's reaction was entirely logical and appropriate. It would not have made sense to accept, without question, the incredible assertion that the One they had watched die on the cross had come back from the dead. This was not the kind of routine occurrence that anyone would be likely to believe simply on the basis of hearsay or second-hand testimony. Before Thomas could believe such an improbable claim, he wanted the same first-hand evidence as the other disciples. After all, Peter and John reacted the same way after the women returned from the tomb and said it was empty: they did not take the women's word for it but went to see for themselves. Truth is discovered, not manufactured, and checking out evidence is basic to the process of coming to an authentic conclusion.

The disciples gathered in the upper room eight days later and, this time, Thomas was with them. When Jesus appeared before Thomas there, he did not reprimand or chastise him, but proceeded to let him see and touch for himself the nail prints in his hands and the wound where he had been pierced in his body. He gave Thomas the same compelling experience that he had given to the other disciples a week earlier. The most beautiful part of this event is that, when the evidence was shown, Thomas knelt down before Jesus and uttered those five words that New Testament scholars agree is the finest single affirmation of Christ in all of scripture: "My Lord and my God!" You won't find a more powerful expression of genuine faith, and it comes from the lips of the one who has been accused of doubting. People of true conviction will change their minds when given reason to do so. It is people of prejudice who don't want to be confused by the facts, or by evidence to the contrary of what they want to be the truth.

Many years ago, a young woman made an appointment to see me while she was home during the Christmas break from the Ivy League university she had been attending. I had known her through high school, and three generations of her family had been a part of the congregation that I was serving. I looked forward to learning how she had been, but the minute I saw her, I could tell by her body language that she had not come to exchange pleasantries. She was tense and somber, and she did not take long to get to the reason she had made the appointment: "I've come to ask you formally to remove my name from the rolls of this church, because I no longer consider myself to be a Christian."

When I asked her what had led to such a radical change, she said, "To be perfectly honest, it is a matter of conscience. I grew up believing what my parents taught me, that God created human beings. However, now that my world has widened and I have encountered other realities, I have concluded that it is the other way around. I think that human beings are the ones who have created God. People just believe what they want to believe. Faith is something that people create out of their own selfish desires, or wishful thinking, then project what they want to be true on to their screen of belief. I see faith as a game of make-believe on a grand scale, and cannot accept that religion is valid." I have no idea how that young woman expected me to react to such a devastating critique of the core beliefs to which I had dedicated my whole life. She may have wondered if I would fall in a faint or attack her angrily in return, but these charges were not new to me.

I acknowledged that the charges she leveled were some of the oldest and most persistent ever made against religious experience, and said I was curious about where she had encountered this approach to religion in college. It was honestly chilling for me to learn that these opinions were promoted in almost every academic discipline to which she had been exposed. In political science, she had learned that Karl Marx said that religion is simply the opiate of the people, used by the oppressors of society to keep the underclass down. She was taught in introductory classes on psychology that Sigmund Freud's title for his classic work on religion was "The Future of an Illusion," in which he wrote that God was an illusion "of human origin." In drama classes one of the memorable lines she had learned for a role in a play was, "Religion is a chloroform mask into which the frightened and the weak stick their faces to avoid reality." Repeatedly she had been taught that religious experience is simply wish fulfillment without validity, manufactured out of one's own whim or need.

I admitted that, although I wished I could tell her there was no truth whatsoever in what she was saying, I could not. Time and again people have constructed their beliefs out of their personal desires and bias, just as she had said. Affirming her seriousness about these important issues of faith and reality, I asked her to do three things before she made an ultimate judgment.

First, I asked her to read the Gospel of Mark in one sitting. I told her, "It is no longer than a *New Yorker* profile and should not take you more than forty-five minutes to read. As you read that shortest of the four gospels, ask yourself if Jesus comes across as a weak and fearful person making up his own concept of God to avoid reality. Or, is it closer to the truth that God allowed him to suffer trial and tribulation, rather than sparing him from it, particularly on the last night of his life? Like any human being in the midst of a dreadful crisis, Jesus poured out his heart to God and begged that somehow he might be delivered. Notice that he concluded by saying, 'Yet not what I want, but what you want.' He conceded that he would accept what this Holy One wanted, even crucifixion. Whatever else you might say about Gethsemane, this is not a religion of wish-fulfillment.

"The second thing I want you to do is read about Saul of Tarsus in the Book of Acts, and take note of how passionately he was concerned about truth. He was a devout Hebrew who became one of the most significant leaders in first century Christianity. When Saul heard there was a group of people claiming that a crucified carpenter had been raised from the dead and was actually the Messiah, he considered their claim to be an appalling affront to his Jewish religion. He used every means within his power to stamp out this heresy and destroy those who embraced such fantasy. In that frame of mind, he was on his way to Damascus when Saul experienced a numinous, overwhelming light from heaven and heard the voice of Jesus. This transcendent force broke into his consciousness powerfully and brought him to a new conclusion of overwhelming clarity.

"Then ask yourself if what Saul experienced on the road to Damascus was something that he *wanted* to be true. Do you think it represented his finest wish that he created out of his own desire? Or, is it much closer to the truth to say that he encountered something that day that was the last thing he wanted to discover, because it meant that his opponents were correct and he was very much in the wrong? It meant that he would have to dismantle everything he had believed before that time, and rebuild his life altogether. Whatever you say about that process, it does not sound like wish fulfillment, nor does Saul seem like a weak and frightened person "sticking his face in a chloroform mask." He sounds more like someone who came in contact with a reality that he did not imagine, or even want, but was honest enough to accept as truth."

Finally, I said, "The last thing that I would like you to do is sit down by yourself, with pencil in hand, and write out the details of the kind of religion that you would create if you were the one who was going to determine the shape of it. Then ask yourself if the religion of your choice corresponds at all with what you find in the New Testament. Let me tell you my answer to that question ahead of time. If I were making up a religion to suit myself, it would not have anything in it about loving my enemies. It would not say anything about denying myself or taking up my cross. It would not mention judgment or forgiving seventy times seven. The beliefs at the core of the Christian revelation are clearly not what a selfish and weak person would want. In fact, the central Christian ideals cut directly across self-interest. No, what you find in the New Testament is not even close to what I think anyone would make up out of wishful fantasy."

To her credit, she was a truth lover just like Thomas, and she did the things I requested over the months that followed. We had many conversations about her vigorous quest, and I am glad to be able to report that she did eventually come to an authentic Christian conversion. This conversion was a result of her thorough process of asking, seeking, and knocking, and it did not come easily. Her reaction to this change of heart was much like that of C. S. Lewis. When he was ten years old, he learned that his mother was dying of cancer. She had been the only warm, nurturing person in his life, and he begged God to heal her and spare her life. After she died, he concluded that there must not be a God, and his prayers had not been connected to anything. For twenty-odd years, he was an ardent atheist, trying to gather information to reinforce his confidence that there was no benevolent reality behind all things.[2]

When Lewis was in graduate school at Oxford, he met religious people whom he admired but could not understand why he admired them. He read books that raised the possibility of

---

2. Dr. Armand M. Nicholi, Jr, *The Question of God* (New York: Free Press, 2002), 46.

the Christian reality being true, and began to wonder whether his atheism may have been a matter of his own wish fulfillment. As he considered that Christianity might represent the truth, he was not hoping that it was true and fearing that it was not, but hoping it was not and fearing it was. When, in his own words, he finally "gave in", he described himself as the "most dejected and reluctant convert in all England."[3] Whatever else you say about that, it is not wish fulfillment, and Lewis's reaction to conversion was similar to that of my young friend.

When Mahatma Gandhi was Prime Minister of India, an idealistic associate was critical of him because he had changed his mind about an important issue. He said to Gandhi, "I've lost faith in your integrity because I heard you take a specific position on this policy last week, and now you are saying something very different. How can you account for that?" Gandhi answered, "It's very simple, my son; I have learned something since last week." A new piece of information had given Gandhi reason to change his mind, and we need to approach actualities beyond ourselves with the same flexibility and adaptability. Thomas did not let pride or rigidity get in the way of his staying open-minded and accepting something new. When he saw for himself what God had done in Jesus Christ, he dropped to his knees and moved to a new level of faith.

So why has Thomas gotten such bad press? I think it is because of what Jesus said after Thomas bowed before him in adoration and declared, "My Lord and my God." Jesus responded by saying, "Have you believed because you have seen me? Blessed are

---

3. Nicholi, *The Question of God*, 85.

those who have not seen and yet have come to believe" (John 20:28–29). The implication of that statement seems to be that true faith does not require evidence beyond itself. Thus, people of genuine faith are those who believe without confirmation, coming to faith without any kind of struggle or questions. In my opinion, that is a bad misreading of that passage.

On the surface, it could appear that Jesus was shaming Thomas for having to see for himself to believe, but I think Jesus was essentially pointing to the way all the apostles were going to have to encounter him in the future. He knew that his way of revealing God through his human presence would be coming to an end in a matter of days. Jesus would ascend into heaven to sit at the right hand of the Father, and come back in the form of the Holy Spirit. No longer would the disciples be able to use their five physical senses to recognize him, because his flesh would become spirit. So I don't believe Jesus was reacting unfavorably to what Thomas said, but referring to his words at their last supper when he was preparing the disciples for the changes ahead. He wanted them to know that he would be with them through the Holy Spirit, instead of a single physical entity that was limited by space and time (John 14:25–29). I think he was explaining that those who received his Holy Spirit in the future would be blessed for doing so, just as the disciples had been blessed by his physical presence. He would not be perceptible through the usual five senses but, as I understand it, through the sixth sense of faith that corresponds to the divine dimension of reality, just as our primary five senses correspond to the physical dimensions of reality.

I remember my second-grade teacher, Miss Ethel Moxley, telling me that I had an "eye gate," an "ear gate," a "nose gate," a "mouth gate," and a "skin gate." I had these five ways through which the wonder of the world could come to me and be recognized. I see color with my eyes, hear sound with ears, detect odor with my nose, taste with my tongue, and feel temperature and texture with my skin. I believe that what the eye is to color and the ear is to sound, faith is to the divine dimension of reality. It is a sixth sense that gives us the capacity to sense God through the Holy Spirit.

When holy realities make themselves known to you in ways that are profoundly authentic, you will know what Blaise Pascal meant when he said, "The heart has reasons that reason cannot know." In the movie, *Contact*, Jodie Foster plays the part of a scientist who claims she cannot accept anything without empirical proof. Yet the man of faith in the movie knows of the deep love between her and her deceased father, and he asks her how she knows that her father loved her. Love is the ideal example of a convincing reality that cannot be proven empirically. God has inscrutable ways of making himself known through faith, just as powerfully as he made himself known to Thomas. Thomas's faith remained so strong that he spent the rest of his life as a missionary to India, telling others about his Lord and God, and tradition holds that he was martyred in Chennai (Madras), where a basilica was dedicated in his name. He deserves to be remembered for his faith, more than for his doubt.

Thomas has much to teach us about how to process truth and come to authentic conclusions. He was perceptive enough to separate desire from reality, humble enough to admit when he did not know and ask to be taught, and willing to change his mind when new evidence was presented to him. Best of all, when fantastic truth broke through to him, he was willing to accept and affirm it from the depths of his being. Faith is an avenue to knowledge, not an alternative to it. Although none of us can make God appear on demand, I bid you to be as open to the great Mystery as you are to the sun in the sky, and to trust that God will be there for you in his own time and way. Most of all, when God does break through to you, I bid you to respond. How? By faith, my friends, by faith. Never set limits on what the Holy One can do. Our spiritual experiences through faith can be just as compelling as the experience of Thomas, when he bowed before the incarnate Jesus and said with the utmost conviction, "My Lord, and my God!"

Simon and Matthew
Unlikely Companions

In this chapter, I have linked together the apostles Simon and Matthew for a reason. If you read about the twelve companions of Jesus without much background knowledge, you might not notice some details that provide clues as to why these two make an intriguing pair to study together. From Scripture, we only know one thing about Simon and three things about Matthew. That is why we have to rely on Christian tradition as well as the biblical record to fill out the portraits of all twelve disciples. All that we are told about the disciple who goes by the name of Simon is that he was identified as Simon the Zealot, and some knowledge of his cultural context is needed in order to understand the significance of that affiliation.

In the time of Jesus, there were three great parties or movements that made up the texture of first-century Palestine. The Pharisees were the primary religious leaders of that time, and they had a great concern for meticulous faithfulness to the religious law. Their name comes from the Hebrew root that can mean "to separate," so they may have sought purity by separating themselves from anything unclean. Opponents of the Pharisees belonged to a second party called the Sadducees. They rejected any belief in the resurrection and were principally interested in the upholding of Temple ritual to safeguard the covenant with God. Sadducees belonged to the ruling elite, who held most of the power of government in their hands. Those who belonged to the third party were called the Zealots, and it was with this party that Simon was affiliated and identified.

The history of the Zealots is very interesting. By 1300 BC, the descendants of Abraham had come out of Egypt, wandered in the wilderness, and then entered the land that had been promised to their ancestor, Abraham. At first, they simply took little portions of that land and settled down. Thus, for the first two hundred years, they were simply another migrant refugee people who had taken root in a land to which they had moved. In time, they grew much stronger, and evolved into a coherent and powerful political state under King David. During the period between 1050 and 1000 BC, David emerged as the principal political figure in the whole Mediterranean basin, at a time when Egypt, Syria, and Babylon were all weak. Israel came to its political zenith under David, and they relished what it meant to be the rulers from the Nile to the Euphrates. However, political supremacy was never the role that God intended for his "chosen" descendants of Abraham. This problem is found throughout the Old Testament, for the Hebrew people always dreamed that being "chosen" meant being on top of the heap and powerful, rather than being witnesses to God's mercy and love.

After the time of King David, the political fortunes of the Jews declined. In 721 BC the northern portion of the kingdom was taken over by the Assyrians, and about 150 years later, in 586 BC, the Babylonians completely defeated the southern kingdom. Then, for the very long period from 586 BC until AD 1948, spanning from nearly six centuries before Jesus was born until after some of you reading this had been born, the Jewish people did not regain political control of the land that had been promised to Abraham. My understanding of their role in history was that it was not destined to be politically dominant, but that was something with which they could never come to terms. They never learned how to be good subjects of the rule of other people, and after 586 BC, they resented increasingly those who came to rule them, remaining rebellious and difficult to govern.

In the second century BC, the Syrian kingdom came to ascendancy, and there were some particularly cruel kings called the Seleucid kings. There was one named Antiochus IV Epiphanes, who particularly loathed the Jewish people. He despised their religious fanaticism and hated especially that they would not eat meat from pigs, would not accept any kind of graven images, and would not work on the seventh day or Sabbath. So he did everything in his power to antagonize them, including erecting a pagan altar to Zeus over the altar of Yahweh and having a pig sacrificed on the main altar of the Jerusalem Temple in 168 BC. These were egregious affronts to Hebrew tradition. Antiochus was flagrant and abrasive in the ways that he showed his contempt, and his extremism evoked violence in response. All Jews who would not renounce their religious faith and accept the Greek idols and forms of worship were murdered on the spot.

Observing the Sabbath and circumcision were forbidden on penalty of death.

Jewish resistance was centered in the Hasmonean royal family, which included Mattathias ben Yochanan and his five sons— all priests who ministered at Jerusalem in the Temple. They are better known as the Maccabees, and they organized a guerrilla-type army. As their father was dying, he said to his sons, "Be zealous, with the law, and do not hesitate to give your life for the holy cause," fostering in them an attitude that prompted the beginning of the Zealot movement. Upon the death of Mattathias, Judas called Maccabeus ("hammerlike") led this army to recapture the Jerusalem Temple, and the Hasmonean dynasty ruled Palestine from approximately 135 to 37 BC, ordaining the annual Festival of Hanukkah to commemorate their dedication of the Temple.

In 63 BC Rome took over Palestine and throughout Jesus' lifetime the Zealots were one of the most extreme of all the patriotic movements of that day. They represented the most radical right wing of their time, and their fanaticism for Israel led them to become urban terrorists, known as "the assassins." They carried knives under their cloaks, and they would take pleasure in plunging them into the backs of Roman soldiers. Their hostility expanded to include any Jewish person who had the slightest kind of friendly relationship with the Romans. Thus, more than anyone else, the Zealots were the ones who were responsible for the Romans concluding that they had no choice but to use force to settle their Jewish problem, once and for all.

There is an old Yiddish saying: "When the chicken challenges the elephant to a fight, the chicken had better be agile." In other words, if a small amount of strength provokes a huge amount of power, it is likely to be bad for the chicken, as it was for the Jews in this case. In AD 70, the Romans besieged Jerusalem and completely surrounded the city. They cut off the Jews from all supplies of food and, when the Jews were weakened, the Romans burned the temple and sacked the city. All that had come from the great legacy of David's period was leveled to the ground, and the Zealots were largely responsible for having provoked this destructive anger from the Romans. The Zealots had the fanatical idea that the end justified the means, and they would stop at nothing to further their cause.

All we know about Simon was that he was a member of that particular party, but we can infer from that information that he burned with zeal for something that he considered to be a positive ideal, had the capacity for radicalism, and was willing to do nearly anything to promote his particular goals. Therefore it is ironic that he is linked with Matthew, Jesus' disciple who stood at the extreme opposite end of the temperamental and ideological spectrum. Matthew was a Jew who worked for Rome, which meant that he had chosen to collaborate with the occupation forces. It is thought that he held the post of tax collector at Capernaum, a village close to Nazareth, where Jesus made his first headquarters. It is located at the northern end of the Sea of Galilee, on the great trade route that goes from Damascus in the east to the Mediterranean in the west. It was Matthew's job to collect taxes at that very important crossroads, and he collected those taxes on what was fished out of the sea and on what was exported and imported, too.

In that time, Roman bureaucrats in Palestine were especially on the lookout for people like Matthew. The Romans were wise colonialists, who were not interested in humiliating the people they had conquered. They were very tolerant of local customs and typically did not try to stamp out particular religious beliefs. They wanted simply to establish control and enable peace to exist around the Mediterranean basin. One of their strategies for accomplishing these goals was to recruit local citizens who had the kind of pragmatism that made them willing to work with them. Instead of sending Roman citizens to establish rule over foreign colonists, the Romans recruited the locals to set up a kind of franchise, in which they paid the Romans a certain amount for the right to collect taxes. Roman authorities gave these local tax collectors the added incentive of having the right to keep whatever they collected over and above what they were required to send to Rome.

It seems clear that most Roman rulers preferred for these locally recruited tax collectors to be reasonable and moderate. The Romans were well known for the sense of equality that was employed in their system of law and justice, and they did not like extremists working for them. However, it was very hard to police the thousands of locally recruited officials that were required to do the ongoing business of Rome, so you can understand how this system might have lent itself to abuse. The Jews who decided to work for the Romans would often use their power to exploit the people. Thus, they were considered the worst of all traitors by their fellow citizens, who felt they had sold out their national heritage by working for the occupation forces. They were viewed as criminals, also, because they would frequently charge exorbitant taxes. Worse yet, when someone could not pay these excessive taxes, tax collectors would offer to lend them the money in order to profit in two ways. They were adding insult to injury by not only exacting high taxes, but also charging interest on loans to pay them, which was forbidden in Jewish law.

From this you can imagine how Simon would have loathed Matthew and wanted nothing to do with him before Jesus came along, because Matthew was exactly the kind of person that Zealots regarded as the scum of the earth. It is easy to imagine that Simon would have gladly killed Matthew with his little curved knife before Jesus came into his life. Similarly, Matthew would have looked on Simon as a hopeless idealist who did not understand the limitations of his situation. Matthew might have expressed himself to Simon this way: "Look, in order to get along, you have to go along. We can do only so much, and I am just going to make a better place for myself in the world as it is. Forget about any impractical ideas of trying to change the world." The two apostles were as different as they could possibly be, both temperamentally and ideologically. They would have had an enormous conflict of personalities and beliefs before they met Jesus. I dare say that, in all probability, neither one of them could have been lured to stay peaceably in the same room with the other because they were so far apart in the way that they viewed reality and in what they were willing to do as a result of their convictions.

Some of you may be familiar with the Jewish playwright Herb Gardner, who wrote a play called *A Thousand Clowns* that ran on Broadway for years and was eventually made into a movie, too. The story involves two brothers who remind me somewhat of Simon and Matthew. One of the brothers, Murray, is an idealist. He was not fanatical like Simon, but he trusted his own intuition more than the conventional rules of the establishment. His brother, Arnold, had sold his soul to the culture, giving up everything else in order to make $30,000 a year, working for an ad agency. One night in their father's basement, they had a terrible confrontation. Arnold said, "Murray, you have to understand that I am willing to deal with the available world as it is. I don't choose to shake it up, but to live with it. I know there are people who spill things and people who get spilled on but, Murray, I choose not to notice the stain. After all, I have a wife and children and, as the saying goes, business is business. So I lie a little, cheat a little, peddle a little, play the game, talk the talk, and stay with things as they are. I guess I'm lucky I have the talent of surrender."[1] Like Arnold, Matthew was willing to simply accept things the way they are and get the most out of a situation without trying to change it. He didn't notice the stains or make any waves. He was a pragmatic realist, and he probably felt contempt for what he thought were Simon's "pie-in-the-sky" goals. In stark contrast, Simon, the idealist, always had his pack on, laboring tirelessly to change things for which he considered the struggle worthwhile.

The miracle in this situation was that Jesus had reached out so far in opposite directions with those gracious hands, grasping

---

1. Herb Gardner, *A Thousand Clowns: A Comedy in Three Acts*, (London, New York, Hollywood, Toronto: Samuel French Inc, 1962).

the hand of Simon the Zealot on one side and the hand of Matthew the tax collector on the other. It is even more astonishing that Jesus wanted two such radically different people to be his close companions, and it illustrates how all encompassing his love was. Something in Jesus drew both of these dissimilar human beings to him. I believe that Jesus offered these opposites a glimpse of the kind of unconditional acceptance and wholeness that gave them a completely new understanding of what it means to be fully human. It was the gift of Jesus to make it possible for people as different as Simon and Matthew to get to know each other, thereby helping one another toward more wholeness and balance.

Simon represented those who were willing to do everything possible to make the changes he thought were necessary, while Matthew represented those who were complacent and willing to "go along to get along." Both of these approaches are a part of the truth, and being made in the image of God means using appropriately both capacities to let things happen and to make things happen. Neither condemnation nor complacency evokes creative vitality. What is remarkable is that Jesus was able to reach out and bring these two together as companions, giving Simon the opportunity to learn more practicality and Matthew the chance to get in touch with more creative energy. In a profound sense, Jesus knew that these two utterly different people needed each other: Simon needed some of the realism that Matthew represented, and Matthew needed some of Simon's idealism.

Jesus said that we are to love our enemies and pray for those that are against us, and these concepts are shockingly difficult for most people to embrace. Yet, as children of God, we are all more connected and more alike than most of us understand. Jesus understood that we humans need the kind of mutual influence and understanding that can come only from reaching across the chasm of "otherness" between people that seem utterly different like Simon and Matthew. Only the spirit of mutual understanding can lead to lasting solutions or wholeness, and only such broadening acceptance can make it possible for us to grow into the fullness of what it means to be made in the image of God.

Apart from the gospel records, legend is vague about Simon, saying that he preached in Egypt, Africa, and Britain. It is said that he is mentioned in *The Apostolic History of Abdias* as having ended his ministry in Persia, where he died a martyr. Legends about Matthew's life and death are even more vague. Since he is mentioned twice by name in the gospel of Matthew (whereas in both Mark and Luke, the tax collector is called Levi), Matthew has traditionally been called the author of this gospel. Although Matthew may have been active in the community where this gospel first originated, scholars now doubt that he actually wrote it. Still, it is appealing to think that because he was accustomed to keeping written records when he was a tax collector, Matthew may have been the first one to record the teachings of Jesus.

Thaddaeus
Three Names and One Question

We know very little about Thaddaeus and we are not even sure what name to call him. St. Jerome, who translated the Bible into Latin during the late fourth and early fifth centuries, called him "Trinomius," which means "a man with three names." In the gospel according to Mark, he is known as Thaddaeus, and that is the name by which he has been best known in church history. In some translations of Matthew's gospel he is known as Lebbaeus, whose surname is Thaddaeus. In lists of the disciples in Luke and Acts, he is called Judas son of James. John has no list of the twelve disciples in his gospel, but during Jesus' farewell discourse to his followers one of them is identified as "Judas (not Iscariot)" who asks, "Lord, how is it that you will reveal yourself to us, and not to the world?" What do you think is the significance of this? I should point out that it was not unusual for a person to have three names in that time, just as it is not unusual now for babies to be given as many as four. So it is possible that this man's full name was Judas Lebbaeus Thaddaeus, and that he was properly known by all three of those names[1]

But I think it is more likely that there were other reasons for him being identified so inconsistently. It is quite possible that he was called Judas in the early years of his life but in later years preferred Thaddaeus to avoid being confused with Judas Iscariot, who was infamous and reviled for betraying Jesus. After Jesus was crucified, he might even have gotten in the habit of saying "I am not Iscariot" whenever he identified himself as Judas, then decided it was easier to introduce himself simply as Thaddaeus, because he was tired of having to explain. Since he had the same first name as Judas Iscariot, furthermore, Thaddaeus became the patron saint of lost causes and desperate situations in the Roman Catholic tradition. He is also called "the forgotten saint" because people who prayed through the saints were afraid to invoke the name Judas and would appeal to all the other saints first, thus making Judas Thaddaeus the saint of last resort.

My southern family considered names very important, and the value of bringing honor to the family name and avoiding shame was a powerful dynamic that was emphasized to me by my parents from the time I was a young child. I imagine that many people throughout the world share a similar heritage, in which there is a high regard for family names and how they acquire special significance. My maternal grandmother's family name was Berry, slave-holders who had owned a large plantation in northern Mississippi. One of the tragedies of her family

---

1. Mark 3:18; Matthew 10:3; Luke 6:16; Acts 1:13; John 14:22.

was that, when the slaves left after the Civil War, my grand-mother's father did not have the foggiest notion what to do to keep the plantation going. He knew how to entertain beautifully, dress elegantly, ride around on his horse and be gracious, but he and the whole Berry family had depended on slaves for nearly everything that was essential—as did many other southern families. The tragedy of slavery is not only does it dehumanize slaves and reduce them to objects, but also makes slave owners relatively useless and dependent. My grandmother's family had not learned how to do even the most basic tasks of life because they counted on slaves to do whatever was needed. Eventually, they lost their family home because they could not pay taxes, which meant that all my grandmother had left was the memory of the grandeur of that former life style and her pride in her family name.

My mother was born in 1890, and she actually remembered her mother telling her stories about her life before, and after, the Civil War. I suppose that is the reason she would say to me whenever I was getting ready to leave home, "Now, remember who you are, what your name stands for, and always bring honor to the family name." Names are certainly not everything about a person, but the way you live your life definitely affects the way others react to your name. The names we choose for our children are usually determined by our reactions to people with whom we have associated those names in the past. For that reason, the betrayal of Jesus by Judas may well have caused Thaddaeus to stop using that part of his name.

It has been said that the Macedonian Conqueror, Alexander the Great, inspired his soldiers with his enthusiasm, but was known to be a very strict disciplinarian, also. On one of his campaigns, a soldier had been given the responsibility of being the watchman through the night, on an outlying perimeter. Without any other means of communication in those days, armies depended heavily on the soldiers who were given the responsibility to keep guard, and nighttime was an especially vulnerable time for an enemy to attack. When this particular soldier was found asleep at his post, his lapse was considered such a serious betrayal of trust that he was brought to Alexander himself, and the nature of his crime was stated. Alexander was on his horse, looking down at the soldier when he asked, "What is your name soldier?" The man answered in a weak voice, "My name is Alexander." Alexander the Great then stated more forcefully, "I said, what is your name?" When the soldier repeated, "My name is Alexander," the story goes that the great general leaned down and slapped this soldier across the face with the back of his hand, knocking him to the ground before he warned him with controlled rage, "Listen soldier, either change your name or change the way you're living!" Even the illustrious Alexander the Great was sensitive to the possibility of having his name dishonored.

In a similar way, there is a sobering challenge inherent in calling ourselves Christian, for nothing can be more powerfully subversive to the spread of the Christian gospel than for people to call themselves Christian without being serious about the way they live up to that ideal. The famous preacher George Buttrick often said, "Some people live the life and don't wear the badge, while other people wear the badge but don't live the life." Of course, the ideal is to "live the life" if you "wear the badge," behaving in congruence with the values you claim. It is more important to be a living example of your faith than to be always talking about it. While the hypocrisy of others is no excuse to neglect one's own spiritual life, the truth is that there are many people who have been turned off by the whole Christian enterprise because of somebody wearing the guise of a Christian without a sincere commitment to living honorably and lovingly.

While Thaddaeus the disciple may have stopped calling himself Judas because he felt that Judas Iscariot had tarnished his first name, there is also the possibility that he changed his name to represent a genuine transformation in his own life. Taking a new name to acknowledge that something significant has happened is a time-honored tradition that is mentioned throughout the Bible. You may remember the Old Testament story of Jacob wrestling with the angel of God all night long, struggling with the unfinished business of his past. After the two had wrestled and Jacob had been blessed, as the angel was leaving Jacob he said, "You shall no longer be called Esau ["the supplanter," who tricked his brother out of his birthright] but Israel, for you have striven with God and with humans, and have prevailed" (Genesis 32:28). Jacob was given a new name to symbolize that a change of great consequence had taken place in his life. Similarly, Saul of Tarsus became known as Paul after his incredible encounter with the risen Christ, which transformed him from a persecutor of the gentiles to a devoted Christian apostle and, eventually, a prominent leader of the very same people that he had tried to destroy before his conversion. Likewise, Judas "not Iscariot," may have become known as Thaddaeus to call attention to the dramatic changes that had occurred through his relationship and experiences with Jesus.

When the disciples are listed in the gospels, the names of Peter, James, and John are always the first three and the same four always come last: Thaddaeus, Judas Iscariot, James the son of Alpheus, and Simon, who is identified as a Zealot. It has been suggested that these four were grouped together last because all of them were associated with the Zealots. It is interesting to note that at least a third of the men that Jesus attracted seemed to have had some connection with this party, coming to Jesus with a passionate nationalism as part of their background. This would mean that Thaddaeus probably had a strong desire for Jesus to share the goal of reestablishing Israel as the national power over the whole Mediterranean basin. The great hero of the Zealots was King David, under whom Jerusalem became the capital of the known world for a relatively short period. The Zealots believed that being the chosen people of God meant that they were to be the rulers of the rest of humanity.

There is only one time that Thaddaeus is quoted in Scripture, and it was to ask Jesus a question on the night before he was crucified. As a Zealot, his idea of Messiah would have called for Jesus to make a public demonstration of power and mount a full-scale campaign to demand loyalty. He must have realized that they were running out of time for that as he asked, "Lord, how is it that you will reveal yourself to us, and not to the world?" Jesus answered, "Those who love me will keep my word, and my Father will love them, and we will come to them and make our home with them" (John 14:22–23). William Barclay wrote, "Jesus was telling Thaddaeus that the only loyalty that was of any use to him was the loyalty of the loving heart and the surrendered life. . . . The way of power can never be a substitute for the way of love."[2] Jesus' response was a summary of his highest principle, the principle of love. Love is never coercive, and people cannot be forced into discipleship. We will do what Jesus taught only if we love him.

Jesus was probably challenged most vigorously by those who wanted to exercise power through force rather than save the world through nonviolent love. The dream of the Zealots was to have power over others, while Jesus had a very different vision of what is of ultimate value and he taught that love is the essence of reality. There may not be any other question more basic or profound: which is of greater consequence, exercising power coercively or raising the whole creation to higher levels through the nurturing reality of love? I imagine that Jesus had intense conversations with these four passionate disciples about this foundational choice between power and love.

In book five of Fyodor Dostoevsky's novel, *The Brothers Karamazov*, Dimitri tells his brother the story of the Grand Inquisitor as a way of searching out the ultimate difference between these two ways of looking at life. The scene is set in Spain during the sixteenth century, when the power of the Roman Catholic Inquisition was at its height. In this fantasy, Jesus reappeared in the Great Square outside of the Cathedral of Seville. He did not say anything, but he radiated the same kind of love that flowed through him in Galilee and excited the common people

---

2. William Barclay, *The Master's Men* (Nashville: Abingdon, 1959), 120.

as he healed and helped others. Frenzy stirred among the crowd in the cathedral square as word spread that Jesus had returned. When the Cardinal Grand Inquisitor of Seville happened to come through the square, he saw immediately what was happening. Instead of falling on his knees to welcome the return of his Lord, as you might expect a holy man to do, he gave the guards the order to arrest Jesus and put him in prison. The people in the crowd fell back in fear because they were used to being cowed by this man's intimidating and unquestioned authority.

The Inquisitor went to Jesus in the prison cell that night, just the two of them, face-to-face. What follows is one of the most profound critiques of the ultimate difference between power and love that I have ever read. He asked Jesus, "Why have you come back to hinder us? Why have you come back to impede what we're trying to do? You were totally wrong in your understanding of human nature. You thought human beings were sons and daughters of God, capable of sharing with God in all of his wonder, but the truth is that human beings are simply slaves and children who need to be controlled. What you did not realize is that human beings cannot be free and be happy at the same time, because they want somebody to provide for them and tell them what to do. They look for some authority to take over the burden of running of their lives. When you take the controls off of them, corruption rises to the surface. Only anarchy and destruction result from setting the masses free. Nothing is more untenable than this notion of yours that freedom is a high human virtue.

"Where you made your great mistake, Jesus, was there in the wilderness after your baptism. Do you remember how the spirit of this world came to you and tried to show you what works in this kind of world? He told you that human beings have three needs, and three needs only. They need to be fed, mystified, and dominated. He suggested that you turn the stones into bread and fill people's stomachs, explaining that if you had done that, they would have followed you anywhere because they are little more than mouths and stomachs. He suggested that you jump off the pinnacle of the temple and dazzle everyone with something spectacular, because people long to be mystified and entertained. They want excuses to believe that they can't understand things, so it seems perfectly fine to turn everything over to somebody else and just stand like sheep in a blizzard. He offered you Caesar's mantle of power and handed you a sword, because people want to be dominated.

"You, in your foolishness, said that men do not live by bread alone. You had the audacity to believe humans can think for themselves and should not be manipulated like objects moved around a board, because they have more worth and dignity than to be treated that way. Well, we have taken those gifts that you refused in the wilderness, and we are willing to conquer this world and rule others as they wish. You didn't love people realistically, Jesus. You expected too much, but we know how they are and we will not let you hinder us or interfere with what we are doing."

Jesus never speaks a single word in this whole episode. When the Inquisitor fell silent, he waited some time for the prisoner to reply. The old man would have liked Jesus to say something, even something bitter or terrible. But suddenly he approaches the old man in silence, takes his head in his hands, and gently kisses him on his lips. That was his answer. The Inquisitor leads Jesus out into the dark alleys of the town and tells him to come no more.

That is the whole answer. By returning good for evil, Jesus seems to say, "I have heard this all before and, while I don't agree with you, neither do I reject you or give you the power to make me less loving." I believe this fantasy clearly presents our most profound human choice, in striking contrast. Love does have power, but power is not love's greatest concern. Love does not take freedom away, but uses power without abusing it. Love is forever working to nurture and lift creation to higher dimensions of wholeness. The great difference between the way the Grand Inquisitor and Jesus viewed human nature was that, although Jesus recognized we do need others to make decisions and provide for us when we are young, he also trusted that there is much more to our human potential beyond our early stages of development.

Expectations are crucial. We humans develop best when we are affirmed, encouraged, and given a sense of our best possibilities. This is how Jesus related to others, especially his twelve closest disciples. He accepted them honestly as they were, but also told them they had more to offer. For example, he told Simon, "You have been fishing for fish, but you have it in you to become a fisher of men." He said to Matthew, "You have been keeping records of the taxes people pay, but you can begin to keep records of what I teach." Jesus was realistic, but the ideal of what we can become was part of his realism. He did not expect too much of people. His hopeful vision enabled them to believe they had it in them to be, and do, grand and wonderful things. The way love does its work is more powerful and unexpected than brute force could ever be.

At the last supper Thaddaeus seemed to have one burning question for Jesus, perhaps to challenge his strategy, or from genuine confusion and the humility of one who sincerely wanted to understand. It appears that he did finally come to understand the answer Jesus gave him because, according to Christian legend, Thaddaeus spent the rest of his life preaching the gospel in Judea, Samaria, Idumaea, Syria, Mesopotamia, and Libya. A lovely legend has been passed on that Thaddaeus also brought about a miraculous healing for King Apgarus of Edessa, in Mesopotamia, which resulted in the king's conversion to Christianity. He is said to have suffered martyrdom in Syria in about AD 65 together with the apostle Simon the Zealot, after years devoted to bringing others to Jesus. The power of Jesus' love transformed his disciple, Thaddaeus, and it is still redeeming us.

Judas
The Traitor

The Bible is very truthful about our human situation, containing not only the positive stories of heroism but also the sullied records of those who used their gift of freedom in destructive ways that were contrary to the spirit of God. That is one reason why Scripture includes the story of Judas Iscariot, the disciple who is recognized widely as the most notorious symbol of betrayal in the Bible. We can learn from both the failures and successes of others. Thus, I look for ways that the story of Judas Iscariot offers wisdom for the living of our own lives.

Failure is always a human possibility. We humans live in the midst of a battlefield of contending forces, and we would be naive to reckon only with the power of goodness and to underestimate the power of evil. The story of Judas serves as a warning regarding the consequences of disappointment and failure, which live on in the shame and disgrace of his reputation. We do not find churches named Saint Judas, nor children who have been named Judas, in his honor. Before the treachery of Judas Iscariot was known, "Judas" was a favorite name that means "praise to God." Judas Iscariot had been given an honorable name, which he defiled with his infamous treachery and disgrace. As far as his last name is concerned, scholars tend to think that "Iscariot" identified that Judas and his father, Simon Iscariot, came from Kerioth, a city in Southern Judea.

It is difficult to find objective facts about Judas, because the only records we have of him were written after his betrayal led to the death of Jesus: "Then one of the twelve, who was called Judas Iscariot, went to the chief priests and said, 'What will you give me if I betray him to you?'" (Matt 26:14–16). The early Christian community was so deeply offended by what he had done, that Judas was judged and described thereafter in extremely harsh and negative terms. For example, he is called "a thief" in the Gospel of John, but keep in mind that John wrote about Judas seventy years after he betrayed Jesus (John 12:4–6). No other gospel writers record any doubts about his integrity or how he handled their money. He must have been considered capable and honest during the period that he was trusted to be their treasurer. Furthermore, it is likely that if any of the disciples had suspected that Judas was disloyal, they would have confronted him and done whatever was necessary to prevent him from doing any harm to Jesus. We know little about the major portion of Judas's life, while he seemed to be blending in as an accepted comrade. He is remembered almost exclusively for the appalling thing he did in the last days of his life. In the Gospel of Luke, he is accused of being possessed by Satan when he went to betray Jesus to the chief priests and officers. (Luke 22:3) Yet,

Jesus told the disciples that one of them would betray him only a short time earlier, and none of them seemed to suspect Judas as the one likely to do it. To the contrary, they "became greatly distressed and began to say to him one after another, 'Surely not I, Lord?'" (Matthew 26:20–22). Judas must have hidden his hypocrisy and traitorous nature well in the three years that the disciples did nearly everything together, for he fooled everyone but Jesus to the very end. However, in hindsight, his reputation makes it difficult to suspend judgment long enough to recall that Jesus would not have chosen Judas to be one of his disciples, if he had not believed initially that Judas was brimming with good promise and potential. He must have been the greatest disappointment of all to Jesus, because Judas might have become one of the great apostles of history, if he had allowed the grace of God to work through him. Why, then, did he betray Jesus?

Many people embrace the Calvinistic notion that everything has been pre-ordained. They think that Judas had no choice but to play out a part that had been designated to him beforehand. Calvin believed that everything was determined from the beginning of time, including the destiny of the unborn, for generations to come. The commentator William Barclay did not agree that God condemned Judas in advance. He wrote, "We cannot and dare not say that Jesus chose Judas in order that he might betray him, nor can we say that Jesus chose Judas knowing that he would betray him. Such an idea would be little short of blasphemy, for it would mean nothing less than that Jesus deliberately placed a man in a position where deadly sin was inevitable."[1]

---

1. William Barclay, *The Master's Men*, 79.

Gaston Foote agreed, adding, "I do not believe Judas betrayed his Lord simply to fulfill scripture that prophesied betrayal. John so indicates when he records the story of the betrayal: 'I know whom I have chosen; it is that the scripture may be fulfilled, . . . He who ate my bread has lifted his heel against me.' However, the Gospel of John was written two full generations after the scene of betrayal. Can God in justice ever rob a man of freedom of choice? If God predestined Judas to betray, he would have robbed him of a fighting chance at salvation. . . . God selects no scapegoats."[2] I have always wondered why clergy who believe in predestination preach sermons to influence others if they really believe that our human choices in life have already been made for us.

As I understand Holy Scripture, I cannot accept that predestination is the deepest truth, nor do I agree that Judas was bound to betray Jesus. If everything has already been "rigged," and we humans have no freedom to alter a script that has been foreordained, then why would Jesus have lamented over Jerusalem and said, "Jerusalem, Jerusalem, the city that kills the prophets and stones those who are sent to it! How often have I desired to gather your children together as a hen gathers her brood under her wings, and you were not willing!" (Matthew 23:37). It is tempting to relinquish personal responsibility for life and blame it on a predetermined fate, but it makes more sense to me that Judas did not become the admirable person he could have been because he abused God's gift of freedom. The French philoso-

---

2. Gaston Foote, *The Transformation of the Twelve* (Nashville: Abingdon, 1958), 115.

pher Simone Weil said, "Creation was that moment when God ceased to be everything, so that we could become something." As an inherent part of the reason for creation, God limited his own power in order for us to know the wonder of being made in his image.

Paul Tillich claimed that he began his own philosophic and religious journey as an adolescent, when someone posed the question to him, "Why something, and not nothing?" Why does anything exist at all? My answer to this question comes from my grasp of the whole sweep of the biblical story. I believe that, in the time before time, in the world beyond this world, when there was nothing but God, something momentous happened. The Holy One became the Generous One, instead of keeping the joy of aliveness for himself. The Holy One created, not because of any need, but out of desire for others to know the ecstasy of being. According to the book of Genesis, God's generosity is the primal reason that anything came into being out of nothing. In one sense creation was profoundly unnecessary. There was no lack in God that creation was to fill. Creation resulted from God's overflowing abundance and desire to share. God's nature is love, and love is not coercive. Thus, we creatures had to have a certain measure of freedom in order to experience God's personal kind of delight. We are divinely empowered, but the same freedom that can be our highest glory can be our greatest peril, too. God took an enormous risk in allowing us to know his kind of existence, because to be genuinely free means we are able to use our power in ways that God did not intend. We are free to behave selfishly and destructively, instead of generously and creatively, but I think God was willing to run that risk to afford us the wondrous possibilities of being. I believe that Judas did not become the saint he could have been because he made choices that were contrary to God's purposes. He used his freedom in the service of destruction, instead of blessing.

We humans have long questioned what causes people with similar backgrounds to react quite differently to similar circumstances. The famous preacher George Buttrick asked why the same sunshine melts wax, but hardens clay, and Oscar Wilde wrote the popular couplet: "Two humans looked through the self-same bars. One saw mud and the other saw stars." Two people looked at an identical scene, but one pair of eyes gravitated down to the grime and the dirt that was there, while the other pair of eyes looked up to the sublime and the celestial. We may never understand such a choice, or why Judas Iscariot used his freedom as he did. I once heard a preacher say, "God votes for you, the devil votes against you, and you get to cast the deciding vote." That is a simplistic and dramatic way of putting it, but it does make the point. Judas had tremendous potential at the time Jesus chose him, but he chose not to fulfill it. That choice was not a monument to predestination, but to the mystery and power of human freedom.

There has always been a lot of speculation as to why Judas betrayed Jesus, after sharing life intimately with him and the other disciples for nearly three years. The most obvious answer is that he did it for the money, and he may well have chosen monetary gain over friendship. There are all too many people whose greed has led them to do dreadful things for money.

However, I do not believe that Judas betrayed Jesus for money because, if he had been that materialistic, he would not have been attracted to spend time with Jesus in the first place. If the focus of Judas had been getting ahead materially, he would not have been willing to live the simple, mendicant life of Jesus and the other disciples. Thirty pieces of silver was not enough to convince me that Judas's motive was financial; in the book of Exodus, it was the price of a slave. If money had been his driving force, he could have held out for a good deal more. The Jewish establishment was extremely anxious to get to Jesus in a way that did not cause a stir, before others realized what was happening. They would have paid Judas much more for the valuable secret as to where they could seize Jesus quietly, if it had been the money that mattered to Judas. I do not believe he was motivated by greed.

Another possibility is that Judas panicked when he saw how quickly the tide turned after the crowd's adulation of Jesus on Palm Sunday, and he realized the grim determination of the authorities to put him away. He could have seen he was clearly on the losing side and jumped ship to keep from being harmed along with Jesus. Fear has the power to dehumanize those in its grip, and any humane tendencies Judas had may have evaporated as he focused only on saving his own skin. The problem with that explanation is that, even if fear and panic had overwhelmed him, he did not have to betray Jesus. He could have easily slipped away, dropped out of sight, severed his ties with Jesus to cut his losses, and disappeared until the furor had subsided. My own opinion as to why Judas betrayed Jesus is admittedly speculation, but I believe the choices Judas made were acts of willfulness that represented the culmination of forces that had been at work in him for a long time before he ever met Jesus.

Judas had been deeply influenced by the Zealots, a movement determined to drive out the forces occupying the land that had been given to Abraham and their Hebrew forebears. They yearned for the grandeur of the days when King David held the power over the Mediterranean Basin, and they dreamed of a time when Jerusalem would become the preeminent political center of that region again. The Zealot movement was a vibrant one and it captured the enthusiasm of some of the most idealistic Jews of the first century. Judas was the only disciple from Judea, which was a hotbed of Zealot enthusiasm, and my hunch is that he was attracted to Jesus because he saw that his extraordinary charisma and influence could be of enormous help in persuading others to combine forces to oust the ruling Romans. Judas could well have joined Jesus for the purpose of using him as a means to his own end, instead of allowing Jesus to shape the ends for which he was to live.

I envision Judas and Jesus having spirited discussions about what it meant to be a true descendant of Abraham, and that Jesus might have said, " Your focus is too small, Judas. The main problem is not that the Romans are here. The real problem is that we humans no longer trust the One who created us. I am much more interested in restoring human trust in God than in throwing out the Romans. As heirs of the covenant, our calling is to witness to God's goodness and be a source of blessing to all the "families of the earth" (Genesis 12:2–3). Driving out the

Romans with the same kind of force and domination that we have suffered from them is not a worthy cause. That is not what it means to be a true son of Abraham."

The trouble with political revolutions is that they are always "revolving": when the people on the bottom have had enough and decide to throw out the people on the top, they are usually willing to resort to anything to achieve their goal. By the time they reach the top, they are likely to have taken on the same qualities that they initially detested, and have become like their former oppressors. The subtle seduction of evil is that it gets us to imitate the very things that we abhor, and to use its own coercive methodology in trying to defeat it. The Quakers have a profound saying: "If, in order to defeat the beast, one becomes a beast, then bestiality has won." Using unjust methods to oust unjust powers simply leaves us without any justice. Jesus was more interested in correcting the injustice of the whole situation, than in simply changing the faces at the top and at the bottom.

Unfortunately, Judas was too determined to have his own way to learn from Jesus. At the core of most evil and wrongdoing is the desire to be God, rather than to serve God. Those whose grandiosity leads them to believe they could handle being in control, are not willing to accept the reality of their human limits. Judas would not let new truth break through to his consciousness. He was narcissistically defended in ways that kept him from seeing anything but his own point of view. When people believe that their way of perceiving reality is the only way, they are figuratively living in a house of mirrors. It is as if they are driving around in a car with the interior lights on, so that their own reflections prevent them from seeing the real world outside the car. In a similar way, Judas may have been so committed to his Zealot ideals, that he could not perceive the greater truth Jesus taught.

If this were actually the case, Judas would have been increasingly frustrated by the ideal opportunities Jesus missed to gather support for starting a revolution against Rome. One day, they encountered more than five thousand people out in the wilderness, whom Jesus helped miraculously to feed. There is speculation that this was a group of Zealots, and they became so ecstatic in response to Jesus, that they wanted to take him by force and make him their king right away, but Jesus showed no interest in that prospect whatsoever. Judas must have been dismayed when Jesus walked away from that chance to rally the crowd to rise up against the Romans and went to pray by himself, instead (John 6:1–15). Then on the last Sunday of his life, as all four gospels record, the whole town exploded in affection when he entered Jerusalem. People shouted hosannas and covered the streets with their garments and branches, while Judas probably thought, "Now is the time to begin the revolution, Jesus! This is the moment to call forth all this energy on behalf of liberating the Holy Land!"

On the evening of that first Palm Sunday, Judas had to be distraught that Jesus would not lift a finger for a military revolution. My theory is that, in sheer desperation, Judas decided to back Jesus into a corner to force him to retaliate. He caused Jesus to be handed over to the Romans, with full confidence that he would be compelled to use his charisma and influence for the Zealot cause, because his Jewish blood would rise to resist the power of Roman conquerors. I do not think that Judas meant for Jesus to be crucified. I believe that he was so intent on his own goals that he used a manipulative ploy to try to bend the will of Jesus, and his plan failed miserably. Even if Judas did not want Jesus to be killed, there was cause for him to be resentful of Jesus.

As the only disciple from Judea, Judas may have always felt he was an outsider, and he may have taken particular exception to being excluded from the inner circle of Jesus, since he did hold the position as treasurer. Then, when Mary washed the feet of Jesus with expensive perfume, Judas protested that the cost of the perfume should have gone to the poor. Whether or not Jesus believed in his sincerity, he rebuked Judas sternly and Judas may have held a grudge afterward. He may have even come to resent Jesus. In the final analysis, Judas remained too worldly to embrace the spirituality of Jesus. He rejected the divine authority of Christ completely, and he did so after years of hearing Jesus teach, watching him heal, and living with him in close relationship. The crux of the matter seems to me that Judas betrayed Jesus because he would not do what Judas wanted. Judas's willful attitude was the opposite of the attitude of Jesus in the Garden of Gethsemane, where Jesus made it clear that he had his own strong desire to avoid suffering, but he stopped short of insisting on getting his own way and said, "Not my will but yours be done."

I admire the self-reflectiveness of one biblical scholar who wrote, "I have great sympathy for Judas, not only because he is a pathetic figure, but because the seed of divine betrayal is in each of us. And while I really cannot imagine myself performing the Judas-deed, I know my capacity for my own kinds of shame and betrayal. Nevertheless, I don't believe Judas was helpless; I don't believe he was simply a divine pawn. I believe he could have resisted evil, and that he could have been a disciple of honor."[3] Judas was his own worst enemy, as he missed every opportunity to learn, to change, and to receive the healing love of Christ. Studying Judas reminds us that it is possible to be close to Jesus in many ways, and still remain sinful and unyielding. We have all heard of church leaders and others who present themselves as devout Christians, but have been discovered guilty of heinous crimes. The great good news is that we can also see encouraging hope in the story of Judas, because our human sins have no ultimate power to overcome the purposes of God.

Judas led the authorities to Jesus to arrest him. If he was counting on this event to motivate Jesus to revolt, he must have watched in horror after his deadly kiss of betrayal, because Jesus did not resist when the Romans took him by force. Instead, Jesus demonstrated that God's way of dealing with evil is not to return evil, but to absorb and redeem it. God responds to our human misuse of our freedom by absorbing it in redemptive love, rather than escalating conflict and destruction. Judas saw Jesus become the suffering servant and use a greater power by giving back goodness in the face of evil.

As the Romans took Jesus away, Judas saw that his determination to have his own way had failed disastrously, and he

---

3. J. Ellsworth Kalas, *The Thirteen Apostles* (Nashville: Abingdon, 2002), 92.

was filled with remorse. He went back to the chief priests and the elders, returned the thirty pieces of silver and said that he wanted them to stop the whole process because he had sinned and betrayed innocent blood. Their response was, "What is that to us? See to it yourself," putting the responsibility squarely back on him. Ironically, after trying to use Jesus, Judas was used by the establishment himself. Although he still had the freedom to make other choices after his plot backfired, he chose to end his own life, resorting to a final act of determination to control his own end. He threw down the pieces of silver in the temple and went to commit suicide. The Gospel of Matthew says he hung himself, while the book of Acts records an even more gruesome end (Matthew 27:3–5; Acts 1:18). Regardless of the details of how he ended his life, it was a tragic conclusion to what could have been a fruitful life.

I am firmly convinced that Judas did not have to commit suicide. If he had opened his mind and spirit to the truth of Jesus, he could have discovered something bigger and better than his own willful way of putting life together. He still had freedom even after he betrayed Jesus and his plans went awry. The story of Judas could have turned out very differently. Instead of giving up and taking his own life, he could have followed the crowd out to the city gates, gone to the place where the three crosses stood, looked up at Christ on that middle cross and said, "Jesus, oh Jesus, this is Judas, and I have been so horribly wrong. I am truly sorry. You kept telling me about the love of God, but I did not listen. Now I understand that, 'all who take the sword will perish by the sword' (Matthew 26:52). I am so ashamed, Jesus. Is there any way that you could forgive me?" Only moments before, Jesus had prayed, "Father, forgive them; for they do not know what they are doing." He had just turned to a criminal on the cross beside him and said, ". . . Today you will be with me in Paradise" (Luke 23:34–43). I have every confidence that he would have said, "Of course, Judas, of course I will forgive you because God's mercy is greater than all the sin in the world. It is not when you learn, but that you learn. Take what you have learned and go be my witness." If that had happened, Judas might have become one of the greatest saints for God, because those who are forgiven much, love much.

The final tragedy of Judas is not what he did, however despicable. The final tragedy is what he did not do. He could have asked Jesus for forgiveness, and received it. He could have learned the error of his ways and experienced the marvelous truth that where sin increases, grace abounds even more. He did not trust that God's willingness to forgive and power to redeem are greater than our power to sin. If Judas had been able to shift his sense of proportion regarding his own performance as less important than the power of God's grace, he could have received everlasting mercy and gone on to do the good things that Jesus had hoped he would do. Simon Peter sold out and betrayed Jesus in his own way, but he was willing to learn from his mistakes, to be forgiven, and to spend the rest of his life serving God in magnificent ways. I believe with all my heart that Judas Iscariot could have done the same.

My friends, it is too late to worry about innocence. If the truth were known, every one of us has failed. There are skeletons in everybody's closet. We have all sinned and fallen short of the glory of God. The astonishing good news is that, regardless of the mess we may have made of our lives, there is nothing too bad or too big for the redemptive clemency of God to handle. God is more interested in our future than our past, more concerned about what we can still become, than what we used to be. C. S. Lewis said there will come a time for each of us when we will either say, "Thy will be done," and we will be invited to enter into the joy of the Lord, or with infinite sadness, God will say to us, "Thy will be done," and we will not enter into the joy of the Lord. The tragedy of Judas was that he did not trust God's love and mercy enough to say, "Thy will be done."

James and James
The Greater and Lesser

James is one of the most popular of all saints' names, and most of us know of at least one church named for him. However, few of us are likely to have much clear information about him because there are actually three different men named James in the biblical record: James the son of Zebedee, James the son of Alpheus, and James the Lord's brother. All three share surprising particulars in common. In addition to having the same name, which was a common one among Jews of this period, each one had a brother—either another disciple or Jesus himself—and all three were martyred in Jerusalem. With these similarities, it is easy to confuse them and, ironically, the James who is best known to us through Scripture was not one of the original apostles, but the brother of Jesus. To clarify their identities, I will describe all three even though only two were among the first twelve disciples.

In Paul's letter to the Galatians he speaks of "James the Lord's brother" (1:19), who became a leading member of the church at Jerusalem after the resurrection. Those family ties did not prevent him from strongly opposing Jesus' sense of his call as the Messiah and criticizing the things that Jesus did during his lifetime. There could be several reasons for James' attitude toward his brother. From the vantage point of a sibling, it would be understandably difficult to believe that someone you knew so intimately as a child could be uniquely special enough to be acknowledged as the long-awaited Messiah. Furthermore, when Jesus decided to leave his carpenter's bench and become an itinerate preacher, responsibilities for caring for the family and their carpentry business may have been passed on to James. If that were true, he could have resented the fact that Jesus had left. In the culture of Jesus' time, sons were simply expected to do what their father did. Apprenticeship was the main form of education, and people did not typically change vocations in the middle of their lives. What Jesus did was most unusual, and James may well have thought he had abandoned their family.

We know from Scripture that Jesus' family members were so upset by Jesus' preaching and teaching that Mark's gospel has them coming to him in Capernaum with the intention of taking him home by force, as if he were mentally deranged (3:21). Their belief that Jesus was crazy, or possessed by a demon, must have caused a painful breach in his relationships with those family members. It is even possible that his brothers and sisters became estranged from their own mother because of her loyalty to him, which could explain why, as he was dying on the cross, Jesus designated the disciple John to be the one who would care for Mary. As far as the relationship between James and Jesus was concerned, it seems that there may have been a rift.

Then something very mysterious happened. We don't know the details, but in listing the appearances that Jesus made after his resurrection, St. Paul stated, "Then he appeared to James" (1 Corinthians 15:7). In the days soon after the resurrection, something profound must have happened in the depths of James's psyche when Jesus made it a point to go to his estranged brother, just as he had reached out to Simon Peter after he had denied he even knew Jesus. In spite of all that James may have done against him, experiencing Jesus' forgiveness could have moved James to see in the resurrected Jesus what he had never been able to see in the earthly Jesus. The amazing truth is that, James, the brother of Jesus, went from opposition to the Christian movement to being one of its primary leaders, rising to become the first bishop of Jerusalem. Some scholars believe that we have Jesus' brother to thank for writing the Letter of James as well.

The story of James' journey from opponent of Jesus to bishop of Jerusalem and a Christian martyr's death is another reminder that people can change significantly. Growth is possible. It is not inevitable and it cannot be forced on us, but there is a better future available to us through Jesus. That is the basis of hope for every one of us, in spite of the problems, addictions, family scars, or wounds we may carry with us. Regardless of what our past has been like, we can become different in the future. James, the brother of Jesus, is an inspiring example of such transformation. The long-standing conflict between brothers was healed, and a harmonious, creative relationship emerged. Do you ever wonder where you would be, if nobody had ever given you a second chance? If everything that we regret having done in the past were held against us, what would our lives be like? We humans are not capable of perfection. We can't even be at our best always, so there will inevitably be occasions when we disappoint and let each other down. However, we are blessed by the grace of a God of many chances and, although James was not one of the first twelve disciples, he is a testimony to the power and potential of new beginnings.

Now, we come to the other men named James, who were actually two of the original apostles. They are both mentioned in every list of the apostles and, strangely enough, they each had a brother who was one of the original twelve as well. You can see why it is easy to confuse one James for the other. Among Jesus' first followers we know of three pairs of brothers: Peter and Andrew; James, the son of Zebedee, and John; and James, the son of Alphaeus, and Matthew the tax collector.

James, the son of Zebedee, was called James "the Great" in early church records because he was either taller or older than James, the son of Alphaeus, who was referred to as "James the Less" or "Younger" in the Gospel of Mark. James the son of Zebedee, was the older brother of John, the beloved disciple, and as the eldest, his name is usually mentioned first when these brothers are mentioned together. Their father was a prominent fisherman who hired many workers in his Galilean fishing enterprise. James, John, Andrew and Simon Peter had all worked for Zebedee, whose employment they left to follow Jesus. The mother of James and John was Salome, and there is reason to believe that she was the sister of Mary, the mother of Jesus. Salome was an ambitious woman who in Matthew's version asks Jesus for her sons to be given preferential treatment in the kingdom of Heaven. In Mark's account the brothers spoke for themselves but, either way, their mother was with them, which means that she was likely to have approved, if not initiated, this bold request. Perhaps Salome thought that her sons should have special privileges because they were Jesus' first cousins, but that is pure speculation.

I imagine that James's father was often absent from his family, tending to his large business, and that his mother was driven to derive her sense of worth vicariously from the accomplishments of her sons. James and John must have been aggressive young men because Jesus called them "Boanerges," which means "Sons of Thunder" (Mark 3:17). There is evidence of their explosive temperaments in their reaction when Jesus and his disciples stopped at a Samaritan village but were refused hospitality because of long-standing religious conflict between Jews and Samaritans. James and John wanted Jesus to call down fire from heaven right then and burn the people to the ground. They could have been remembering that in the Book of the Kings, the Prophet Elijah called down fire and destroyed two groups of men that were sent by the king of Samaria to meet him. However, they were not remembering that Jesus had been teaching them to be merciful and make peace. So Jesus "rebuked" James and John before going on to the next village. They had not yet learned that the saving way of Jesus was one of love and forgiveness, not revenge and destruction.

James, the son of Zebedee, was clearly part of Jesus' inner circle. He is always listed among the disciples—along with Peter and John—on whom Jesus seemed to rely the most. There were three occasions when Jesus was accompanied by only those three. They were present at the healing of Jairus's daughter, when he brought back a young child from the dead, and they were there to witness Jesus' glory on the Mount of Transfiguration while the other nine disciples were left in the valley. On the third occasion, Jesus turned to these three special companions to pray with him privately as he agonized in the Garden of Gethsemane, before his trial and crucifixion. Yet, while James was clearly part of Jesus' closest inner circle, there is no individual reference to him apart from the other disciples except the fact that he was the first of the twelve to be martyred. (Acts 12:2) It is odd to me that his own brother wrote nothing about James in the Gospel of John, especially since the only scriptural information we have about Philip, Andrew, and Nathanael Bartholomew is found in John's gospel.

I imagine that it was not easy for James to be the older brother of John, because John had a special capacity for being lovable that made folk instinctively feel close to him. As one of the three upon whom Jesus relied the most, James must have had abundant affection for Jesus, and I cannot help but wonder what he felt as he watched his younger brother enjoy an even closer relationship than he had. Since it appears that nothing he said or did independently was considered worthy of recording in Scripture, we can assume that James was not a person who typically took the initiative. In contrast, bombastic Simon Peter was a natural leader, who emerged to the forefront by force of his dominant personality. James had been called to follow Jesus at about the same time as Simon Peter and John, but he must not have been viewed as a leader. He was not the one Jesus asked to sit by him at the Last Supper. I am suggesting that it could not have been easy for James to be one of Jesus' three closest companions, but not to feel that he was special enough to distinguish himself. In his heart of hearts, he must have wished for more. It is human nature to want to be recognized and appreciated for one's own unique qualities and the striking lack of any individual mention of James leads me to conclude that he was not.

We know that James stayed close to Jesus right to the very end, and that he was first to die for his beliefs. I believe that he deserves high credit for his unwavering commitment, in light of the fact that he was not considered a leader as was Simon Peter, nor the beloved intimate friend of Jesus that John was. Nonetheless, he remained loyal and did not let a comparison of himself to others become determinative. It is more likely that he felt lucky to have been with Jesus at all, and that sense of gratitude would have made it possible for him to make the most of his situation.

When you make any kind of interpretive evaluation, the choice of criterion by which you make judgment is crucial. One of my uncles returned from vacation one summer and was having coffee with his boss on a Monday morning, when he asked rather ritualistically, "How's your wife?" He was shocked when his boss shot back, "Compared to what?" Well, my uncle was no philosopher, and he was not used to being questioned in response to his own question. Yet, the more he thought about it, the more he realized that the answer to his question was truly determined by the answer to his boss's second question!

Compared to Mother Theresa, or compared to Angelina Jolie? Nearly everything is relative. James could have become quite discouraged if he had focused on comparing himself to Simon Peter or John, or his relationship with Jesus compared to theirs. Then he would have had no cause for gratitude at all.

The sidelong glance of envy distorts our ability to see ourselves realistically, because there will always be people in every category who are better or worse than we are. James may not have gotten much individual attention, but he must have developed a healthy self-acceptance that enabled him to be a valuable part of the group. It seems clear that he was transformed by the power of Jesus from a "son of thunder" to a "team player," who did not push to get attention merely for himself. That is a remarkable change for one who had boldly said to Jesus, "Teacher, we want you to do for us whatever we ask of you" and wanted to be sure he and his brother would be sitting right by Jesus when he came into his glory.

Instead of that glorious end, James became a martyr for his faith. Herod Agrippa, the nephew and successor of Herod Antipas, who put Jesus on trial, "laid violent hands upon some who belonged to the church. He had James, the brother of John, killed with the sword" (Acts 12:1–2). In his book *The Apostles*, Gene Getz comments insightfully, "Why James and not John? After all, John had become very prominent in Jerusalem as Peter's right-hand man. Together they had confronted the Jewish leaders . . . on numerous occasions. . . . Was he even more daring as a witness for Christ than John?"[1] These are provocative

---

1. Gene A . Getz, *The Apostles* (Nashville: Broadman and Holman, 1993), 35–37.

questions, and if James did become a more courageous and vocal witness for Christianity as he matured, it would be a further sign of his spiritual growth. James was willing to die for what he believed, thus fulfilling his agreement to drink the cup from which Jesus drank.

There is an inspiring legend about the way James responded when Herod abused him as Caiaphas and the Roman authorities abused Jesus. There had been a time when James had wanted to call down fire on the Samaritans who had refused him hospitality. Now he did not call out for revenge in the face of being treated like an animal but was compassionate and dignified instead. He did not become a beast in reaction to the beast, but—as did Steven when he was being stoned, and Jesus when he was crucified—looked up to heaven and asked God's forgiveness for the people who were putting him to death. This was the great witness of the martyrs when, in the worst of times, they did the best of things. In the legend of James, it is said that Josias, who was his accuser, was so impressed by James's faith and conduct in the face of being treated terribly that, as James was being led to his death, Josias shocked everybody by asking for Jesus' forgiveness and declaring that he was a Christian, too. Thus, Josias was beheaded and accompanied James to martyrdom because the witness of his forgiving love drew in even his captor.[2]

The other apostle named James, has been referred to as "the lesser," "the less," or "the younger" (Mark 15:40). We don't know as much about this disciple as we do the others, because his

---

2. Kalas, *The Thirteen Apostles*, 31–32.

name is mentioned in Scripture only five times, and each time it is part of a list. All we know besides his name is that he was the son of Alpheus. Since Matthew was also the son of a man named Alpheus, many scholars believe that Matthew and James were brothers. They were both natives of Capernaum, from the northwestern shore of the Sea of Galilee. We know nothing more about this particular disciple, so he is a symbol to me of all the wonderful unsung heroes and heroines whose names are forgotten in spite of their great efforts and accomplishments. We know of nothing negative that has been written about him. It is encouraging to me that he was included as one of Jesus' close companions, to represent that silent majority of admirable people who have not received tribute or accolades.

James, the son of Alpheus, will always have the honor and distinction of having been chosen by Jesus to be his apostle. I like to think of him as one of those special people who have the kind of humility to do whatever they can quietly, without any need to call attention to themselves or be recognized. We all know people like this, and we usually like them for their gentle, dependable, and steadfast ways. They usually show up to help when there is a job to be done, or someone in need, without asking much in return. Thus I think of James "the less" as James "the humble," ministering in an unassuming way, concerned only with doing God's will whether or not he got credit or praise. The world needs people like this even more than it needs leaders.

One other interesting note is that this James was always listed in the gospels as one of the last four disciples, and the other three are believed to have had ties with the Zealot Party.

Some scholars believe that Judas Iscariot, Simon the Zealot, and Thaddaeus had all once belonged to the Zealot party, the first-century political movement intent on throwing out the Romans, and it is reasonable to suppose that James the Less was listed with that group because he shared their Zealot sympathies. It could have been that James was passionately idealistic, while his brother, Matthew, was willing to work for the Roman occupation and do whatever he had to do to get ahead. Although they had grown up in the same family, these two brothers may have taken diametrically opposite paths, with one becoming a tax collector and the other becoming a Zealot.

There is a mystery as to why people with similar back-grounds often turn out so differently. The Austrian psychologist, Dr. Alfred Adler, was intrigued by the following story. A well-dressed businessman got off the train in Vienna, walked through the lobby, and was stopped by an alcoholic beggar. The beggar said, "Please give me enough money to buy breakfast." The well-dressed man said, "I don't usually give money to beggars, but I'm going to give you some money on one condition. Tell me how somebody as intelligent looking as you appear to be, has allowed himself to get in such straits of dependency?" The beggar got red in the face and said, "Listen, if what's happened to me had happened to you, you wouldn't be asking such a question. You'd be begging for your breakfast, too."

The beggar continued, "I've never had a chance in life. My mother died when I was young, and my father was cruel and irresponsible. Things got so bad that, finally, my brothers and sisters and I were taken away from my father and put in a state run orphanage. I was getting along pretty well when World War I broke out and, one evening, a battle developed around our orphanage. A shell hit my dorm, and I had to flee to save my life, in the middle of the night. I have never seen anybody in my family since that time. It has been like that from the beginning. Every time I manage to get to my feet, circumstances knock me to the ground. If what has happened to me had happened to you, you wouldn't be asking me such a question."

The well-dressed man said, "You know, it is strange to me that you should say that because, as you tell your story, it does parallel mine. My mother died when I was young, and my father was cruel and abusive. The authorities had to take me and my brothers and sisters away from him to live in an orphanage and, when World War I came along, a bomb hit the dorm where I was living. Yet," he added, "I always had the feeling that I wasn't a victim. I always believed that I could fight back, somehow, and not just make the best of things, but make the most of them." Well, they began to talk, and you have probably guessed already that they discovered they were blood brothers. Separated for years by the accidents of war, their lives had mysteriously intersected again.

Adler used that story to illustrate how individuals can respond so differently to the same parents, similar circumstances, and a similar context. One brother allowed events to overwhelm him, while the other found a way to tack into the wind and use the forces against him to move him forward. This different choice of responses to the same situation is the ultimate mystery of the freedom and power to choose that each of us is given. There is no way of accounting for why one son of Alphaeus would have sold out to Rome, and the other son would have fought vehemently against Rome as a Zealot, but that may have been the case.

I will never cease to be amazed by the capacity of Jesus to reach out in extremely diverse directions, to very different kinds of people. He came not only to reconcile human beings to God, but also to each other. He can heal the deep wounds that exist in families. All of us are flawed and our mistakes from the past can lead to an avalanche of condemnation. We gain incredible hope and encouragement from knowing that Jesus can bring healing to even the deepest divisions. None of us was born to angels. All of us have been wounded and have inflicted wounds along the way. Yet Jesus attracted disciples to his own inner circle that had taken opposing paths in life, such as Matthew and Simon the Zealot, and even brothers who may have been estranged, like Matthew and James. Their reconciliation offers us a vision of the healing of our worst enmities.

Of the twelve original apostles, I believe that these two named James, "greater" and "less," are the most likely to be confused not only with each other, but also with James the brother of Jesus. Both of these men called James were distinct and each has something to teach us. I hope this chapter gives you a clearer sense of the unique significance of these two followers of Jesus.

John
The Disciple Whom Jesus Loved

The disciple John was a significant part of the inner circle of Jesus' closest companions, and I like to refer to him as "the disciple whom Jesus loved." He has been called "the beloved disciple," too, and I will elaborate on how he came to be identified in these particular ways. But first I will tell you what we know about this apostle, mostly drawn from Scripture and also from Christian tradition.

John's father's name was Zebedee, and he was the head of a thriving fishing business on the Sea of Galilee. One tradition holds that Simon Peter worked for Zebedee, which would explain how Peter became a close friend of Zebedee's sons, James and John. John's mother's name was Salome. His older brother was called James, and it appears that these two siblings were part of a prominent family in Capernaum, a village to the east of where Jesus grew up. Furthermore, there is good reason to believe that John was actually a first cousin of Jesus, a relationship that has been gleaned from what is written in the gospels. Matthew's gospel says there were four women standing at the foot of the cross at the time Jesus was crucified, three of them named Mary and the fourth, "the mother of the sons of Zebedee" (Matthew 27:55–56). Mark's gospel includes the same women named Mary at the foot of the cross and then adds that a woman named Salome was there also (Mark 15:40). Finally, John's gospel also mentions the three women named Mary and adds, "Jesus saw his mother and the disciple whom he loved standing beside her" (John 19:26). Since it appears that Matthew and Mark are referring to the same woman as "Salome" and "the mother of the sons of Zebedee, Salome may well have been the sister of the mother of Jesus, which would have meant that James and John were Jesus' first cousins.

We know that John was a fisherman, following in the footsteps of his father as nearly every male in that culture did, learning the trade from his father as an apprentice. Also, it is clear that John was part of the inner circle of the disciples because, when Jesus was really in a crisis, he would turn to his three closest companions: Peter, James, and John. It could have been through their family ties as first cousins that John and James were especially close to Jesus, and we know that John was seated next to Jesus at the Last Supper. Because of his tremendous impact on the early church, tradition ascribes authorship of five of the books in the New Testament canon either to him or to the circle of people who followed and learned from him: the Gospel of John, the three epistles of John, and the book of Revelation.

From the information that we have about John in the Bible, it is pretty clear that there was a genuine shift in the personality of this particular disciple across the years of his life. In Matthew, Mark, and Luke, the first three glimpses we get of John are not very favorable. In fact, these little vignettes give you some insight into the kind of person he was when Jesus first encountered him, and it was not an altogether flattering picture. For example, John and his brother, James, stand out in the biblical record as being consumed with ambition. There was a particularly revealing occasion toward the end of Jesus' ministry, when many still thought that Jesus was going to be a political messiah who would effectively drive out the Roman occupational forces, establish Jerusalem as the new Rome, and would himself become the equivalent of Caesar. James and John took Jesus aside one day and said, essentially, "We have a favor to ask of you. When we take over and come to power, we are anxious that one of us will be on your right hand and one on your left. We want to be right up there, close to you." The context in which James and John made this request makes their self-centered request even more shocking, for it was their first response to Jesus' prediction of his own betrayal and death. Concerned only about their own ambitions, they show they have completely missed the point of Jesus' mission (Mark 10:35–37).

The other disciples were infuriated when they heard about what James and John had done, probably not because they were much nobler, but because the two brothers were trying to beat them at a game that they were all still playing. I am sad to say that too many of us continue to be involved in a destructive process of striving for power and status, looking for ways to climb over everybody else's back and become "king of the mountain."

When James and John told Jesus that they wanted to be elevated to places of superiority, he used the occasion to tell them that they had still not gotten the point he had come to make. Abundant life is about service in the name of love, not acting superior to "lord" it over people. It is the willingness to humble oneself and serve others that brings ultimate fulfillment (Mark 10:41–45). Jesus demonstrated his own willingness to serve repeatedly, particularly on that last night when he got up from table, wrapped himself in a towel, and washed the disciples' feet. Jesus came to teach and model such love and humility, but John was not even close to having that kind of serving heart in the early stages of his life.

The second unbecoming aspect of John's personality in his youth was his violent temper. He tended to blow up when crossed, and we get a glimpse of this tendency when Jesus and his followers were going through Samaria on their way to Jerusalem. The Jews looked down on Samaritans for a number of reasons, and particularly because of religious differences: Samaritans claimed that their holy mountain, Gerizim, rather than Mount Zion was the true place of worship. There were not many public inns during that era, so travelers had to rely on the hospitality of others, regardless of any prejudice. As they journeyed along their way, Jesus asked some messengers to go ahead and ask the people in the next village for hospitality through the night. When the Samaritans refused hospitality to Jesus and his followers, James and John were so angry that they asked Jesus to call down fire from heaven to destroy them. In other words, "Why don't we just take a scorch-the-earth policy here and do away with them completely!" (Luke 9:51–56). In this event, we see how James and

John came to be called the "sons of thunder," because they could be quite combative when they did not get their own way. Again, Jesus "rebuked" them because they did not yet understand that he had not come to condemn the world, but to save it. It was very hard for them to comprehend that the purpose of Jesus was not to bring down the wrath of destruction, but to spread the gentle rains of rescue and redemption upon all God's people.

It is sobering to ask yourself the question: What do I do when my will is crossed or I can't have my way? Not long ago, I read an absolutely chilling report that a sixteen-year-old boy had recently gotten his driver's license and had asked his mother if he could use the family car one afternoon. For her own reasons, she told him that he could not use the car at that time. He became so infuriated at her for not giving him what he wanted that he got his father's rifle and shot her in the back of the head as she was getting food out of the refrigerator, killing his mother in cold blood because she would not let him drive her car that day. I know this example is extreme, but the same kind of violent unwillingness to be thwarted was part of the make-up of young John and his brother James.

A similar unflattering characteristic of John in his early adulthood was his arrogance and intolerance for anybody who was not in step with him, doing exactly what he wanted. There is only one place in the gospels in which John is speaking solely by himself, for he is usually described as being with either Peter or James. On this occasion, he saw a stranger casting out demons in the name of Jesus. (Remember that Jesus had said he would empower others to do the works that he did.) When John saw an outsider performing miracles in Jesus' name, however, he was incensed. So he went back to tell Jesus that he had seen somebody casting out a demon in Jesus' name and that he had told him to put a stop to it as quickly as possible, because he was not one of disciples. But Jesus said, "Do not stop him; for no one who does a deed of power in my name will be able soon after to speak evil of me. Whoever is not against us is for us" (Mark 9:39–40). Jesus taught that he came for us to have more abundant life, and John was slow to grasp that Jesus wanted his teachings to lead everyone to do good in his name. He had to tell John repeatedly that the gospel was not something for the disciples to keep for themselves, but was good news to be shared as widely as possible.

I have always wondered how some Christians can arrogantly claim that their way is the only way, and that their interpretation of truth is the only possible truth. If I have been cured of cancer, I have every right to tell everybody who will listen, "I want you to know the good news about a medical treatment that has had a marvelous healing effect on me." However, I have no right to say that my experience means there is no other medicine or treatment that can cure cancer. The fact that one person's cancer is healed by surgery does not mean that others cannot be healed by radiation or chemotherapy. No one knows all the ways that the grace of God may assume in the saving of creation. We are called to be witnesses to share the good news of our own experiences, not to dictate the beliefs and choices of others. I believe Jesus is overjoyed whenever good is being done and love is being shared.

So John was slow to learn what Jesus was trying to teach him, and when we first see him we see a person with consuming ambition, an explosive temper, and intolerance. Realizing how far John had to go to change his life makes it all the more impressive when we find later descriptions of John becoming a remarkably loving and capable leader in the Gospel of John, the epistles that carry his name, and in the traditions that surround him. It is evident that the great emphasis of the Gospel of John is on God's love. The theme of the epistles is to love one another as God has loved us, and we are told in the last two chapters of the book of Revelation that we can look forward to the ultimate triumph of love. It seems clear to me that John's worst traits were gradually purified, and that exquisitely loving, spiritual qualities gradually permeated his personality.

When Jesus was dying on the cross and knew that the time left to him was very short, one of the last things he did was to tend to the care of his mother. She was probably a widow by then, and she may have even become estranged from her other children because of her loyalty to Jesus. Jesus went to special lengths to make sure that she would have a guardian, and it is significant to note that the one he chose to care for her was John. It may have been because they were kin, but I don't believe that was the only reason. Something had happened within the spirit of John that Jesus saw as worthy enough to entrust to him one of the most important people of his life. So it was to his mother that Jesus said, "Woman, here is your son" and to his beloved disciple, "Here is your mother." It was a very tender exchange, as Jesus committed the care of his mother to John, and it was a sign that something of great value had surfaced in the heart of this disciple (John 19:25–27).

John was one of the few disciples who were not martyred, and he is said to have lived longer than the rest. One tradition has it that he lived to be one hundred years old, staying in Jerusalem to keep his promise to take care of Jesus' mother until her death. This arrangement makes even more sense if she was John's aunt. Later in his life, John was persecuted and banished to the isle of Patmos, where most scholars think he wrote the book of Revelation. After he was released from Patmos, he went to the thriving city of Ephesus in present day Turkey. In Ephesus, John became the spiritual leader of the church and was known especially for the loving quality of his spirit. As John became weak and senile as he aged, one tradition holds, he had to be carried by others into the places where the church in Ephesus would convene. The old man was almost past being able to make himself heard because he was so weak, but those who revered and cared for him would bring him in and lay him down in the center of the church, where he would rise up on his elbow and say, "My little children, love one another." When asked, "Master, why do you always say this?" John replied, "It is the Lord's command and, if you love, it is enough."

John is remembered best as one who came to be consumed by the reality of love, which is a marvelous contrast to the way we saw him at the beginning of his life. That is the encouragement and wonder of the Christian gospel: we don't have to stay the way we are. God is much more interested in our future than in our past, more concerned for what we can become than what we used to be, and the essence of the good news is that we have the possibility of becoming more Christ-like through God's grace. What do you suppose happened between the time when John was a young, ambitious man with a quick temper and his later years, when he became a magnificent embodiment of love? I believe that the crucial pivotal hinge that marked the turning point of his life was his encounter and experience with Jesus of Nazareth, and he was probably stressing that fact every time he referred to himself.

You may have noticed that in the Gospel of John, he never refers to himself by his given name. Whenever it is obvious that he is talking about himself, he does not use the name that his mother and father gave him but instead refers to himself by using the enigmatic phrase, "the disciple whom Jesus loved." He does this on four separate occasions: at the Last Supper sitting close to Jesus (John 13:23), at the foot of the cross watching Jesus die (John 19:26), when Jesus appeared to his disciples and helped them catch fish on the Sea of Tiberius (John 21:7), and later that same day when Jesus was talking to Peter (John 21:20). From this you might get the impression John was boasting that he was the special favorite of Jesus' companions, but I don't think this was an expression of egotism. I believe those were words of humble testimony that came out of a nearly unspeakable depth of awe and wonder as John's way of saying, "The only way to understand how I came to be who I am now is to know that the most amazing, life-changing thing that ever happened to me was receiving Jesus' love and incredible grace. The most important way to describe me does not involve who my mother and father were or how they named me. The greatest single thing that made the difference in who I am today is that I was loved by Jesus." That is a profound and remarkable claim, which leads me to wonder why John would have found Jesus' love so unusual and powerful that he would have reached the point of identifying himself in terms of that relationship. I admit that I have to speculate and use my imagination about this, along with what little information we have, but we do know enough about John's family of origins to be able to appreciate why the love of Jesus was so significant to John that it became the very foundation of the way he thought about himself.

We know that John's father, Zebedee, was the head of a successful fishing operation, with enough business to have a "branch office" in Jerusalem. His status and reputation are validated by the tradition that he was the one chosen to provide the High Priest's family with their food supply. This could explain why John was allowed to enter the home of Caiaphas, when Jesus was taken there on the night he was arrested and John and Peter followed Jesus and his captors. Somebody there probably knew John because he had delivered fish to the home of the High Priest.

It is reasonable to imagine that keeping a huge business going kept John's father very busy, and that Zebedee was so invested in his work that he did not have much time for this son. Many times the cost of being professionally successful is that a busy schedule leads to neglect of family life. You and I may be different in many ways, but we are exactly alike in that we all have the same 168 hours a week. We are absolutely equal in the amount of time we have available to us each day, and Zebedee was no exception in being limited by those time constraints. It is not hard to understand that Zebedee could have been too busy to have much occasion to be with his son or to give him that sense of his value that is so crucial as children are developing. Thus, John may have gotten used to being ignored by "the big people," people like his father who were in places of power and importance. If his father was too busy to show much interest in John, he could have concluded that he had little value.

Young John's situation may have been similar to the plight of one of my friends who told me that he did not remember one time in all of his life when his father chose to be with him over doing something else. He added, "My father was never abusive or physically hurtful, but what felt even worse was that he treated me as if I were a glass window that he could see through, hardly noticing that I was even there." The opposite of love is not hate, but indifference, because we do not hate something that is of no importance to us. Hatred always has a component of interest in it. The worst way that we can show disrespect for another person is simply to treat them as if they do not exist. Do you remember the parable of the last judgment in which Jesus described how the human race is finally going to be judged? He said that it is not the abuse of power, but the neglect of power, that is the opposite of love. To paraphrase, Jesus said, "I was hungry and thirsty, but you acted as if I did not even exist." (Matthew 25:42)

Now, John's mother was completely different from his father. No one could ever accuse her of being indifferent or uninvolved with her boys! John had a mother who cared deeply about him, but she did so in a way that promoted her own hidden agenda, in which her sons became a means to her own ends. It is important to remember that for many centuries women had very few ways to express themselves publicly or professionally. One of the only ways that they could channel their energy and derive a sense of significance vicariously was by investing in the success of their husbands and sons. The ambitions of James and John are much more understandable when you consider the behavior and needs of their mother, Salome. However, that kind of family dynamic can be extremely hard on a young person's self-esteem. If you feel like your parents love you only when you do well, or that they can give you affection only when you are fulfilling their dreams, such conditional love is more like emotional blackmail than nurturing love.

It could be that my interpretation of John's relationship to his mother is biased by the way that I remember my own very ambitious mother. My parents were both thirty-six years old when they met each other and neither had ever married. They had a whirlwind romance, fell in love, and became engaged the third time they ever saw each other. They were married the eighth time that they were together, to the utter dismay of both of their families, who were absolutely aghast when this seemingly confirmed bachelor and spinster decided so impulsively to marry without any family support on either side. After they were married, my father brought my mother to live in Nashville near his family members, who were not at all pleased that my father had married so quickly. They were neither accepting nor hospitable toward my mother, who had been the principal of a junior high school in Mississippi but gave up her work because married women could not teach in that era. Although I never heard her say so publicly, I have reason to believe that my mother soon questioned the wisdom of her impetuous decision to marry. Her life changed radically when she suddenly left her work, as the respected principal of a junior high school, to go live where her in-laws did not like her and her husband's business required him to travel from Monday through Friday of every week.

In response to that harsh reality, I believe my mother decided that she would have children and that, by God, they would have to be perfect in her eyes so she could feel better about the decision she had made. For the entire time that I was growing up, I had the feeling that I had to achieve for my mother's sake. She used to say to me, "If you are ever going to amount to anything, you have to make something of yourself." Since she had been an educator, she was extremely anxious for her children to do well academically. I can still hear her voice, sounding very much like the teacher she had been, saying, "Bring me hundreds, and you'll see me smile." God knows I wanted to see her smile!

The American psychiatrist and educator, Rudolf Dreikurs, believed that children are keen observers but poor interpreters, and my interpretation of my mother's admonition was that I must not have amounted to anything as I was. I kept thinking that I had to get something from somewhere outside of myself, and make it part of me so that I would finally amount to something in her eyes. Most of us want very much to please the one who brought us into the world, but you will have to admit that the benchmark can be set awfully high. I was constantly striving to please her, but if I brought home a ninety-eight, she would frown and ask what had happened to the other two points. That kind of parental pressure can do terrible things to a young psyche or fragile ego, but many parents do not understand that. They truly believe that it is good to push their children to strive for perfection, without realizing that they are asking the impossible.

Years ago, I had a friend who was one of the most successful people I have ever known. His father committed suicide when my friend was in college and he had to take over the failing family business at a young age. He was a genius at this task and built that business into a flourishing enterprise. By objective standards, I don't know anyone who achieved more, yet I don't think that man ever drew three consecutive happy breaths in his life. He was one of the most driven, dissatisfied persons I have known. He told me that his father put him in the tightest double bind imaginable when he told him repeatedly as he was growing up, "Should you ever think that you have succeeded, then you know that you have set your goals too low." This is a trap out of which there is no escape. No matter what he did, it would never be enough.

Against that background, it is easy to imagine that John was amazed when Jesus came to the boat where he was working for his father, saying, "I want you to come, follow me, and share your life with me." He must have appreciated every bit of the respect and genuine affection he received from Jesus, which led to that life-changing self-definition for John, "the disciple whom Jesus loved." The Catholic priest and author John Powell said that we are shaped both by those who choose to love us and those who refuse to love us. The ratio of love to lovelessness is the crucial equation. Jesus blessed his disciple, John, by giving him the sense that he was truly lovable and by showing him how to be loving in return. Many of us have forgotten, or never even realized, that each of us is God's beloved child. That is our primal and deepest identity, and the story of John reminds us of the transforming power of that love.

The author and professor, Sam Keen, told a poignant story about going out west to see his father as he was dying. He said that he had been sitting in the hospital room with him one afternoon while his father was trying to sort through his life and thinking about how he had done with his days and nights. This gave Sam an ideal opportunity to say something to his father that he had wanted to say for a long time. He told him, "I don't know how you feel about everything you have done with your life, but I want to give you the highest marks for what you did for your four children. I don't ever remember a time when I did not feel that you are glad I am in your life and that I am who I am. You gave each of us the finest single gift that any parent can give a child by taking delight in us, and I am truly grateful."

I think that is the way it is with the One who loves each of us as if there were none other in all the world and who loves all as he loves each. I think that is a description of how Jesus related to John. I believe the significance of the way Jesus sparkled on John with the gift of delight took on an increasingly deeper significance as it gradually dawned on John that Jesus was not just another good man finding his way to

God, but that he was the good God himself finding his way to humankind. Remember those beautiful words in John's gospel, "And the Word was God. . . . And the Word became flesh and lived among us . . . full of grace and truth" (John 1:1, 14). John went from being amazed that Jesus really cared for him to the amazing knowledge that Jesus was the Son of God himself. To that mystery Jesus gives a human face and on that face is a smile of love.

Lo and behold, John came to understand that Jesus' love was like the powerful love that first called creation into being. He knew the Old Testament as well as any good Jew did, and he was familiar with that magnificent picture of the One who is life and has life in himself, wanting to share with his creatures the ecstasy of being. As that wonderfully reassuring passage unfolds, it says again and again, "God saw everything that he had made, and indeed, it was very good" (Genesis 1:31). Perhaps, John was also claiming the Holy One's delight in all creation when he defined himself as the disciple whom Jesus loved. He must have been astonished as he fully realized that the love of Jesus turned out to be the love of God.

I believe, with all my heart, that this healing reality of God's love is available to every one of us. I don't have any idea what kind of road your life has taken. I don't know what kind of parents you had. I have no idea what your childhood, adolescence, or adulthood has been like, but I do know that life works all of us over if we live long enough. We have all been in tough situations and come in contact with people who, for whatever reasons, have been cruel, neglectful, or abusive. Yet, before any human hand ever touched us or said anything to us, God called us his beloved.

Our greatest need is to make God's love for us the foundation of our self-understanding. We need to know that we are beloved—not because of anything that we have done, but because of what God is. This is the extraordinary gift that Jesus gave to John, and it is the life-changing gift he has for every one of us. All we have to do is open our hearts and receive. The best description of the way God feels about us is the word that Jesus heard as he came up from the waters of baptism. Imagine yourself coming out of the waters of your own beginning, out of whatever situation into which you were born, through all the experiences you have passed in this fallen world, and coming into God's view and hearing God say, "You are my beloved child in whom I am well pleased. You are my precious girl, my precious boy, the apple of my eye, and a chip off the old block. You are my exquisite child in whom I take delight!"

Sources

Barclay, William. *The Master's Men.* Nashville: Abingdon, 1959.

Becker, Earnest. *The Denial of Death.* New York: Free Press, 1973.

Brownrigg, Ronald. *The Twelve Apostles.* NewYork: Macmillan, 1974.

Click, E. Dale. *The Inner Circle.* Lima, OH: CSS Publishing Company, 2000.

Covey, Stephen. *The Seven Habits of Highly Effective People.* New York: Free Press, 1989.

de Mello, Anthony. *The Song of the Bird.* Chicago: Loyola University Press, 1982.

Dostoevsky, Fyodor. *The Brothers Karamazov.* NewYork: Alfred A. Knopf, 1992.

Foote, Gaston. *The Transformation of the Twelve.* Nashville: Abingdon, 1958.

Getz, Gene A. *The Apostles.* Nashville: Broadman and Holman, 1993.

Kalas, J. Ellsworth. *The Thirteen Apostles.* Nashville: Abingdon, 2002.

L'Engle, Madeleine. *A Live Coal in the Sea.* New York: HarperCollins, 1996.

MacArthur, John. *Twelve Ordinary Men.* Nashville: Thomas Nelson, 2002.

McBirnie, William Steuart. *The Search for the Twelve Apostles.* Carol Stream, IL: Tyndale House, 1973.

Nouwen, Henry. *Life of the Beloved.* Lanham, MD: National Book Network, 1992.

Powell, John. *The Christian Vision.* Allen, TX: Argus, 1984.

Ruffin, C. Bernard. *The Twelve.* Huntington, IN: Our Sunday Visitor, 1984.

Wiederkehr, Macrina. *Seasons of Your Heart.* New York: HarperCollins, 1991.